The Metanarrative Hall of Mirrors

The Metanarrative Hall of Mirrors

Reflex Action in Fiction and Film

Garrett Stewart

BLOOMSBURY ACADEMIC
NEW YORK • LONDON • OXFORD • NEW DELHI • SYDNEY

BLOOMSBURY ACADEMIC
Bloomsbury Publishing Inc
1385 Broadway, New York, NY 10018, USA
50 Bedford Square, London, WC1B 3DP, UK
29 Earlsfort Terrace, Dublin 2, Ireland

BLOOMSBURY, BLOOMSBURY ACADEMIC and the Diana logo are trademarks of
Bloomsbury Publishing Plc

First published in the United States of America 2022

Copyright © Garrett Stewart, 2022

Cover design by Eleanor Rose
Cover image © Shutterstock

All rights reserved. No part of this publication may be reproduced or transmitted in any form or by any means, electronic or mechanical, including photocopying, recording, or any information storage or retrieval system, without prior permission in writing from the publishers.

Bloomsbury Publishing Inc does not have any control over, or responsibility for, any third-party websites referred to or in this book. All internet addresses given in this book were correct at the time of going to press. The author and publisher regret any inconvenience caused if addresses have changed or sites have ceased to exist, but can accept no responsibility for any such changes.

Library of Congress Cataloging-in-Publication Data
Names: Stewart, Garrett, author.
Title: The metanarrative hall of mirrors :
reflex action in fiction and film / Garrett Stewart.
Description: New York : Bloomsbury Academic, 2022. |
Includes bibliographical references and index. |
Summary: "A profound and entertaining new work on contemporary narrative in film and literature from celebrated literary critic, Garrett Stewart"– Provided by publisher.
Identifiers: LCCN 2021047863 (print) | LCCN 2021047864 (ebook) | ISBN 9781501388798 (hardback) | ISBN 9781501388781 (paperback) | ISBN 9781501388804 (epub) | ISBN 9781501388811 (pdf) | ISBN 9781501388828 (ebook other)
Subjects: LCSH: Narration (Rhetoric)–Philosophy. |
Motion pictures–Philosophy. | Fiction–Technique.
Classification: LCC PN212 .S74 2022 (print) | LCC PN212 (ebook) |
DDC 808–dc23/eng/20211202
LC record available at https://lccn.loc.gov/2021047863
LC ebook record available at https://lccn.loc.gov/2021047864

ISBN:	HB:	978-1-5013-8879-8
	PB:	978-1-5013-8878-1
	ePDF:	978-1-5013-8881-1
	eBook:	978-1-5013-8880-4

Typeset by Integra Software Services Pvt. Ltd.

To find out more about our authors and books visit www.bloomsbury.com
and sign up for our newsletters.

For D.A. Miller,
fellow tiller
across unfenced fields of storytelling media

Contents

Preview \ Beveled Planes of Response   1 /

1 \ Picture Shows   25 /
2 \ Cross-Fade to Prose   49 /
3 \ Understories   79 /
4 \ Wording Unbound   105 /
5 \ Writing Unpent   139 /
6 \ Reading: In Decent Exposure   179 /

Afterthoughts \ The Angle of Incidents   219 /
Index   227 /

Preview \ Beveled Planes of Response

And yet, a man's speech should exceed his lapse, else what's a meta for?
—Richard Powers, *The Gold Bug Variations*

Powers isn't just punning, in the mode of that dated bumper sticker popping up during the early *Star Wars* craze over a decade before his own 1991 big hit with *The Gold Bug Variations*: namely, "Metaphors Be With You." His two-pronged word play suggests another whole theater of textual attention, one attuned to the vagaries of "man's speech" more broadly, metaphoric in cast or otherwise. Given such expressive contortions in both the "lapse" (the loosened "grasp" of the torqued cliché) and the "exceedings" of routine human language, the "force" a reader may sense to "be with you" in reading prose of this layered stamp cannot be taken for granted. The mental work of negotiating the license of such incautiously energized narrative writing—in a dynamic apart from, or underlying, plot momentum—is felt in verbal "reflexes" by no means limited to the typical knee-jerk recoil from supposedly dumb puns. Dumb sometimes, yet even then anything but mute in their attention-grabbing—and response-refracting—slant. Across a far broader range of verbal tensility than just the piggy-backed wordplay of this opening snippet, such are the self-framed shocks of recognition at which this book is taking aim in appreciation—via an analysis already half-drafted, in effect, in being funneled by the text itself.

And so my subtitle. By way of definition and proposal at once, *reflex action*: in literary encounter, a text's means of mirroring back to you the implicit terms of your own response in the event of reading, terms tangibly phrasal first of all. In a complementary sense, though at a more encompassing scale, self-reflexivity is typically understood as a case of story reporting on itself more or less wholesale. Reflex action locates instead those nodes of reading, in or apart from plot, and by association those modes of screen viewing, that are framed in advance for the immediate—but medium-determined—performance of response. Far less condensed and farcical in Powers's usual style, of course, verbal inflections like those of the epigraph offer the broached spans and breached gaps, the leaps and bounds and brief phonic bleeps, that can at any turn serve to extrude a lexical substrate prodigiously his to tap at its restless phonetic and syllabic base. And yours to recognize in the medium-primed energy and inference of its phrased effects. On immanent call in such turns is the verbal fundament as undercurrent—or, as we'll come to identify it, in borrowing Powers's own botanical vocabulary from *The Overstory* (2018), certain twists and tendrils of wording comparable to the tangled floor cover of forest overgrowth: its so-called *understory*. These are verbal thickets so thick on the ground at times that they sprout into outcrops of open comedy. More often they just seed an internal ecosystem of phrasal intertwine and echo. In and beyond the epigraph's corny comic nugget at the end—with its interrogative fissuring of one word into two—it is just such canny linguistic density, in thinner doses, that makes for Powers's unique and curious music, at once odd and inquisitive, and makes us muse on it in quick, and quickening, reflection. Beneath the malaprop comedy of that first citation, in other words, from exactly those skewed other words glimpsed at an oblique angle, a principle emerges all but bent out of shape by compression.

For what the *meta is for* in the fiction of Powers—in his explicitness on this point, a resulting standard-bearer among contemporary writers for the emphasis of this study—is just such a split-second (though not necessarily split-word) recognition. Yet his prose is hardly alone in this. The effect results from a wedge driven into the lexical infrastructure, or say the underlying organic loam, of a narrative turf—one whose best effects in his case root themselves in recursion and rhythmic echo. Often involving the pattern recognition of various specialist vocabularies, such verbal energy in Powers can, of course, be otherwise channeled in contemporary writing. At issue is a mode of a self-mirroring textual impact in which reading finds its own true image as well. And finds reason, in the process, for an instructive cinematic comparison with screen viewing. For any such wonder about the *meta* and its uses resonates with and against not just the postmodern fictional moment in which Powers came of age but, in that same period, a previous quarter-century of high modernist metafilm from Ingmar Bergman, Alain Resnais, and Federico Fellini on. This is a book about the aftermath of all this for the medium of prose, as well as for image projection, in the default tendencies—as well as genuine experiments—of contemporary narrative form.

Tested on the pulse of our own attention is the keyed-up *reflex action* of our reading or viewing. At base is the assumption that fictional exposition *means what it says*: many a seeming "lapse" or "excess" serving to trace—if often a bit edgeways—what a text, whether verbal or visual, really has *on its mind*, however we understand any such personified "self-consciousness" within the relays of response. The result for this study is a double axis of comparison: first, between the differently tooled gearboxes of screen montage and prose's narrative grammar; then, within the latter, between two of current American fiction's leading prose writers at their fictional genre's most antithetical extremes, Powers and Nicholson Baker. The first is a scientifically venturesome maximalist devoted to something like a broad-ranging historiography of our bio-technical and aesthetic present. The other is a detailist of such visceral immediacy in the account of objects and bodies that his notorious turn to, and verbal turns on, hardcore pornography would seem an all but inevitable outgrowth of his prose's indiscriminate libidinal attachment to perception's everywhere caressed material surfaces. Each author precise and exacting in his stylistic experimentation, and with similar demands on reading in the details under description, Powers's ultimate revel in the expansive terminologies of evolution and cognition, musicology and cybernetics, is to be immediately contrasted not just with Baker's love affair with dirty words but with a whole whittled-down fixation on everyday objects rather than on the theoretical systems they instance. The vagaries of descriptive phrasing, therefore, when taken up in response, are naturally enough the first measure of this contrast.

And not just immediately contrasted, Powers and Baker, but *diametrically*—raising the question of the closed polarized circle within which such different writing delimits the broad space of readerly engagement in contemporary letters. There is no aesthetic priority implied here in the ranks of recent American fiction. No guiding preference for the taut, spare, adroit, and mostly undecorative prose by which these two writers prosecute their quite separate claims on thematic participation, over against the lyrical sonorities of a Toni Morrison, the baroque Faulknerian cadences of a Cormac McCarthy, the colloquial wit and pace of a Colson Whitehead, the swirling euphonies and ensnaring macropolitics of Don DeLillo, the demanding grammar of sentence and plot in David Foster Wallace.[1] The list is yours to enlarge. In any case, with the authors here paired for antithetical case studies, Powers and Baker, a certain sparsity of *rhetorical exertion* in each—a sense of language's own material density apart from colorist display—has its way of bringing the reader's textual reflex into sharper light.

Even in this polarized literary phase of the argument, then, once we have brought a lineage of screen experiment into the orbit of this contemporary writing, certain shared tendencies emerge between Powers and Baker. With the different texture of their equally close-grained lexical invention, the ingenious scientific flights of the one author can seem almost parodied by the downbeat sci-fi porn of the other, given especially the erotic time-control magic vested in the narrator of Baker's *The Fermata*. Scientific speculation rendered in fictional form is "answered" by a sci-fi carnality; it is up to analysis to find the questions to which such divergent writing seems rising in response. But the very contrast brings into mutual disclosure the verbal force—and, in reception, reflex counterforce—of a prose stretched beyond any normal expertise, on the one hand, and, on the other, a wording set on rubbing your nose in new concupiscent terms for what you know all too well. The way in which each mode of writing constitutes a kind of reading lesson in the power of wording per se, per saying—knowingly (self-consciously) turning a given text inward on its own transmissive *function*, even while outward to *effect*—is what links these writers across the axis of their antithesis. And, again, across the diameter of that circuit of potential response they so oppositely cultivate.

But that's too much, perhaps, too soon. Stepping back, we recover questions more fundamental yet to the shaping of this study. How best to rethink the idea of "self-consciousness" in fiction, on either page or screen? Whose really is it? Or start the inquiry more historically. What is usefully left to ponder about the notorious postmodern concept of the self-reflexive metatext? Who, you ask—and who better to be asking the question, you as potential reader of this book, let alone of such novels—could be interested still, for more than the course of a few passing acknowledgments, and if so why, in the time-encrusted concept of metatextuality: a formal orientation falling somewhere in narrative analysis between a hoary crux and a cliché? So many years after the canonization and graying of this concept, and its enfeeblement by overuse (in both fictional and critical practice), why should there be a book newly devoted to a sampling of certain residual commitments to its imaginative leverage in contemporary narrative on screen as well as page? Why set about beating a dead warhorse as if one were calling it a drum?

The start of an answer only generates more pointed questions about given instances. But the broader utility of cross-medial thinking can be insisted on. Perspective often comes from adjusting the magnifying lens of contrast. Motion pictures can give us a new picture of prose fiction, and vice versa, when comparison—so strikingly rare—is arranged to emphasize their own separate media of (and in) transmission. But that may be easier to say than to see—when attempting to summon up exemplary cases for comparison. In just this last narrative decade, for instance, what does the Hollywood franchise blockbuster *Spider-Man: Far From Home* (2018), in its hypertrophic digital effects, have in common with the Pulitzer Prized ecological novel by Powers of the same year or with the latest porn picaresque by Baker, the flagrant and unabashed *House of Holes* (2014) about a theme park edifice as monument to the human orifice? Or with the metaphysical puzzlements and trick imagings of Christopher Nolan's film *Tenet* (2020)? Although that four-way query, in its set of drastic contrasts, can scarcely seem meant to cordon off some definitive narrative field in assessing current fictional initiatives, nevertheless a certain overview comes through in addressing with this kind of comparative question that crowded intersection of texts. The cross-medium scope of *The Metanarrative Hall of Mirrors*, advertised by subtitle, signals this as the first book in years to bridge storytelling forms between prose and cinematic modes in a way that might at least offer the considered *terms* of an answer from work to work.

And to such terms we can therefore helpfully move, including the first of that subtitle. Three dictionary usages loom over that central noun, whether the generative medium is optical or verbal: two of them convergent, one ruled out. Reflex: (1) response to a stimulus and (2) a reproduced image. Such is the double function appearing, for our purposes, both to trigger and to mirror (or enact) reaction in the viewing or reading mind—a function in each case verging on automatic, or at least nearly instantaneous. Yet this returned image of attention does not occur at the so-called (3) reflex angle, defined as greater than the 180 degrees even of a mirror plane, let alone the 90-degree axis of strict orthographic reflection—as when confronting one's own cued response in texts of either medium. But hold that last phrase. A so-called self-reflexive work, in the classic sense, tends to confront and reframe head-on its determinate structural features for a more decisive window on its terrain and constitutive horizon. At stake here instead, a more localized reflex action in viewing or reading tracks the underlying prompts to deciphering first hand—with all effects conditioned on themselves as in process medial rather than just narrational operations, whether cinematographic or linguistic. Such is the discerned energy of time-based production when read at the pace of a certain resistant textuality. Confronted, yes, head-on, but as an activated medial interface.

But if that brief dictionary recourse may help clarify certain hopes for the fuller scope of an adjusted reflex model, freed quite completely from an art-about-art rut, it doesn't yet ratify the need. Rephrasing the initial question more pointedly: what in inventive current writing, film aside for the moment, can make a suspiciously vestigial impulse toward fictional reflexivity newly compelling—and this partly in regard to abiding tendencies it might help to elucidate in hindsight? As that version of the question implies, it all depends on the angle—what I am evoking here as the *optically* figured angle, the evident bevel—of approach: the proverbial new (though often rear-view) slant. But what has changed over time to facilitate a new perspective? What might metanarrative vigilance invite that exceeds, even if underwriting, the hoary metatextual paradigm? In literary terms, how are we better positioned lately, via what kind of contemporary writing, to consider the way a fixed and inert text can reflect not just on itself but on its own induced performance in the reading act? One instinct behind this book, and dictating now its comparatist point of departure, is that recent developments in popular cinema—under the escalating self-display of computerized effects, including the sometimes metaphysical tricks they both instigate and then motivate as narrative in the "mind-game" mode—shed a certain (pixelated) light on the granular lexical entailments (in this sense, the infrastructure) of fiction reading. Mediation itself becomes the median term in the comparison. In assessing what the *meta* might still be *for*, the very etymology of "metaphor" (*meta-ferein*) may be of incidental help: a ferrying-across (or "beyond") that—although strictly ticketed only from literal to figurative in the work of fictional phrasing—might have other aptitudes in play. Its transfer might also designate, at the scale of plot itself, a certain carry-through from narrative roadmap to structural blueprint, from story to the architectonics of its discourse. At which point form may still remain in touch with the formative at pressure points of self-leveraged recognition. It is in this way, at scales small as well as large, that narratives in fiction as well as film can become parables of their own process.

Reflexivity Redux

Rich, rigorously mined, and some may have thought thoroughly played out, the sedimented veins of metanarrative self-reference in literary and image media have a durable fertility that might well surprise. And certainly if films and novels find continuing ways to innovate explicitly on their own conditions, scholarship needn't protect its own originality by ignoring this continuing or revamped trend. One path forward, then, as proposed, is to compare the intersecting logics of this metanarrative longevity across alternate narrative media—and this in the transformed cultural context of their latest articulations: fictional "omniscience," if not always actual plots, caught up in the computerized blitz of global data streams; cinematic imaging gone over from the transparent cellular frames of filmic materiality to the electronically coded generation of the digital image. To that end, this is the first extended study of its kind in the almost four decades since the postmodern apotheosis of metatextual literary structure—together with its cinematic counterparts in the art-house Modernism of the 1960s and 1970s—was taken up by Robert Stam's book on that comparative topic.[2] My renewed effort is to bring popular screen fiction and literary narrative together under the still-open umbrella, or more like the capacious tent, of the *meta*. What this approach also brings together is a field of investigation in my work over the last two decades, mostly along separate lines until now, in the "narratography" of literary narrative and the "apparatus reading" of screen fiction, each concerned less with the broad armatures of plot than with the "graphic" microplots, phrasal or optical, of narrative sequence.[3] This is where inferences of the medium, its machinated "channel characteristics," are found—are felt—delivered as a factor of the narrative message itself. And such technical or formal determinants, best estimated *in contrast* I now find, locate in each medium separately an immediate, even when unconscious, audience reverb. Viewing, reading: these, not montage or narrative pattern, are the true zones of what I am highlighting as reflex action. But that only makes an alertness to slow motion on the one hand, anaphoric loops on the other, here tracking shots, there serial syntax and its comma-spliced variants, optical superimposition and metaphoric equivalence—or, with the epigraph in mind, the shock-cut of a disruptive word break—all the more suggestive in the work of investigation.

Of course any preview like this of the coming evidentiary finds—and theoretical findings—could only offer vague inklings for the reader at this point. Still, jumping the gun may help us take a more closely calibrated aim at the target as we go. One broad proposal, then, to be tested only by individual readings, seems worth floating front and center. Against the backdrop of Brian McHale's influential distinction between the *epistemological* orientation of a fragmentary aesthetic in modernist writing and the subsequent *ontological* problematic of imagined world space in the postmodernist novel (between forensic and existential ironies, we may say) falls what evidence to come may well suggest as a definitive third term—and turn.[4] And nowhere more systematically than in the contrapuntal scope and shifting scalar perspective of Powers's novels—as well as, from the margins, the contrastive frame through which Baker's eccentric porn, with its explicit metanarrative episodes, helps us to see them. Writing of Powers's omnivorous intellectual caliber shows its surest colors amid the complex structure of cross-sectional multi-plots rather than across the paranoid uberplots dear to earlier metanarrative fictions. His prose—manifesting the diverse scientific schemata behind it—is marked by discrepant shifts of scene and association rather than by the panoptic centering that characterized so many postmodernist classics. In this his plotting registers, in its manifestation of a variant narrative paradigm, a stance that has evolved well past both a quasi-cubist epistemology and a dubious global ontology to an aggregate—and sometimes aggravated—*phenomenology*, where the world is now filtered for consciousness through ever more complex, abstract, and increasingly digitized grids.

Operating with new prominence in such recent fiction is not the *what* or the *whether* of reality (epistemology or ontology) so much as the *how* of its imaginative manifestation in (and as) narrative: a felt measure of those means (still stylistically modeled, as in the previous literary-historical stages) by which the story comes through to us in narration's either hazy or polished mirror. And coincides there, less or more, with the world on which the mimetic mirror is trained and meant to report. As much as those of any current writer, Powers's novels read not just as learned but as researched and all but hyperlinked texts, a dazzle of digested information headily cross-referenced in their scientific and technological intertexts. And whatever brainy spontaneity is implied by these polymath *infofictions*, one upshot of their reading—even as the terminological flights of fact take wing in stylistic wit—is often to send us privately webward. It is in this respect that their maximalism of cross-reference—though thematically driven rather than easily distracted by digressive sidebars, as in Baker's more contingent specialist riffs both in and beyond his porno experiments—does nonetheless link the two writers. Such technical density in Powers's work—to borrow the kind of punning liberties evinced by the epigraph—leaves no specialist stone *untermed*. And in this respect it connects with the more ad hoc data obsession of Baker's "inclusivist" tendencies, as spelled out in a well-known essayistic critique of the inimical "deletionist" approach characterizing both the in-house policing of Wikipedia entries as well as the jettisoning of libraries' paper archives.[5]

But the prose alone of these writers tells its own story. And it is under a phenomenological description of its effect, regarding how *it comes across* to us word by word in the manifestation of event, and becomes its own event in the process, that Powers and Baker can so revealingly interpret each other. In confronting the former's gravitation to a not-unfamiliar mode of contemporary narrative often kaleidoscopic in form, though certainly maximized by Powers's multifarious plot vectors, one reader imperative comes clear. Long before closure, the need for bringing a plot into interim "resolution"—in the sense of mental focus—is itself a wholly narrativized rather than a passive aspect of the reading act. And it is just here that the continuous demands on an analytic attention stylistically cued and coached—regarding, for instance, the potentially shared narrative terrain of at first discrepant fictive events in Powers—bear comparison, not just with cinematic reflexivity in broader historical terms, but with the duped frames of reference manipulated by trick narration in the flourishing turn-of-the-millennium genre of the so-called "mind-game" or "puzzle" film.[6] Comparison only though, with no final equivalence. These films typically rely on undermined realities that replace one (often narrowly subjective) plot with its repressed corrective double in a surprise ending, rather than educing a looser system of narrative secret sharers across the scope of story. Ontological *upendings* of this sort set these films apart, in their trick-mirroring of expectation, from the composite objectivities of prose in Powers as well as Baker.

In this literary comparison, Powers's omnivorous "inclusions" are the more daunting—or better to say, regarding their reader dynamic, the more demanding. This is a matter not just of scientific outreach but of structuring set up. Technical intertexts aside, even when we remain entirely engrossed within Powers's own narrative covers, greedily reading on, plot comprehension must wrestle, tested thereby, with disjunctive zones of textual event not easy to coalesce in reception. Reading is guided only by the often elusive infrastructure of textual grammar and its reflexive rhetoric. The best clue to the potential link between otherwise-isolated characters in far-flung locales—and between the plot turns that might ultimately interrelate them—is often the laminated doubleness of a pun. Again and again, the act of reading these fictions of Powers—reading them into an often dialectical coherence—constitutes a fashioning of the narrative's own interpretive metaplot. In Powers's debut book, though not admittedly commenting *about* it, the postmodern habit of metanarrative design, to be examined in Chapter 2, is dubbed "constructivist fiction." His own novels since then, incidentally laced as they are with cinematic devices transposed to fictional syntax, have evolved beyond novels whose plots openly floorplan their own structure. Increasingly, his fiction, his *writing*, has refined a mode of oblique auto-inference that turns instead—outward—away from how such novels are constructed to how they are to be construed. This, I'm suggesting, is a typifying turn from inbuilt system to the post-postmodern implications of response: from the architecture of fictional reflexivity to the reflex actions of embodied reading in process. Beyond the demands of immediate narrative structure, this reading is at work, or even play, within the new cognitive surround of global cybernetics and its informational densities, overloads, and attenuations.[7] Here is where current post-filmic cinema also comes into the picture—as if from the underside of the screen—whenever it offers openly paraded computer-age evidence of digital generation, mediation, and transmission all at once. After tracing, in the first chapter, a technological as well as narrative arc from *Citizen Kane* to the latest franchise blockbusters in their sci-fi thematization of computerized special effects, and with it the elicited complicity of audience reflex, the main weight of discussion then shifts to prose as medium. Evidence moves to narrative's synthetic comprehension and its infrastructural cues in the contrapuntal build of Powers's "scientific fictions" (as they are widely identified). And turns next and last to the more obsessional lexical triggers—the gaudy dirty words and their reflex responses—in Baker's ongoing fantasies, also cinematically inflected, though operating at a far (and normally ostracized) pole of the contemporary genre spectrum.

The main claim of literary-historical transition here is that the broad encyclopedic penchant in Powers—along with whatever degree of thesaurus fever we diagnose in Baker's dirty and always specialized words—is the sign of something relatively new. These terminological preoccupations are not simply coextensive with what amounts to a mega- as well as meta-textual agenda in the previous synoptic mode: that branded postmodern overtext of totalized, quasi-paranoid inclusivity. To which of course specialist vocabulary was no stranger. If we consider Don DeDello's twelfth novel, *Underworld* (1997), as a late instance of the once-dominant mode—in that case a kind of cyber epic in the author's technological update of a Dantesque *Inferno*—we can nonetheless track, even there, another and more granular dimension of his narrative writing, a deliberately textured cast of his prose. This is his admitted tendency to foreground style over narrative, if only intermittently. Or one might say signage over extra-lexical design: sound over structuring sense. In a 1993 *Paris Review* interview at the height of his renown, DeLillo explains that being a writer means, for him, the *writing of sentences*—phrasings acutely attuned to the syllables of words: "I'm completely willing to let language press meaning upon me," so that "I might want *rapture* matched with *danger*—I like to match word endings."[8] In this rhyming poetry of prose itself, matching words to each other first and foremost, rather than to the meanings that supposedly authorize them: that's the writer's craft at rock bottom for DeLillo—as well as (in different valences, though at similar lexical scale) for the related prose we'll be examining under the sign of narrative's beveled effects. On this view, fiction writing is the making of words happen—whatever events, whatever narrative happenings, they are enlisted to recount or even mirror. Diction at one with depiction, under the "press" of "language" either "upon"—or as a further force of—"meaning." And thus the press of language upon recognition. In response to such pressure points arises exactly the reflex action of the reading event. Same goes—goes forward in turning back on itself—with the weight of optics upon plot in screen "reading."

Dividing this book's medial attention, as I am, across markedly divergent test cases—screen kinesis versus prose, as well as two very different verbal stylists—analysis means to consider more closely the seductions of uptake (erotic or mostly otherwise) in prose narratives, including their self-flagged attention to worded form. It goes about this by juxtaposing them with a cinematic spectatorship elicited in full view, often exacerbated lately, of the historically evolved machinations of screen mirage. Both the materially reflective plane (and narrative frame) of cinematic projection and, from there out as well, the rhetorical field (and yield) of the page's imprint rectangle are recognized in part through a salient common denominator. This is their medium-unique, but structurally equivalent, means of catching attention in the very mirror of mimesis: refaceted by some glancing aspect of narrative's own stylistically articulated logic along the framing slant, or bevel, of representation. Refaceted, yes: more than, in the stricter language of prismatics, refracted.[9] At off-angles to their own plots, such reflexes can serve to clarify and even analyze each other—cinematographic over against lexigraphic effect—in the engineering of narrative response across the micromanaged gauges of cultural, political, and erotic registers in either medium of delivery. All to the end of asking again—from differing perspectives, and with by that point the earned expectation of an answer—"What's a meta for?" As in cinema study, so in literary reading: the use of that prefix—when soldered either to "fiction" or "narrative," or just as pertinently here to "text"—is only as fruitful as the use made of its operations in a given piece of literary writing. The fact that, on inspection, it does help isolate something tangibly at stake at the far extremes of contemporary fictional practice—not only in the bioetheical and geopolitical grip of Powers's mercurial erudition but in the hothouse of Baker's obsessive parodic eroticism—testifies in particular to the use of this authorial contrast in triangulating certain common moves, and commotions, in the shaping of narrative prose.

Words in Action

Mirror, mirror, off the wall. Hamlet's mirroring chiastic reminder to the players—to "suit the action to the word, the word to the action"—is comprises its own words to the wise about dramaturgic gestures in holding "the / mirror up to nature" (III.ii). Such are words that become all but tautological if translated to the time-based medium, not of classic theater or its cinematic descendants, but of fictional narrative: where the self-performed symmetry of the action/word match takes on a different sense when all action is in words to begin with. Words *are* the literary deed—seen at times to mirror the response their performance instills, to reflect on the demands they make in reading. That putative mirror of reflection is only a metaphor, of course, and misleading at that if it is allowed to imply some virtual simultaneity in the angle of incidence by which its illumination, of whatever sort, reaches us. Rather, the reflex action this book tracks is always a matter of cognitive time-lapse, however minimal. Unlike the closed anatomical circuit of stimulus-response, a metanarrative reflex requires at least some momentary lag time for recognition, if only for a split-second's second thought on the run.

If such reflection's microtextual markers have a *catalytic* effect on the narrative progress, they are nonetheless *analytic* first: a tacit parsing, even while channeling, of reaction. Or put it that, in such texts, cogitative reading encounters its own anticipatory write-up in the cogs and gear shifts of inscription itself. And if this is not just a period habit and trademark—the special province of postmodern metanarrative, say—but rather an abiding instinct of the writer/reader (performance/audience) circuit, then it is worth continuing to weigh, for a measure of their ongoing vitality, the surviving, refined, and replenished texture of such effects in contemporary fiction.

And on fiction's screen as well as page—where in each case reflex action is a mode of interpretive traction. If the medial (rather than plot) reveal is thorough enough, the formative yield from a blockbuster Hollywood spectacle may far outbid any niche-marketed interest sustained by its storyline, its merch, its gamer tie-ins. And can thus help us to name and investigate the very different measures of the meta in a literary writing that has long outlived the postmodernist zenith of the mode. So a movie doesn't have to be good to be revelatory. Further, and quite apart from aggressive special effects cinema arising alongside the puzzle-film trend, if narrative self-reference is having a low-profile comeback lately in the mainstream novel, that's only incidental to these concerns as well. The dominant interest of the medial comparison underway rests with what it *means,* in given instances rather than in a period trend, for narrative to go *meta*—and where exactly that is when arrived at. It is only then of interest, once the dynamic is specified, to wonder why again now—and in a longer view than usual. On that last point it would be silly not to admit—regarding a sensed trend toward the allegorizing of reader reaction, rather than fictional architecture, in turn-of-the-twenty-first-century American prose—that the author of a book on the apostrophized audience of Victorian fiction, *Dear Reader,* has something of a vested interest in "conscripted" attention."[10] Long ago researching such a topic, as it happens, in the heyday of autotelic postmodernism and its paranoid rather than endeared complicity with structural patterning, that earlier book's author (yours truly, Reader) might well have had his latter-day antennae out for this more dispersed recent return to encoded response. A return quite purged, however, of open reader apostrophe in the vocative case. As the novels under analysis ahead will demonstrate, the *meta* has found ways to "address" a pending fictional impact—as if to inhabit and micromanage it—rather than, in obtruded second person, calling out "in person" to its attending and endeared reader.

And thus the ongoing etymological subplot of this study is here usefully rejoined. Few terms in literary criticism, at least few big and lumbering buzzwords, may seem by now more shopworn or ho-hum than "metatextual" and its polysyllabic kind. Not just dated in their flourished examples but rusty in their tool use for even more intermittent notice. Who still cares? Though the terms can often strike one as dreary, instances can still surprise or blindside, thrill or chasten, awe or daunt. Or at least beg for estimation in their resurgence in a given swath of writing. Metafilmic too—a term too canned already, it might readily seem, even when the canister has been replaced now, under digitization, by a sleeve or disk case. This book is not devoted to, though it can't escape, revisiting these unhyphenated but decidedly two-ply terms. It needs to begin not by dodging them—these designators so intractably, even if blandly, useful in their shorthand, as many critical writers have discovered—but by exonerating this vocabulary from cliché. The effort to do so can begin by the oddly little-attended route of the prefix's own philological lineage. Such terms, yes and alas, can be pasted on indiscriminately to any fillip of confessed fictionality in literary storytelling: often dulling down the moment in question—let alone the category of effect—rather than animating a sense of its vital function. Yet given what is often being done by recent fiction (as by some of its most strenuously inventive predecessors)—done in regard to our cued engagement with the page—no other terminology, no truer blanket account, will do, at least for starters. But, then again, once spotted, the question follows about how far—or deep—the *meta* can still take us.

So etymology, again, before epistemology. In film as in fiction, the spread of associations attached to the marker *meta* slides over into a "beyond," a superplus, an over-reach from representation to the terms of its presentation. These are terms optical, formal, exhibitionary, whatever the scale of estimation involved—rather than, as commonly misunderstood, straining toward some *above*-and-beyond associated with the everyday spatial trope of a "metalevel." More like the structuralist concept of "metalanguage," the realm of language *about* language, than like the latest coinage "metadata," screen reflexivity is fully cognate with a term (withheld till now, but everywhere implicit) like "metafiction," as coined in 1970, in a book called *Fiction and the Figures of Life*, by a philosopher-novelist, William H. Gass, familiar with the *stretch* of metaphysics when probing beyond and behind the material terms of physics.[11] Such is the etymological model, with metaphysics not subsuming the world to categories but rethinking entities and fields of force at a new depth of generality and attempted principle: being, event, time, will, and the rest. In novels, such an ontology probes the being of prose fiction itself as well as its fictional beings, the latter as in one sense (recalling Gass's title) mere figures (figurations) of life: people manifested only as characters, lives as roles, and then by association careers as plots, episodes as chapters, finality as closure, and, everywhere in between, progressions as mere *passages* in prose. It is in this sense that a metafiction exceeds its own manifest parameters in some added apprehension of process itself, not rising *above* the fray of narrative but pushing beyond—and finally back behind—its surface tension to its propellant mechanism.[12] As Gass stresses in regard to such metafictions, in the brief paragraph denominating them, their function is not that of an "anti-novel" but of a more essentialized structural template upon which "other forms can be imposed" (25): not the negation but the explored condition of storytelling, including its so-called way with words.

With "realist" fiction, any look—on our part as readers—into its mirror of representation tends to see mostly straight past our reflection as performing agents to the social nature of worlds like the one we inhabit. But it is still the case, in certain slants and opacities of phrase, that we may catch a glimpse of our own attention as such. To italicize again the emphasis of this Preview's title, these are bordering slivers of envisaged reading found rimming event just "beyond" its essential narrative frame, angles of verbal incidence as mimesis grades off into disclosed semiosis, action into textual reaction, reflected picture into the reflex of processed depiction. Think of it this way: the *meta* as the *beyond* in its function as the more nearly *about*. Something is *about* when it circulates *around*, not necessarily encircling but operating in the vicinity, potentially involved, available, implicit. Regarding the *meta* as a proximate *beyond*, an activated *about*, there's a two-way pull of etymology haunting the lexical field of that very word *about* at every philological turn of its career. Open any dictionary to its entry on this preposition: "Old English *onbūtan*, from *on* 'in, on' + *būtan* 'outside of.'" X is about Y. In and out at once: approximate and respecting, orbiting and delimiting at once. And this is manifestly the case with metamedial gestures in fiction and film alike, turning the text back upon *and about* itself as function, but recognized as doing so only by the sparked engagement of interpretation.

That is why—not to dodge the buzzword but to explicate one facet of its effect—I have come to think of the reflex action of such moments (as if finding mirrored, in the representation itself, a given angle of uptake on the reader's part) the work of the *extratext*: riding in on the immediate wake of inscribed verbal event to reframe, equivocate, or escalate its reception. But this still doesn't respond to the question (nothing but examples finally could) about what recognitions in particular this extratext—or near-simultaneous aftertext—might precipitate by supplemental inference. And how it might do so in a fashion more nuanced than the closed-circuit postmodern tendency to equate "this is only a novel" with "the world, too, is only a fictional construct." Or—short of such an ontological equation and its paranoid ripple effect—but in yet another variant of the postmodern mode: "this world-building is only the work of words." The latter—as we're to see below, operating in a first and last example of this quintessential trope from an author, Powers himself, who has left it mostly behind in recent decades—is a tendency to privilege form over responsive function. Typical here is the way in which the hermetic architecture of the narrative construct in his *The Gold Bug Variations* (1991)—however polyphonic and even ultimately collaborative it may appear in that one landmark novel—remains an imposed formal pattern (theme and schematic variation) rather than the naturally unfolding account of an independently imagined world. If not plastered on, the thirty subdivisions are hardly intrinsic either. It is a case of intertextual format getting lifted to prominence over the plotted action of character or the invested activation of scene by reading.

Even in briefly revisiting the multiplex work of *Variations*, it is easy to see the novel's watershed status at the start of the 1990s on the cusp of—whatever we are to call it—metafiction's aftermath or its posterity. This most famous novel by Powers—while featuring the usual technological savvy, radiant scientific learning, musicological and mathematical flair, and intense information-age saturation of his prose—also represents one of his most resolute metanarratives. And thus represents itself as such. In this respect it is bound up, as book form, in its unfolding structural composition as roving biographical narrative: site-mapping its own hybrid architecture—rather than being turned back (troped) in reflex upon its verbally charged phenomenological force as read. Announced by title alone, the novel's own novelty is both derivative and a reshuffling: a structure metatextual by way of intertextual mash-up. For *The Gold Bug Variations* puts Poe's tactical code-breaking in the famous story of cryptanalysis, "The Gold Bug," back to back with Bach's aesthetic version of the permutable, the famous thirty-stage Goldberg Variations, is a narrative rumination upon their shared mathematized progeny in the DNA code. It plays out as a plot divided across a parallel terrain to Bach's thirty recursions, begun and ended with an "aria" that, on Powers's page, seems not just an integral part but an anagrammed inset of the work's own plural, its incremental and recursive *varia*.

The principles Jan and Franklin, estranged lovers, have both become obsessed with retrieving the unheralded saga of genomic pioneer Stuart Ressler, whose story—we're slowly let recognize—we've been reading from their divided perspectives. In Jan's voice at first, about the scientist's childless death: "The trial run is over, Dr. Ressler dead, his molecule broken up for parts, leaving no copies" (11). If he is to be traced, it can only be in words. And it turns out, nearly 600 of our pages later, that the plot's former lovers, separated because Jan refuses children, have each produced their transcripts instead. Code-shifting, yes, from DNA to prose—and flexing its springs for an extra and encompassing release. For here Franklin proffers—not in so many words, but the trope is entirely forthright—that they merge their linguistically (rather than genetically) coded fecundity in order to disseminate their findings about Ressler in a collaborative text. The hero stresses, as if with the Powers title in mind, that his former lover is "sitting on a gold mine" (637). The time is right: "Come on. Let's do it. Let's make a baby" (638). In illustration, he has just mimed an interleaving of the two projects as a dynamic textual coupling: "He made a great show of collating, a little courtship-dance of paper-shuffling to win me again" (637). The proposed result would indeed resemble a novel like the one we've just read, fugue-like in its own way, that has textured its interleaved storyline in highly variable units of discursive focus dealt out in alternate patterns and emphases. Proleptically, then, as if the lover's plea were the foregone conclusion of our own reading so far: "Come on," cajoles Franklin: "A few edits, a little cut-and-paste… " (637). At which point Jan refigures his vision of such scissoring in the idiom not of editorial metaphor but of genomics itself: "I believe 'splicing' is the bioengineers term of choice" (637). Regardless of lingo, the hint that we have been deciphering, in effect, a pastiche of two commemorative biographies in one, via a process dialogic, multivocal, and generative, offers up the very idea of this would-be aftertext as in fact the novel's belated user's manual: retrospective guide to its own variable point of view in a dual-focus hybrid mode.

Operating here as a kind of swan song to the postmodern metatext, this work by Powers leads, nonetheless, almost three decades later, to the eight-part plotting of *The Overstory* (2018), which negotiates its portrayed botanical ecosphere in order to thematize—as if under cover of its more conventional metafictional title—a radically broader agenda of materialized linguistic reading and nonverbal decipherment. This includes the implicit ethics of legibility in the transhuman system of biology's message circuits, the epiphanies of their asemantic decoding, and what one is ultimately tempted to read as the *echology* of their prose manifestation from phrase to cross-fibered phrase. It is here, as a kind of summa for Powers's *scientia* of storytelling, that one recognizes, even more forcefully than before, how it is—among the insurgent technical energies, and resulting interpretive urgencies, of his "scientific fiction"—that what claims real priority in his prose is the organic (and evolving) science of language itself. As obliquely sign-posted by title in this case, the reflex action in a Powers novel is typically metalinguistic in the inferences of its overview. When William Gass speaks of the *meta* at large, in and beyond prose fictions, as a case of "lingoes about lingoes" (24), he thus helps us understand how the specialized botanical term for the often thickly compacted (and even sometimes composted) underlay of a forest floor, in the entwined storage of its "understory," could, without any explicit fanfare, serve in *The Overstory* to generate a reflection on the intricate plotting of the novel itself. And not least in this most lingocentric of all contemporary novelists.

In the work of writers coming of age, or into their own, since Thomas Pynchon, then Don DeLillo (again to name but two canonical placeholders in the precincts of metafiction), certain structural ingenuities have grown looser in expression, more vernacular, though with recognition still exerted back upon text in the maintenance of both plot and thematic impetus—but less in the solemnity of metanarrative world-building (however paranoid or black-comic) than in the slipstream of search-culture and its proliferating encyclopedic terminologies. Amid the continuing ambition of American writing in a certain intellectual tradition, Powers does clearly, along with the equally intrepid, droll, and occasionally recondite Baker, represent—and in this respect sharing in one aspect of DeLillo's legacy—the novelist as sentence-dedicated *writer*, as verbal maker. This is an authorship devoted not to the "poetry" of the novel, or even its drama, but to its narrative medium as such, where languages colloquial and arcane jostle each other—sometimes within a single phrase, even a single syllabic turn of word—so as to snare unawares, and captivate, the attentive response that plot may not yet have caught up with. In the case of Powers and Baker as anchors as much as polar contrasts, then, this "second wave" study of the literary *meta* is written out of a revived sense of the mode's inherent critical fascination—but only in light of recent narrative writing that is itself committed to resuscitating its pleasures at an unexpected stylistic scale, where the knowing phrase is cast up in the emphasized frame of its own transmission. And this in initial comparison with equivalent technical disclosures in screen reception. The fact that such different medial reflexes could exert themselves with comparable force, at the level of narrative's molecular production rather than its received mimetic depiction, goes to show how vulnerable the substrate of each medium is to revelation, to self-disclosure. This book plays on just such vulnerabilities as reflexive tests of attention.

And it does so against the logic of bibliographic chronology in the laboratory of Powers's prose. It attempts instead an interpretive paring down from that late multi-plot structure of *The Overstory*, through the earlier double-plot conception of *Plowing the Dark*, to the third example (and fifth chapter), where a more linear novel is rendered deliberately unstable in its very through-line. This is the oddly named *Generosity: An Enhancement*, developing its conflation of writing and plotting around, at first, the teaching anxiety of its failed-writer hero in the creative nonfiction classroom. What results is impossible to miss as a writer's deep storytelling *animus*—this in both the positive and negative valences of that Latinate term: motivation and hostility alike, eros and resistance. So it is, for the sequencing of this study, that the verbally echoic multi-plotting of Powers's latest work in *The Overstory*, taken up first, offers more a clarifying anatomy than a culmination: a schematic regridding of the novelist's typical considerations that can help guide us through a staged crisis of coherence (in the bifurcated plot trajectories of *Plowing*) to the uneven energies of story's immediate scriptive force as its own kind of *generosity,* its own mode of temporal *enhancement*. It is by this route that plot, or say overplot, however global, however manifold and overweaning, can nonetheless be tracked for its verbal "understory" in the extratext of its uptake. At which point the illuminating metalingual contrast between Powers and Baker can be fully brought to bear in the final chapter. From the learned scintillations of the one writer to the lewd and lurid titillations of the other, verbal invention does the heavy lifting. From the *syntactics* of each, so to say, and always in the grain of their saying, what emerges is an oddly demanding *reflexicon*.

On another question of sequence, suffice it to say the entitling conjunction of "fiction" and "film" in these chapters, despite the predominance of the former mode of prose narrative, came to seem most instructive in reverse exemplification. This is because the conceptual reframings of montage now summarized in the first two chapters—effects designed quite literally to reflect upon the optical faceting of cinema as a medium in reception—serve best in economically distilling the technique\text/context template for what follows regarding the "apparatus" of prose as well. More specifically, it is by the path of such comparative clarification—with film's medial reveals considered before those of prose narrative—that we can best track many of the more subtly self-flagged phrasal anomalies of our paired test-case authors over the evolving invention of their long careers. More specifically yet, given the risks of temporary narrative dismantlement run by such prose, these often blindsiding verbal turns align intriguingly with the common micro-dimension of image generation entailed in a post-postmodern strain of puzzle films—with their strategically imploded screen conditions—proliferating during these same years.

In the narrative phenomenology of invested attention, words may thus be found to deliver the same wrench to unexamined narrative succession as images can manage in default of transparent optic continuity in the corkscrew twists of mind-game cinema—or the paler surprises of their cousin digital blockbusters. When I spoke earlier of such moments as parables of their inherent process, that was to suggest, as well, their function as an ongoing monitor of your own participation. It is in this way that attention's most oblique prompts may be reflected back to you, from page or screen, as the very event of wording or imaging within the implicit picture—or say the variably faceted mirror—of response. At the height of a postwar literary Modernism constellated around the *nouveau roman*, Roland Barthes meditated famously on the "pleasure of the text," its potential joys narrative and realist on the one hand, linguistic and granular on the other.[13] What in the wake of postmodernism (this book may be taken to ask) are the residual pleasures of the metatext, lingering and refigured? And what happens when any instigated delight becomes less a structuring frame than an aftertide of prose motion—or sometimes, on the recent digitized screen, in its own right a tech-heavy disappointment and dead end?

Such a study isn't on the scent of some radical new dimensions or parameters of the *meta* since Pynchon or DeLillo, Fellini or Bergman, or even just a lower-voltage continuation of the same. It concerns instead what has always gone on in reading and viewing around and between any deliberate signposts of fictive superstructure. This tightly framed scale of attention is certainly prolonged into a new century with subtle intent and various intensifications at the level of prose rhythm itself by Powers and, quite differently, by Baker—each less hampered, of course, by industrial imperatives than even the most independent and inventive recent filmmakers. But none of it is unprecedented. Worth repeating, then: well before the texts in either medium to be examined in the following chapters, it was always the case that "around and between" the obvious scaffolded signage of generic metafiction circulated the quieter force of other metanarrative signaling on screen and page. Even in the heyday of cross-media reflexivity, that is, one wasn't only on the lookout for those this-is-just-a-movie moments—as for instance in a given director's 8½ such movie (Fellini), or another's manipulation of star actresses as one shared persona (Bergman). One was more intimately primed by subsidiary screen effects as well, in these same films and others: primed for noticing the ways in which just that intrinsic movieness was being extruded and mused upon in process. In the hinged space of print text, of course, the imagined "world" of a brandished and bracketed metafiction, or some expansive postmodern Underworld, is only a book-bound terrain to begin with: without the mimetic conviction of cinema. Yet the readerly act of traversing it means noticing, and noticing meanings in, particular and curious textures underfoot. Such is the ground of verbal process that at once traces and impedes all pretensions to any experienced horizon farther afield than the vanishing point of the bound pages' own crevasse.

No radical new dimensions or parameters, as I say. The plan is instead to proceed by scrutinized samples—but contrastive ones, and at different, mutually illuminating scales. Two of our reigning media, two of our reigning literary experimenters, are on both fronts chosen to triangulate certain reflex impulses of recognition incident to the thrown switch of "reading" by any name. Whether or not enhanced by bifocals or 3D glasses, this is a reading whose very image of attention tends to be caught off angle in any demanding metanarrative's hall of interpretive mirrors. A study like this gets its tailwind, then, not from the distance behind it of any similarly themed monograph, decades back now, about metafictional films and novels, still less from the aerial overview it might achieve on such a transmedial landscape since. The grounds of comparison between viewing and reading are in this case more closely mapped and site-specific, since ultimately this is not so much a comparative media study as it is a cross-sectional approach to the reading of mediation itself in the quite different texts it generates. The issue is not the avowed metafiction but the discernible turn within the execution of any plotted text when fictional inscription, optical or verbal, goes, however momentarily, metanarrative. Those last five syllables are thus more useful here as an adjective than a noun. In this call-and-response of story's mirroring surfaces, it is a double sense of *reflection*, then, material and mental, that identifies both what text seems picturing back to you of your own coached response and, in the very process, the work you do in making this out.

Notes

1 Or one might add—in addition to McCarthy among the prose writers (more recent than Cather and Nabokov) whose styles are explored by Lee Clark Mitchell in *Mere Reading: A Poetics of Wonder in Modern American Fiction* (New York: Bloomsbury Academic, 2017)—his attention to Marilynne Robinson and Junot Diaz.

2 The dominant literary focus of the present study has in fact set out to reverse the priority of its closest (and historically distant) predecessor—as well as redefining the terrain for more recent decades. Originally published in 1985 (Ann Arbor, MI: UMI Research Press), and later reprinted well into the waning of the mode, film scholar Robert Stam's *Reflexivity in Film and Literature: From Don Quixote to Jean Luc-Godard* (New York: Columbia University Press, 1992) is concerned primarily, despite the literary anchor of its subtitle, with films of the European modernist tradition from the 1960s and 1970s, taking up literature primarily via its film adaptations in the case of *Tom Jones*, *Lolita*, and *The French Lieutenant's Woman*.

3   For my sense of "apparatus reading," see *Cinemachines: An Essay on Media and Method* (Chicago, IL: University of Chicago Press, 2020) as well inferences for a "cinematographic style" in the narrative manipulations of "Fframe-advance" [*sic*], macro and micro, in *The Ways of the Word: Episodes in Verbal Attention* (Ithaca, NY: Cornell University Press, forthcoming 2021), where I mean to evoke in that coinage the linked scales of photo frames on the celluloid strip and the screen Frame (upper case) they generate. In light of the convergent approaches represented in those studies, and to account for the residual effects of medial reflexivity in (by now) a half-century's afterlife of metafictional reverberations, my discussion here moves to the text-triggered audience registrations of style itself—verbal and visual technique alike—involved in the reflex action called upon at times in the process(ing) of fiction's ingrained microplots. Such operations of "narratography"—coined not by way of a scientific or philosophical suffix like "narratology," but on the inscriptive or technical model of "cinematography" or "seismography"—operates as the mapping out of such minimal textual signals in the responsive cartography, as it were, of viewing or reading. The scale of this intuitive micro-reading is the subject, for separate media, of my earlier "companion volumes" *Framed Time: Toward a Postfilmic Cinema* and, with a fuller articulation of the concept, *Novel Violence: A Narratography of Victorian Fiction* (Chicago, IL: University of Press, 2007, 2009).

4   These are claims about the transition from epistemology to ontology—as literary-historical markers in the transformation of twentieth-century literature—first launched by Brian McHale in *Postmodernist Fiction* (London: Methuen, 1987), as adjusted and pursued in *Constructing Postmodernism* (New York: Routledge, 1992): the earlier book stressing a period tendency, the later a historicizing construal (to some extent arbitrary) of the period itself. For a subsequent anthology looking back on major position papers from the period, see Mark Currie, ed., *Postmodern Narrative Theory* (London: Longman, 1995).

5   Baker's case for the "inclusionist" versus "deletionist" approach appears in "The Charms of Wikipedia" in the March 20, 2008 issue of the *New York Review of Books*. For his diatribe against the digitization of library archives, see *Double Fold: Libraries and the Assault on Paper* (New York: Random House, 2001).

6   Thomas Elsaesser's much-cited essay on "The Mind-Game Film," in *Puzzle Films: Complex Storytelling in Contemporary Cinema*, ed. Warren Buckland (Oxford: Blackwell, 2009), 13–41, to which discussion returns in Chapter 2, has since appeared in a posthumous volume: Elsaesser, *The Mind-Game Film: Distributed Agency, Time Travel, and Productive Pathology*, ed. Warren Buckland, Dana Polan, Seung-hoon Jeong (New York: Routledge, 2021). Most of the turn-of-the millennium sci-fi releases discussed in Elsaesser's original 2009 publication had been treated in similar terms, though with more emphasis on digital effects, in

my own *Framed Time: Toward a Postfilmic Cinema* (n. 3 above), with two major additions since, Tony Scott's *Déjà vu* (2006) and Duncan Jones's *Source Code* (2011), taken up in Stewart, *Closed Circuits: Screening Narrative Surveillance* (Chicago, IL: University of Chicago Press, 2015).

7   Under a title nicely designed to capture both the volume and the valence of the intellectual energy behind such work—as the prolific output of identified prodigies, with a special emphasis on the information-age complexity of Powers's scientific meditations—see Tom LeClair, "The Prodigious Fictions of Richard Powers, William Vollman, and David Foster Wallace," *Critique: Studies in Contemporary Fiction* 38, no. 1 (tandfonline.com), 12–37.

8   Don DeLillo, 1993 interview, www.theparisreview.org/interviews/1887/don-dellilo-the-art-of-fiction-no-135-don-dellilo (accessed October 1, 2021). For a fuller discussion of his phonetic aesthetic in this interview, see Stewart, *The Value of Style in Fiction* (New York: Cambridge University Press, 2018), 122–6. Yet DeLillo's sense of the sentence as a field of play rather than a structured element is to be contrasted with a stricter sense of its determining grammatical format in Jan Mieszkowski's *Crises of the Sentence* (Chicago, IL: University of Chicago Press, 2019).

9   A comparable set of metaphors in cinema scholar Timothy Corrigan's *The Essay Film: From Montaigne, After Marker* (New York: Oxford University Press, 2011) accompanies a very different emphasis on discursive reflexivity. Instead of the fabled mimetic "mirror," Corrigan's avowed model for certain kinds of essay films is a multiple and interlocking "chain of mirrors" (191). Corrigan's fullest analogy: "Like the beam of light sent through a glass cube, refractive cinema breaks up and disperses the art or object it engages, splinters or deflects it in ways that leave the original work drifting across a world outside" (191). By contrast, the oblique "deflection" involved in the present study's stylistic "angles of incidence" doesn't skew image or word directly into prismatic refractions of context so much as slant such indicators, on the bias, back upon their own self-reflecting terms of interpretation: say glints rather than "splinters."

10 Garrett Stewart, *Dear Reader: The Conscripted Audience of Nineteenth Century British Fiction* (Baltimore, MD: Johns Hopkins University Press, 1996).

11 William H. Gass, *Fiction and the Figures of Life* (New York: Knopf, 1970), 24–5. His coinage was widely taken up by studies of narrative form in the period, first (a prolific decade in such fiction writing later) with Linda Hutcheon's notion of a period-defining "historiographic metafiction" in *Narcissistic Narrative: The Metafictional Paradox* (Waterloo, ON: Wilfrid Laurier University Press, 1980), and then in Patricia Waugh's *Metafiction: The Theory and Practice of Self-Conscious Fiction* (London: Methuen, 1984), each a spur to Brian McHale's ongoing work (n. 4 above), as summed up in his chiastic quip that "where once we had theories

about narrative, now we have stories about theory" (*Constructing Postmodernism*, 4). There is scarcely a purer example of this, as Chapter 2 will sample it, than Richard Powers's own 1983 first novel *Three Farmers on the Way to a Dance,* an extended ekphrasis on a famous photograph whose meditations are tucked into a Benjaminian philosophical and historical treatise on automatic imaging. In broader terms, apart from that pointed irony of McHale's, the period's self-conscious ontology of plot formats was particularly amenable, it should be noted, to structuralist models in narrative form that dominated discussion during the reign of this metafictive genre—especially the discourse/story paradigm—whereby the reflexive moment can be understood to mark a leveling overlap of pictured world and the flagged maneuvers of its depiction.

12 The tendency toward a solidification of the vertical model, with its notion of a meta*level* (rather than my alternate sense of a bevel) is apparent by mid-decade, five years after Gass's coinage, with the "sur" ("above") of experimental novelist Raymond Federman's anthology *Surfiction: Fiction Now and Tomorrow* (Chicago, IL: Swallow Press, 1975).

13 Roland Barthes, *The Pleasure of the Text* (New York: Hill and Wang, 1975), trans. Richard Miller, to be returned to in more detail in Chapter 6 in conjunction with Baker's strange antiseptic eroticism.

1

Picture Shows

Mirror Mirror Mirror. It is surely among the handful of most famous shots in American film history. And single shots at that, taken in by a slowly drifting camera. Charles Foster Kane (in the person of Orson Welles—or vice versa, in the mirror of screen impersonation), deserted by his wife and destroying her bedroom in a blind fury, then trudges robotically past the byzantine arched moldings of a vast hall of mirrors in his mansion as the camera tracks his rightward dead march ("cited" below[1]). But wait—back that up, not in reverse action but in the retracing of its flamboyant optic recess in those Xanadu mirrors. Rather than lumbering numbly past the camera in a steady rightward motion, Kane immediately disappears frame left behind a pillar, the camera holding in place until his mirror image emerges from that stone occlusion into the drop-back of its optic recess. It is only then that his actual body (though it is one existential notch harder, now, to think of it that way) follows behind, and up on, the reflected double into a nearer close-up on his stricken person as sole (but already visually compromised) anchor of this infinite regress. After its initial lateral glide, the clean-edged rectangular bordering of the camera aperture is stabilized only at this turning point in the record of external motion. Its mediating lens is now passively asserted against (though in figurative association with) the inset Moorish framing of the other reflective surfaces receding inside its own light-receptive mechanical portal. And what is reflected upon first of all, cinematographically, at this late point in the film—"beyond" and "behind" (those crucial *meta* positionings by preposition) the psychological irony of the splintered subject—is the character's optical as well as human superficiality. The titular protagonist is thereby satirized in this one shot by an inspired lampoon of the narrative's whole deep-focus aesthetic, a true shallowness exposed by replication in plane.

This gripping two-stage ocular parable of subtracted spatial presence—and its renewal as embodied image—has remade the abyssal hall of mirrors on the spot. These momentarily imprisoning parallel mirrors take their place not just as a generalized figure for cinema, in its function as an apparatus for secondary imaging, but as a metanarrative mirror of the film's abiding irony as fictional biopic. In this way the famous emblematics of this late camerawork joins earlier ironies of just this sort, narrative but also optic. The film's antihero Kane—seldom more than a mere image, even to himself—has earlier been mirrored in dancing celebration (phantom-like, as mobile vanishing point) in the reflective window glass of his newspaper office between the flanking heads of his two chief minions in debate over his motives and methods. Moreover, this redoubling (even while thinning) of image is a motif of derivative rectangular depiction that has been with the film from the beginning of its real plot. It is sprung there from the jump-cut launch of the narrative's epistemological quest by our drastically sudden side view of the screen on which the working draft of Kane's documentary obit (for "News on the March") is blaringly projected in the production screening room—in all its superficial thinness, material and journalistic. And beyond a first sense of the iconic mogul in repeated ironic reduction to a skin-deep optic mirage, this film-before-the-film is one to which all subsequent montage answers as *meta*cinema—in deep-focus tropes *about* its own contrastive powers of penetration. So it is that this canted angle on the newsreel screen delimits, by synecdoche, the whole outward field of the movie's beveled narrative mirroring. This is the frame of reflex reference through which we see not just the eponymous American tycoon but, at our own spectatorial off-angle, the exposed celebrity fetish of a mass attention that the imaged fictional Kane shares, for instance, with movie stars (like Welles) in their larger-than-life aura, optic duplication, and limitless visual distribution. All these camera-angle trick reframings (in reverse order across *Kane*'s plot: mirror, window, screen) serve in this way to anticipate the template proposed and developed below. For in these optic ironies, medial *technique* directs each episode of narrative *text* toward its reflex *context* not just as machinated specular object but as part of a star-gazing American mythography in visual realization.

When mapped from fiction onto supposed biographical forensics in the documentary picture show within *Citizen Kane*, what can such a mere set of edited pictures really show? And show forth about their own process in doing so? How, within the larger frame of *Kane*'s narrative fiction, do we understand thematically the actual trajectory of optical replication, including the place of both reflective glass and that earlier sideways screen within the broader pattern of iconic newspaper shots and election posters? The vectors of irony are quite pointedly ours to track: from inaugural inset screen *acutely* viewed, even if obliquely read—debunking the metaphoric windowed vista on history it might be thought to simulate—through the enforced reminder of superimposed reflection rather than transparency in that triangulated office shot midway through the plot. From there, with that ocular pivot point of public man versus mere image, visual narrative drives on down, right before the end, to the synecdochic nadir of Kane's disintegrated authenticity in that later hall of mirrors that *is* Xanadu. Dead-ending there, however, is not just the stark replication of a factitious public profile in multiple optic delivery. Although the mirror recession is angled just barely to miss the camera operator's exposed position in our mediated place, what we see all but "captured" nonetheless—at a calculated angle of viewer implicature—is the raw fascination of our own spectatorship at risk of being thrown back in our face: in reflective recognition. A reflex that this book's "Afterthoughts" will borrow the technical term "angle of incidence" to identify as a case of incident taken up on the slant by reception, in prose as well as on screen. What we're teased with the chance of seeing in *Kane*, at a just deflected angle, is not of course our own personal image in this nesting of mirrors. Implicated instead, in any such near-miss breaching of the film's so-called fourth wall, may be no less than a *glancing* reminder of a certain naïve hope. Restaged in this suddenly focalized zone of our own tacit watching, such is the expectation we may have long been harboring about this narrative film, if not the skin-deep "News on the March" inside it: that it may somehow manage to single out the "real Kane" from his mass media image.

Terminology is of no decisive help in all this—except when placed under investigation in its own right. Metacinema? Even for starters, the tired quip (unlike Powers's canny metalinguistic twist in the Preview's epigraph) takes us nowhere: I never met a cinema I didn't like. For one thing, its categorical ambiguity gets immediately in the way: cinema as place versus visual event, movie palace versus motion picture, screen site versus screened sights. Though preventing the jejune wordplay, *metafilmic* will no longer do, either, in marking certain moments of self-reflexivity in motion pictures, since the pictures move via pixels now rather than filmic frames, algorithmic code rather than celluloid units. More flamboyantly all the time, movies are post-filmic. Even in the consideration of mainstream cinema, then, a sense of the *meta* needs to be more specific (medium-specific) about material causes as well as narrative gestures or their extra-textual reverberations. More medium savvy—as the first step toward answering, in Powers's terms, the nagging "what," in a given case, "is the meta for?" Any one "film" (as such projections are still atavistically called), or say each movie, is of course unique—even as it may choose to avow, or generalize about, its own status as image system, narrative format, or cultural artifact.

Adducing just those three aspects in adjacency and overlap—image flow, storyline, sociopolitical or commercial embeddedness—is the agenda of this establishing chapter in its promotion of a technique\text/context model. Parsing the traditional picture show in this way focuses on how cinematic motion, with its machine-gunning of images, pictures its dramatic narrative show only by a typical elision of exactly the separate frames that nonetheless sometimes show through. It is in this sense that the anomalous manifestations—these apparitions of the apparatus—seem to have exceeded what they narratively constitute: to have become *meta*. But even then the unique nodes—rather than just modes—of such acknowledgment or generalization are too various to categorize, and sometimes too intertwined to isolate. Increasingly in Hollywood blockbuster cinema, for instance, the palpable force of "production values" tends to collapse a narrative's admitted status as socially lodged commercial product into its material generation as heavily capitalized digital composite. And quite apart from brandished CGI (computer generated images) in cases of their manifest financial outlay, cinema has often tipped its technical hand in more traditional ways as well. Familiar forms of dissolve, match cut, slow motion, rear projection, what have you, are to be numbered, especially when exaggerated, among the most pointed local triggers of cinema's reflexive recognitions in the movies-about-movies vein—when that category is understood more broadly than just to include backlot narrative storylines. And to speak of such a tipped hand is, of course, to imply the kind of narrative reflex that, in the momentary override (or revealed underwriting) of plot, often gestures back to the structuring technical image even while beyond it to supplemental cinematic inferences for the sociopolitical setting—or reception—of the story thus visualized.

A question is therefore left open. What "about" the movies—in such metacinematic recognition—is being noted or negotiated? About which conditions of their existence as motion pictures do the techniques of visual generation, the arcs of plot, or some third term of socioeconomic context tend to deliver a reflexive inference? Or ask again what, in the first of the threefold distinctions floated above, a given film can (to repeat the triad) work to manifest about "its own status as image system, narrative format, or cultural artifact"? Put otherwise—though still with an emphasis on that orienting division of labor—to what possibilities does a given screen effect, text, or cultural (as well as corporate) product tend to revert, turn back upon in reflex? The issue can't be determined in advance, but the embedded structural mirror—if that's the way we envision it—is likely to be angled in one of those three suggested directions: toward pronounced visuals, narrative pressures, or industrial dissemination within a monetized social arena. Optical process, story, manufacture and distribution: these, then, anchor the artifact in its theatrical display—even while, with that prototypical scene from *Kane* in mind, mirroring our own implicated interest if not captured gaze. Materiality, narrative depiction, exhibitionary circuit in its full social intent: such a cross-section can, of course, be variously sliced and tested. Traversing at once the image function, the plot generated by it, and its public interface, one may therefore cut the distinctions, if seldom cleanly, this way: screen *technique* as medial delivery system, narrative *text* as audiovisually articulated storyline, and circulation *context* as communal space of reception. This division pertains even as that third public dimension may open out by allusion to the broader surround of its own spectatorial moment in relation to mass culture or political climate at large, let alone to the spread of technologies, suspect or otherwise, closely akin to cinema's own computer visualizations.

In my four books on narrative cinema in particular, rather than on the broader aesthetics of time-based imagery, few episodes of concentrated discussion have ever been more than a page or two away from some measure of metacinematic uptake or speculation of this sort: regarding first, in *Between Film and Screen*, the technological evolution of celluloid film from its chemical and mechanical basis in photography, as evinced by the recursive returns of that still medium within the screen image; next, in *Framed Time*, concerning the transformation of screen practice in a post-filmic cinema's new orientation (among other cognitive adjustments, both in frame shifts and in narrative topics) toward the much-debated "time-image" in the work of Gilles Deleuze; then, in *Closed Circuits*, focusing on the relation of fictional visualization to surveillance—frame to frame-up, montage to espionage, passive spectatorship to bodies spy/eyed upon inside the narrative world—including all the inset secondary screens (increasingly the banks of remote digital monitors) arrayed to thematize just this correlation; and then, in *Cinemachines*, involving an explicitly methodological reassessment, under the name "apparatus reading," of the approach I had come to call "narratography."[2] In this mode of applied narratology, the apparatus itself becomes legible in tracking the microplots articulated by disclosed gestures of cinematographic device—what Stanley Cavell calls "assertions in technique"[3]—and not least in their reflexive connection to the wider inferences of screen imaging as cultural production. After that book's renewed emphasis on the machinations of the celluloid, then digital, apparatus in sustaining and inflecting the cinematic mirage, the present effort is to widen further the purview in categorizing the basic threefold range of metacinematic features that this shifting image system tends to foreground. And to do so in preparation for the cross-mapping of this template, in the more extensive readings of later chapters, onto the manner by which verbal technique as well, in the form of literary style, inflects narrative text toward the extralinguistic issues of historical and social context in and beyond the delimited fictive world.

Metamedial: A Sliding Scale

Again the partitioned but interpenetrating template in this spectrum analysis: the materiality of *technique*; its manifestation as *text* at the narrative level; its *contextual* reverberation in industrial production or programmed reception (contemporaneous allusions included, where text finds its dominant terms of interpretation). Traditional narrative cinema can actually be understood as *medial* (because mediating) in all three dimensions—and directions: whether pointed inward to the technology of its material support, forward along the narrative arc of its storytelling conveyance (genre included), or outward to mediating context (industrial distribution, on the one hand, or political topicality, on the other). Increasingly, as noted, this third register may also appear to be pointing back again—inwards—at the same time, via the manufactured audiovisual composite, to scrutinized material conditions: as when a movie is found adverting to—and advertising—its own implicit CGI budget in relation to a broader spectrum of computer technology in social deployment. (Much more below.)

So it is worth stressing, up front, the slippage not just from technique to text to context, but the comparable drift, exerting a reverse pressure upon narrative textuality, when some tacit contextual surround is understood first of all via technical reflex: edging the inference of the narrative toward a zone of auto-imaging that connects in that way with the round and *about* of metacinema as structuring given. So what sort of thing does narrative have to project, if not explicitly to say, about the medium by which it is manifested, either technically or industrially? (It is, one should anticipate here, this same question that we'll be asking about wording in prose fiction as this study proceeds: how it isolates itself for scrutiny in the name of the world on which it reports.) Once plastic and electric in the era of celluloid mechanics, since then electronic and pixel-driven—and often showcased as such in either phase—this technical aspect of the motion picture medium has perhaps never been more baldly asserted than in recent franchise cinema. Canonical formalism speaks of "baring the device," exposing the works of a given work. That sense of device isn't limited to technique. All three dimensions of reflexivity proposed here have their way of devising their own bearings in response, orienting us as we go. In the exponential computerization of the Hollywood action picture, certainly, an overt subterfuge of CGI in the deployment of VFX (visual special effects) can be readily exposed, then reincorporated, by some denaturalized twist of narrative sequence that may also incorporate a knowing sidelong nod at genre slotting or cultural intertext. All may reflect back on cinematic operations in a formative if not formalist manner.

Even if one were to force the proposed dovetailed triad involved in metacinematic registration (technical\textual/contextual) into the more familiar formalist dichotomy of form versus content, style versus substance, all subtlety of gradation would not be lost. When movies are found reflecting on either their manufacture as image system or their manifold narrative infrastructure, the either/or doesn't stay put. In undoing this dichotomy, for instance, there is always the "content of the form"—where densities of style spill over to narrative increments in their own right; or, in turn, the form of the content—where broader structuring functions of genre and social coding come into play. So we're back with the triadic schema after all: call it, under a specifying adjustment, technique\text/intertext, with that third term locating the very process of contextual inference—and with the narrative reflexes of the textual system pointing either out toward it or back upon the material and montage *techne* of plot's own composition. And while we're at it, in this consideration of a formative versus a formalist logic, note how one may rethink another structuralist touchstone in cinema studies that folds any bared device back into narrative as an adjunct of operational process. In David Bordwell's influential definition of screen *narration*, as opposed to the extractable narratives it transmits, "Narration is the process whereby the film's *sjuzhet* and style [sequential structure plus technique] interact in the process of cueing and channeling the spectator's construction of the *fabula* [the fable, the story]."[4] Under the adjusted lens of the threefold refraction I'm proposing, style can momentarily divert structure, away from its ongoing story function—and thus back to the reflexive exhibition of screen narration's own technical provisions. So, too, may screen story at any moment reveal, by metanarrative aside, its shaping conditions in certain contextual rather than technical "cues" that also operate in "channeling" further inferences—industrial and social alike—beyond the formatting of plot. But not without reflecting (upon)—with those "cues" turned clues—the viewer's intrinsic and "constructive" role in the generation of image as event. As Richard Powers will be quick to notice in his remarks on contributory viewing in early cinema, as noted in the next chapter, montage is both the mirage of action and the mirror of viewer involvement.

In all this, one level of self-reflection may well transgress upon and energize another. The reactive leverage entailed can give new purchase on theme or its cultural memes. That leverage, that "moment" in its sense from physics, is precisely the reflex exertion at stake in metacinematic detection. But "precisely" is too easy there—except on a case-by-case basis. How does one really think the *meta* in self-reflexivity? As already tested in the Preview, an etymo/logical consideration is one suggestive step: yielding (in one random dictionary case) a definition of "meta" as "'after,' 'along with,' 'beyond,' 'among,' 'behind.'" When translated to the field (or plane) of the screen's material origins and effects, that array of prepositions samples the various pre-positioning (or premising) aspects of the cinematic condition (however defined) in regard to the multifaceted screen object. This is the *meta* in its full shifting spread of manifestation. *After* but *along with*: the so-called internal supplement, where some cinematic self-acknowledgment completes the narrative picture. *Beyond, among, behind*: exceeding while underlying and interleaved: a certain broad sense of underlay or support (electronic substrate, generic format, financial backing, cultural moment, etc.) made immanent on screen. We may well ask of a given optical crux or trick, for instance, "What could be behind that effect?" In so doing, we are not necessarily hoping to separate technical process from surface result. Rather, we may seek to weld them more persuasively at the level of discerned inference.

Recall here the rhetorical device of metalepsis—as when authors suddenly appear in the role of speaking characters in their own stories, intervening to interrogate another character or to redirect the action. First cause is thereby manifest in a secondary effect, at the narrative rather than stylistic level in that mode of author interpolation—or its more common kindred effects on screen. Famously in film, or infamously, a character's breaching the "fourth wall" by apostrophizing the audience is one way to expose the public-address system of cinema at large—as a set of directed narrative messages, couched ordinarily in dramatic enunciations, and rendered commercially available in the transmit of projection. But there are, of course, other disclosures of cause in effect, technical rather than overtly rhetorical, that pivot cinema back on itself in reflexive twists within the narrative flux—and then outward at the viewing, the viewing function, if never of course the individual viewer, that brings these to notice. Other disclosures: many, innumerable, and not easy to categorize. But the effort alone can be clarifying.

So far, this chapter has been organized to correlate related terminological distinctions across several sliding triadic scales, all of them parallel to each other in their linkages. With each triad separately, the adjacency—or tangency—of emphasis locates a latent transposition from one zone of notice to another: call it an internal "othering" of cognitive strata. Such an othering of effect from within its own manifestation is what may well give rise to a sense of these metacinematic nodes as allegorical: not just figuring forth some cinematic given but emblematizing it in the form of a circumscribed minor parable. The dictionary's received wisdom once more: "*allēgoria*, from *allos* 'other' + *-agoria* 'speaking.'" And since, etymologically again, the "behind," "beneath," and "after" of the *meta*, as well as the "among" and "between," are all versions of the other within—operating as flashpoints of resident alienation on the dematerialized underside of unfolding process—it should be clear how metacinema often comes across as a mode of auto-allegory.

The variable bandwidths of registration distinguishing the technique\text/context nexus are not hierarchical or even topological; they are logical, categorical, and thus permeable—open across each other's delineations (not borders) to a perception analogical or metaphoric. One may best think of the schemata here in terms of Venn diagrams. Such is the unique interpretive value of the metacinematic when conceived according to this overlapping triadic model, where the turns of its reflexes may coincide with—or incur—each other at certain points of perceptual friction. So that when the reflexive axis of a given dimension of response reverts, for instance, from the immediacy of generated image or event—optical manifestation as narrative text—to its inferred technical parameters as such, its "turn" may also at the same time be outward to context (to commercial, social, or political conditions as well as to genre norms) along a linked scale of calibration and implication. Linked—and interpenetrating. It is in this sense that one stratum of apprehension "tropes" the other in the etymological sense, *diverts* into it, or, by another etymological route of figurative understanding, is *carried over, trans-ferred* (*meta-ferein*) to it. An obtruded technical gesture often, that is, becomes not just a nudge to plot, or a roughening of its route, but a metaphor for some organizing dynamic or building theme in the storyline. At the same time, a narrative paradox may trope some political contradiction in the contextual (become intertextual) field. Such, then, are the metatropes at play across continuous dimensions of response, trans-ferried from one field of recognition to another in an auto-allegorical circuit of inference. Think (by viewing) *Kane* again. As far as the eye can see via incremental distortion, there are still far fewer visible mirror duplicates of Kane on screen in the Xanadu shot than are required in near-duplicate photograms, or photo cells, on the strip (technique) to track these few seconds of irony (text) in their epitomizing of a narrative motif—self as image—whose capitalist valence (context) is the very world of media circulation in which Kane and Welles together participate.

Testing: 1941, 1979, 2019

To clarify further, in its metamedial scope, the scalar triad technique\text\context in screen narration—or, if preferred, to offer an alternative formulation as substrate\structure/intertext—let me briefly subdivide such terrain in examples from three motion pictures approximately four decades apart across the technological eras of celluloid, video, and CGI. These initial exhibits are, to say the least, technically invested screen narratives—ranging from the prewar *Citizen Kane* again (1941) through the topical Vietnam epic *Apocalypse Now* (1979, dir. Francis Ford Coppola) to the post-filmic dystopian spectacle of *Blade Runner 2049* (2018, dir. Denis Villeneuve). Substrate in each case, the materiality of audiovisual record, sets off a kind of figurative chain reaction in their variable cinematic allegories.

In *Kane*, we can back up now to the beginning rather than the end of the "News on the March" film, the latter marked with that diminishing side-angled screen view just as the projector was gratingly turned off. In contrast, the first moving footage of the newspaper magnate is introduced to viewers (to us and to those, within the plot, privy to this rough cut of the documentary metafilm made just after his death) only once a dossier of headline photographs and a childhood daguerreotype have been filed past, along with the loot of his wealth, in a series of rapid cross-fades and wipes that figure—in a deliberately clichéd rhetoric of transience—the blatant ephemera of his fortune. The photo-journalistic ironies of these two montage sequences are, in their tumult, also mixed with quick cuts between static images of his discrepant material aggregations. All told, three distinct techniques of cinematographic punctuation, serial and fixative, operate in a correlated intersection of media metaphors. All is *image*, display, including the simulated paparazzi shots of the title figure under the contradictory voice-over "aloof, seldom visited, never photographed," its shaky footage filmed through the forbidding X of protective wire fencing. Internally reframed in this way, (1) the figurative reflexivities of technique are then immediately equivocated by the metatext of filmic access to the private confines of wealth and power. This happens when the flat grainy images of invaded privacy are put in contrast with the deep-focus treatment of the "News on the March" production team in the screening room, to which we cut abruptly across that satiric view of the documentary's skin-deep scrim. At an emerging metanarrative level, then, with the reflexive ironies of technique behind it, this is where (2) the first-draft storyline of the film-within-the-film is postmortemized along with its human subject. From here out, the commercial journalistic purpose is explicitly to deepen its narrative charge. It is this motive that precipitates the five-part frame structure of separate investigative interviews that organize the rest of the main narrative, with no return to any screen-within-the-screen. The resulting puzzle-piece ensemble of subsidiary points of view (3) tropes in turn, and not just through the intertext of William Randolph Hearst's similar career, the broader social context of fame and overexposure in pursuit of the American dream. Such is the public face of a national mythography where the superficial trappings of notoriety are realized, metafilmically or otherwise, in a showiness that invites no stable explanatory gaze.

After Kane, Kurtz, where (quite apart from the fact that Welles wished to play both Kurtz and his double Marlow in a film version of Conrad's *Heart of Darkness*) we can trace out a metamedial domino effect that ends up manifested in Coppola's version of the same classic novel. Crucially, an early reflexive flashpoint in *Apocalypse Now* is ignited from a clutch of mere images divorced from recorded voice. Even before this, however, in the technical salience of the opening scene, (1) an unorthodox blitz of figurative jump cuts submits Captain Willard (the new Marlow as narrating character) to the fracturing of his screen image after he bloodies himself in smashing its (and his) mirror equivalent in a Saigon hotel room. From there we move to an equally thematized technology in that crucial—because technologically primal—dichotomy of image and sound, where Willard, recruited for a new murderous assignment, is made privy to separate visual and audial information regarding a proudly uniformed Colonel Kurtz. On the one hand, he is offered dossier photographs (actually

8×10 publicity shots of Marlon Brando's previous roles as disturbed or brutal military officers); on the other, he is unnerved by reel-to-reel tape (spinning in close-up) of the Colonel's intercepted mad ravings (this, historically backdated, before mainstream digital recording in Hollywood production, and thus invoking the spools of film that will finally fuse voice with image in the plot's climactic phase). These definitive medial ingredients in picture and speech, divided against themselves, thus pass from technical conditions to the guiding terms of (2) the ensuing narrative text, where it is only with the vanishing point of closure in sight hours later, after the ongoing fissure between Willard's sometimes violent expedients on screen and his own intermittent voice-over in the reading of Kurtz's dossier, that convergence will have been achieved. Only when plot's trajectory has brought Willard into Kurtz's compound—and quite literally face to face with the soliloquies of his rogue derangement, through sutured chiaroscuro close-ups and their bifurcating shadows—will the divided audiovisual matrix of that launching scene have been dialectically resolved. And only then to have both dialogue and voice-over suspended together in the intercut execution montage to follow. All of this, of course, in its Vietnam update of the imperial violence in the African colonial setting of Joseph Conrad's source novel, operates as revisionary narrative text within (3) its contemporary context of genocidal conflict and the ravages of American power. Moreover, this outward turn is punctuated reflexively by a pointed intertextual trope. This is a famous fleeting moment of documentary metalepsis (rather than, as in *Kane*, affording an entire framing motif of the plot as the hero's replicated self-image). Whether we tag it as contextual or intertextual, the moment transpires when Coppola himself, cast as a video documentarian, appears on a beachhead instructing his own cast not to look *at* the camera, but just to look *like* they're fighting. As a dramaturgic more than a technical turn—a medial irony cinematographic, yes, but only because on camera as such, as a second-order filming—the effect lodges within the plot a metanarrative reminder of the Vietnam mayhem and its video spectacle as the "first TV war."

After Kane and Kurtz, K, the replicant hero of the *Blade Runner* sequel. He negotiates a world of futurist audiovisual technology well beyond the screen-encased pleasures of the cinematic, whether filmic or digital, being solaced in his humanoid emptiness only by a hologram housewife more penetrable than desire necessitates. His fleshly satisfaction remains balked at the level of the audience's own before her sheer (both senses) scintillating image. (1) The uneven shimmer and variable transparency of Joi's digital manifestation in the inhabited space of the film's 3D world, whether she is beamed from a "home entertainment" projector or later streamed remotely, comments via contemporary media options on the post-millennial telos of optical technology as well as AI. Her speaking image, her hologram, serving K his dinner, represents the phonorobotic kitchen helper as erotic surrogate. At the same time, the riveting metamedial (or auto-allegorical) specter of her CGI hovering and break-up is a reflex that, we may say, *tropes over* into (2) the vexed cyborg narrative of K's existential crisis, the hero clutching at the possibility of his lone humanity among a cadre of replicants—with Joi only a more pointed reminder that you can't tell by looking (on screen or off) what someone really is, or even whether, in an anthropocentric sense, they really are. This is a sustained dramatic irony centered, in terms of classic narrative epistemology, on tactical flashbacks to a human past that are discursively real for us (as a staple of narrative anachrony) whether they are the hero's own or an implanted memory. It is the inherent "mind-game" tendency of this film to reveal them finally as the latter—in the mode of a trick flashback. At the metatextual level, this technique of montage insert works to expose the inevitably constructed storyline that makes up any supposed autonomous lifeline in retrospect. But the narrative reflex is sociocultural as well as biographical and existential. This is to say that the plot-bound ruse of false memory as visual illusion in the text is at the same time (3) rendered further metaphoric—in contextual extrapolation to the exponential electronic infrastructure of our own social systems—for the proverbial crisis of authenticity in a wired culture of rampant simulacra, prosthetic virtualities, and vicarious affordances. To say nothing of VR's reflex action in regard to the Hollywood audience's ongoing inculcation into the ruses of post-filmic screen imaging—in ways that come to a seeming point-of-no return in this chapter's final exhibit below.

In summarizing the sliding scale of these three differently "medial" examples so far, before looking more closely at the latest extravagance of metamedial CGI, we may say that (1) the manifestation or emblem of the material medium—at whatever stage in its evolution from photography through celluloid projection, then on past videotape to digital and laser streaming, and by however dramatic an eruption of technique—may at the same time become (2) a metaphoric reflex within the encompassing textual structure of the narrative medium as plot format. And it is there that (3) an extra contextual torque may further evoke a specific cultural intertext or zone of association (the opacity of fame, the artifices of staging in photojournalism, the corruptions of power financial or military, the fragility and lurking misnomer of electronic "presence") in the media surround of a given historical moment—as typically exaggerated in the sci-fi genre by its futurist projections. Projections often in the double reflexive sense: optical and historical.

And thus media-historical—and hence industrial. In one of the most obvious ways of limning the text/context slant of recognition in recent screen experience, the production company logos are increasingly enrolled into plot. This has gone way beyond the diegetic match cut from the Paramountain to its jungle equivalent in *Indiana Jones and the Temple of Doom* (Steven Spielberg, 1984). In the latest iteration, for instance, of this branded corporate icon as "mount," abstract geometric stars sweep into view from the sky behind its gleaming peak, orbiting as a kind of halo in this upgraded industrial imprimatur. Such is the case, for instance, in the first four films in the *Transformer* series, with only tantalizing hints of alien cyber noise on the soundtrack accompanying the whizzing astral shapes. But by 2017, for *Transformers: The Last Knight*, with its chivalric throwback twist, the same cookie-cutter star-shaped forms now hydroplane toward the mountain on a reflective body of water extending out toward the theater audience before creating the logo's star-power aureole. Then suddenly, from the distant zone of these astral graphics, a barrage of meteor-like forms rocket toward us from behind the mountain—easily mistaken for asteroid visitations or, of course, extraterrestrial weaponry on the attack. But they are actually catapulted balls of fire vaulting not just the mountain but straight into a flashback on a medieval battle field—as millennial prequel to the alien invasion masterplot. Primitive aerial weaponry undergoes digital manifestation (of course) in order to snap us out of our high-tech expectations—only momentarily (of course)—and then only at the plot level, doing nothing (of course) to impugn the credibility, just obtrude the ingenuity, of those impinging CGI fireballs. Again imploding the threefold nexus of the metamedial spectrum: collapsing its sliding scale into a self-confirming circuit. What results in this case (and others like it) is that a *text*, as if jumping its own narrative gun, has broken through—by foregrounded *technique*—into the framing corporate *context* itself as an extra advert for (and to) its own high-tech finesse.[5]

Looking back for a moment to the latest *Blade Runner*—and returning there all the way to its opening credits as well, we note how, more histrionically than ever, they manipulate the production company logos that flash past—Warner Brothers, Alcon, Sony, and Columbia. Each seems to be invaded in anticipation by the diegesis—this through a digital glitching easily read as leaked in advance from the instabilities of a high-tech dystopia in the plot to come, with its repeated evocation of optic data fields and their fragile electronic manifestation. Here, as the industrial advertising logos seem themselves to advertise, is a plot so intense that it can't be contained, its metatechnical blowback already felt on merely routine corporate approach. This familiar trope of a narrativized paratext, so to say, together with its thematized technique—foregrounding the electronic apparatus at its inaugural apparition—is in danger lately of becoming a distribution cliché: in our terms, the studio imprimatur already imprinted with the technical traces of a text still in promotional abeyance.

Yet such slick involutions of corporate "investment" in the narrative's own technological intensity find understandably little place, up front, in one of the latest overblown and metamedial VFX spectacles. It would be too much, too soon, by way of CGI chicanery. As it unfolds, the film in question marks a quantum leap in thematized technique even beyond Villeneuve's *Blade Runner 2049*, risking as such a kind of dead end for this mode of showcased computer graphics—even if not, of course, for the Marvel franchise already proleptically rebooted by the film's final credits with an inbuilt teaser. I refer to *Spider-Man: Far From Home* (Jon Watts, 2019), which settles in its precredit logo for the cycle's routine kinetic montage of graphic frames from the comic series, digitally shuffled but bearing no electronic wear and tear. Never in the familiar studio-branding of this franchise, however, has this quarantine of pulp source from CGI plot been more apt, even tactical. We'll soon see why. The only logo irony this film can sensibly permit itself seems based on that famous match fade of Spielberg's, in *Raiders of the Lost Ark,* between the signature Paramount pinnacle and its imposing diegetic double in the exotic precincts of the launching scene. In *Spider-Man*, we fade even more quickly from the statuesque Columbia torchbearer to a briefly glimpsed outsize statue of the Virgin Mary, driven rapidly past, at the site of Mexican devastation after a recent and mysterious weather disaster. Any erosion of the female Columbia icon by digital noise, for instance, would have compromised too soon another kind of optical faith—with which the film narrative is multiply caught up through its timely story of a manufactured global menace facilitated by electronic data subterfuge.

Reflecting the escalating CGI aesthetic of the Hollywood action film over the last two decades, here is a movie that comes down to the wire of this present media-reflexive commentary almost by being cornered on the ropes of its own technical expertise, slapped all but silly in the ricochet of the special effects ironies it unleashes. And it can best be comprehended in this framework under one final rephrasing of the sliding scale of such reflexive functioning—with technique\text/context translated on the spot to apparatus\plot/production. Each of these zones of response is shot through—as a further zone of contextual reverb—with intertextual links to the epidemic of mass manipulation in contemporary politics. This outer range of contextual reference is secured only once a midpoint reveal has reset our terms of engagement with the film: namely, that in regard to (1) the digital bravura on display so far, we've been watching the medium's computer apparatus generate, as in the normal operation of VFX, a cataclysmic series of trick effects to materialize (2) narrative threats that are in fact, diegetically, just that: deceptive effects, tricks—or, in other words, (3) explicitly projected illusions of Hollywood-style industrial technique, as well-funded but unreal as the self-styled superhero who vanquishes (vanishes) them.

The overriding trick of the plot, then, in this attenuated and soon-truncated mind-game mold, can only be to banish the risk of tech disaffection by a metaphorics of damage control within a familiar genre pattern of unrest and restoration. To summarize this way, however, is to recognize that the particular slant or bevel given to medial inference in the lateral flanking of the apparatus\plot/production model is pointedly rooted in the hermeneutics of recognition: namely, in what reading for the plot can still help us to read about narrative constitution both before and beyond it, now reverting to generative machination, now adverting to commercially geared cultural impact. This matter of perspective is an important proviso. For it is equally, or reciprocally, the case—if understood as picturing in formative terms what puts pressure on narrative material in giving it shape—that our template could be installed instead as the inward slanted technique/text\context. In that form it would schematize the way story's manifestation is determined by, as well as reflective of, pressures now behind, now beyond it, now technological, now sociological.

Optical Allusion: Causes and F/X

One rule of action genres—western, detective, and sci-fi especially—is that they melodramatize broader cultural anxieties before laying them to artificial rest through some variety of heroic intervention or sacrifice. Franchises, a kind of subgenre all their own, work somewhat differently. In this they resemble serial TV. With the "tag scenes" familiar from the final credit rosters of the Marvel series, these loose ends—despite intermittent narrative plateaus of resolution in a single film plot—keep refueling the cycle from within its own peripheral flexibility. It is all the more likely, then, that broader cultural parameters of intended audience response, rebooted with each new wrinkle of geopolitical anxiety, will coincide with narrative and technological reflexivity in a franchise devoted almost exclusively to digital "marvels" at the cutting edge of technological empowerment—or its revenge upon us.

Certainly this is the case with this latest *Spider-Man*, including its implicit critique of Trump-era demagoguery linked directly to global technological deception (think Russian hacking) in a plot of nefarious VFX technique. The distinction this chapter began with, between cinema as mediatized spectacle (once filmic, now digital) and cinema as designated site of exhibition, has perhaps never been more reductively addressed than in this film's plot about Hollywood-style illusionism in its strategically remote deployment. Plot, did I say? Intertwined with a thin rom-com story about a high school trip through European tourist sites—attended, among the usual typecast suspects, by our secret spider-boy, a goofy nerd sidekick or two, and a would-be girlfriend—is the frail narrative thread of the story's thriller premise. According to which: a maestro of technological illusions generates and projects the CGI mirage of monstrous urban catastrophes (Venice, Prague, London) that only he can fend off, becoming in the process a global hero. The unleashed Spider-Man, with all his teen powers on offer, is recruited to the villain's assistance before the former, our true hero, discovers the ruse. Reduced to the simplest logic of genre showdown, and to near pun on the prosthetic efficacy of the eponymous hero (his *web*-spinning miracles included)—as well as backed in turn by much repeatedly loaded dialogue to this end—the auto-allegory of *trucage* (what Christian Metz saw as the "special effect" that is cinema all told[6]) is impossible to miss. The panic fostered by high-tech "propaganda" (in this case the illusory images of elemental forces out to destroy the world as we know it)—a paranoia to which a self-styled fascistic superman and avenging scourge is the fake antidote—can in the long run be bested rather than abetted, in its campaign of big-budget illusory disinformation, only by the spidery net of our webmaster hero.

Anything we might call the apparatus disclosures of the metacinematic spectrum in all this are so surfeited and manic, almost comic, in their Hollywood overtones that one feels compelled to work backwards from (3) the production end of the sliding scale we've been contemplating toward (2) the plot-transacted sense of its own (1) generative electronics. Though deliberately avoiding any logo contamination by a glitched d/effect—precisely the pixel break-up that will be climactically incarnated in the plot—this latest *Spider-Man* enterprise wallows in an almost uncontainable level of digital reflexivity. Computerized technique has swallowed all action. Which is just where the overarching paranoia plot must kick in, displaced from its own comic-book source, so that now the updated glancing barbs at fear mongering and fake news never let up for long. When the wunderkind Spider-Man—fostering in his own right a false cover story to keep one of his heroic interventions under wraps so as to protect his empowering anonymity—suggests that people should always believe what they see on the news, the audience's mild sniggering is merely de rigueur. In the age of "post-truth," the plot's whole premise, including a villain pretending to hail from a supposed parallel universe within a wide array of "multidimensional worlds," feels pitched at the idea of Trump-era alternate realties—and not just when this fake superman is anointed as patron saint of terrestrial *border defense* in coming to society's collective rescue. Duping the news outlets with his announced arrival from another version of Earth, where Elementals have slain the populace, the con artist Mysterio is the embodiment of group-think mystification. And what he promises, one simulated alien invasion after another, is only a protective ballistic scrim, exposed eventually as a mere CGI interface, between the spectacle of encroaching horrors and its riveted but vulnerable public audience.

With climate change unsaid but inescapably pressing in the allegory, the worldwide elemental disasters—explicitly subdivided as those of air (emissions), earth (quakes), water (floods), and fire (exponential heat)—all "have a face" in Mysterio's artificial mobilization of their threats. All are incarnate as oversized demons. But here, as so often, is where sci-fi dystopias can get caught up in inverted transpositions of the anxieties they are manifestly extrapolating from. Paranoia is a double-edged sword. The enormity of Mysterio's trumped-up threat is rendered with an enormous and vaguely humanoid form, that is, not because rampant cataclysmic forces are the embodiment of human-induced meteorological disaster, but rather because in this case (phew!) they are all fake: staged flashpoints in a climate of fear itself, stoked with advanced electronic enhancements by the wannabe Avenger. In a no-doubt accidental facet—and fallout—of a typically lightweight political parable, climate deniers may thus take some cold comfort even from within the denigration of their parodied hero. "I control the truth," boasts Mysterio (a.k.a. Beck, who thinks he has the world at his beck and call). "It's easy to fool people when they're already kidding themselves." Finally overmastered by the "web"-adept Spider-Man once the latter wins back his billion-dollar experimental upgrade of Google Glass, it is up to Mysterio to repeat one more time, with his dying words, his earlier confidence in mass gullibility. "People need to believe," says this vicious genius of a computer-boosted confidence game, and "nowadays they'll believe anything."

Especially their own eyes. What tucks all this limply scripted topicality back into the coils of cinematic self-reference in the cognitive force field of the post-filmic screen apparatus is that Mysterio is, in fact, a maestro of what one of the teen heroes calls, in knowing industry lingo, "illusion tech." So designated is the whole panoply of marauding demons and heroic resistance that gets staged—make that virtually screened—before gullible mass crowds in Mysterio's digital enactment of his own image as savior. He accomplishes this sci-fi feat by manipulating, from a remote electronic hub, a collaboration of weaponized drones (military-industrial anxiety du jour) and gargantuan laser holograms. These we see him testing out under laboratory conditions in the CGI rendering room—and then implementing in real-world capitols by the remote voice-activation of such Hollywood argot as "cue the lightning" (with a genre precedent taken up in the next chapter in connection with the rudimentary "mind-game" plotting of *Groundhog Day* exactly a quarter-century before).

Beyond narcissistic megalomania, Mysterio's particular vendetta stems from a festering resentment against his ousting by onetime boss Iron Man. This detail marks the film's most obvious strategic dodge, at the plot level, in avoiding what would have been too explicit a corporate reflex if drawn from the villain's actual backstory in the Marvel comic source. In his original paper incarnation, Mysterio's perverse illusionist credentials are more, so to say, medium-specific in their visual deceits than the film would be likely to withstand without toppling into satire or black comedy. In the original serial pages, Mysterio is an unlikely double-threat as maverick agent: having lost his Hollywood jobs as at once a top FX engineer and a valued stunt man (combining Christian Metz's separate categories of visual and invisible tricks: the fantastic illusions you do see, and the substitutions you don't). In that original commix premise, Beck's deceptive tech becomes the incarnate revenge of the system against its own benign commercial spectacles, turning them to a new kind of conviction and notoriety as global terrors. But the movie doesn't offer up such Hollywood employment practices to be sacrificed on the altar of plot, just its hallowed VFX technology to be implicitly borrowed from—and, of course, signally misused. In his filmed version as antihero, Mysterio's CGI stunts, both physical and pyrotechnical, are nonetheless studio signatures: feats of motion capture, green screen, CGI infill, and the rest. Incautiously enough, in this version of the Marvel Universe, everything keeps reverting to a reflex of its own electronic marvelous. So it is that form and content implode upon each other, with any clean delineations in the matter of social or political critique being the first victims of this collapse. Unlike in his film incarnation, Mysterio in the comic version feels guilty, and, staring into an ornate mirror of introspection, thinks he should maybe just make a "short film" and then retire.

Even the immediate narrative backstory (rather than comic-book genealogy) of the franchise confirms such metacinematics—and does so explicitly at the border between technological and corporate contrivance, CGI and the casting department. Explicitly rehearsed, early in this *Spider-Man* plot, is its position in the wake of *The Avengers: Infinity Wars* (2017), where superpower heroes suffer pixelated dissolution along with half of the human race. Five years later in narrative time, though only one year in the fast turnaround of the lucrative franchise, we learn of a remission in this galactic "Blip." The chronological mismatch is itself, one suspects, part of the metanarrative inference. The fact that many other victims of the Blip have been restored (after this half-decade hiatus) to their former stations, their bodies unaged, and thus lagging behind their cohorts, is a kind of industry in-joke. It doesn't take much to see this as a reflection of such franchise filmmaking at large, which can only keep rebooting itself (the James Bond cycle being quintessential and exemplary) if it replaces plot agents every few years with younger actors in comparable roles.

The film wants us to remember the special effect itself of this cosmic devastation as it fills in this backstory. A simulated video newscast by amateurish student anchors in the film's second scene—begun in elegy for the disappeared Avengers, and broadcast on video screens to a high school audience—is the film's genre link to the previous year's *Avengers* installment, where we are reminded of the way the superpower heroes are summarily "retired" from the franchise by seeing, through cellphone images, the pixelated evisceration of students and athletes vaporized from the school gym. These vanishing ash-gray digital variants of a dust-to-dust paradigm in mortal disintegration remind us, of course, that the splintered, then obliterated, heroes in the *Avengers* saga have in fact been constituted, in their flashiest exploits, by piecemeal CGI simulation to begin with. So that the dissipated victims here anticipate the consolidating splintered nemesis of London at the end.

Moreover, what turns out to be the ultimate threat to Mysterio's computerized disinformation campaign is also part of the closely calibrated Hollywood metatext, around which the last phase of the plot revolves. The closest friends of Spider-Man have come to learn, along with him, that the humungous Elemental predators are just digital simulations beamed by what they guess, when finding one detached from a downed drone, is a "very advanced projector," whose results are "real, very real." At this point the film cuts abruptly, clumsily, to an explanatory episode of Beck in the computer rendering studio, assessing the holographic files of his derring-do at several yards remove from his own image, with the illusion-backing drones next seen hovering behind the optical data banks that are transferring these illusions to the magic upgrade of Google Glass spectacles. In the final siege of London, however, by a kind of trivialized avant-garde "glitch aesthetic" built into the thriller plot, Mysterio learns by remote warning that his looming CGI hallucination is "coming apart" by explicit pixel break-up at the very seams of its interlace—and thus confirming, for all to see, its basis in mere optical trickery.

But there is more Hollywood reflex action yet. Before the spectacle quite literally decimates into bitmap graphics, the teens in the know need to be kept from spilling the beans. As agents of a potential debunking—in a kind of tacit generational parable—they serve to concentrate the audience demographic whose aggressive doubts (as opposed to merely suspended disbelief) would demolish the electronic fabric of the whole Marvel Universe, let alone the thrills, however deceptive, of this one plot. If these kids don't fall for the spectacle, who will? They are in this regard, aptly enough, the intended victims of Mysterio's final lethal retaliation: in this weaponized illusionism, and in an unsaid but deeply organizing metaphor, the once target audience as now renegade target. And as if to make this inference unmistakable, there is the final turning point in the action plot when a lone drone, stripped of its trappings as part of the murky pixelated illusion ravishing London—tracks those-who-know-too-much into the Crown Jewels vault, the remote technology reverting here to its standard operating procedure as surveillance and lethal take-out. It is at this point, given the angst of dialogue, that mind-game reflexivity has unmistakably turned the corner into a gamer-mind logic. Cornered in this way, one of the kids about to die whines in regret that he's wasted his life playing video games, another that he's posted stupid videos to get people's attention. But ludic interactivity and amateur production are now both redeemed, in this era of corporate tie-ins, with the assurance from Spider-Man's handler (former head of Stark security) that this is all that might still manage to save them—a way for the hero to have tracked a digital footprint to their present location. Ah, yes, the nonparanoid upside of involuntary GPS, won back for universal computerization—and by explicit association with gameplay. Spider-Man's Web to the rescue after all.

Again, in the variable interchange of this chapter's threefold template, we find the corporate logic (video adjuncts and tie-ins included) enfolding (3) the political intertext of fake territorial invasions and their self-appointed superman of nativist resistance. And from there the inferences of plot circle back via (1) the CGI screen's own technical apparatus when "read"—that is, when figured or troped in the plot, or say allegorized—toward (2) a textual reflex, at the narrative level, of aggressive computer manipulation (not just on Facebook or in the voting booth, but as the very *specte*r of mass paranoia).[7] At the plot level, of course, redemption is pure Hollywood celebration in the formulaic happy ending—yet, in this extreme case, wrung from within the surprise vilification of its own industrial selling point in compelling special effects.

In my earliest writing on cinema, I had occasion more than once, in identifying the reflexive escalation of visual technology in the sci-fi genre, to observe that "movies about the future tend to be about the future of movies." If one were tempted to update this for the transition from the hologram in 1956's *Forbidden Planet* to Mysterio's digital demons, in positing that "VFX cinema is about the future of illusions," the question would remain, in the face of a present dead end, what future? In the normal run of CGI spectacle, we in the audience, like a credulous public at large, will believe anything too, as long as it's expensively enough generated on screen—and not least, in the closed circuit of the fan appreciation sublimated here, when it parades itself as such. In the digital poetics of the Marvel franchise in general, cinema loses nothing in brand loyalty by adverting to the artifice of its own signature effects. But the risk exposed by an unavoidable "apparatus reading" of the pixel substrate in this hypertrophic case has been, if almost too obvious to mention, all the more serious for that. Where can sci-fi screen invention possibly go from here—in bringing VFX along in motivated genre tow—when plot has become all apparatus?

What persuasions remain once the tail has wagged the dog in this blatant way—or the metatale been so egregiously flagged: exposing the frayed heels of narrative originality dogged by exclusively industrial resources in "illusion tech"? What story is left to tell, what narrative challenges left to face, but those of industrial production and its self-congratulatory sleights of hand? That's one question such an exacerbated case of pop metacinema can't avoid being met with. Looking forward now to prose fiction from this elucidating dead end of the screen mode, we note the contrast, certainly, between illusionist sci-fi and the technological curiosities (both senses) of Richard Powers's roving scientific narratives. These are fictions whose verbal courting of the low-profile *meta—* in the richly distributed reflex actions of language as medium triggered by his prose—turns up one inventive way after another to refresh the energies of storytelling rather than stifle them. But to rescue the structural from the judgmental, clear the mind's eye of *Spider-Man* by thinking back to Coppola, or to *Kane*: to the genuine force of their optical flashpoints both of cinematography and of near-miss viewer address by the camera. And here's the main point to stress. There is no way to specify in advance what exactly "about" fiction the classic metafictional moment, whether on screen or in prose, is destined to be about—or what, in respect to narrative form, the self-referential narrative, even at its postmodern cynosure, tends to put under tacit study. So, too, with this book's attention to the localized "reflex action" of incorporated stylistic response, audiovisual or verbal, and especially in recent literary initiatives. The node of cued intake—as self-conscious uptake—reflects back on itself in ways not just ad hoc but already incorporated by form. Yet not disappeared into it.

Less abstract and categorical than is metafictionality at large, more dynamic, more narrowly and intensively gauged, the immediate reflexive event of viewing or reading—within its oscillating closed circuit of intuition, mental playback, re-cognition—can seem (which is its whole point, its perceptual pressure point) already accommodated by theme as its very materialization. Not only in the grain of image or montage on screen, this "picturing back" of meaning through medium also inflects, every bit as specifically, the track of emergent wording in a prose text's own, so to speak, reflexicon. To recall that coinage from the Preview is precisely to speak again with the phrasal (including syllabic) give—and take—of such writing's frequent alphabetic transfusions. It is our look so far at kindred cinematic effects that should, from here out, help in pinpointing—and decoding as narrative checkpoints—an ingrained range of comparable prose events. And one ground of this comparison has already been prepared, anticipating an alignment across media. On the one hand: digital recognitions of the sort just tracked—as they also inflect, and often redirect, what has come to be known as the "mind-game" film (with *Spider-Man* an attenuated version of such structuring deception; another example coming from Christopher Nolan). On the other hand: exemplary "trick" convergences or subversions, including surreptitious parables of storytelling itself, in contemporary prose fiction—in particular, the dissociative narrative structure of our three examples from Powers's fiction and the explicit trope of stop-time magic in the descriptive dilations, the narrative monomania, of Baker's *The Fermata*. Bridging the evidence for such intermedia comparison is what the following chapter has metaphorically in mind by a "cross-fade"—or call it an overlapping dissolve—in our analytic transition from digital cinema to the microstructures of narrative prose.

Notes

1 "Quoted" here in its full "textual" complexity: https://www.youtube.com/watch?v=4iQSr-aDuow

2 Stewart, *Between Film and Screen: Modernism's Photo Synthesis*; *Framed Time: Toward a Postfilmic Cinema*; *Closed Circuits: Screening Narrative Surveillance*; *Cinemachines: An Essay on Media and Method* (Chicago, IL: University of Chicago Press, 1999, 2007, 2015, 2017), with a subsequent turn to motion picturing as a gallery aesthetic in *Cinesthesia: Museum Cinema and the Curated Screen* (Montreal: caboose, 2020). Regarding the media-focused method of *Cinemachines*—with its stress on the techno-historical factors of the apparatus in the "reading" of its technique as text—I'm not promoting that study (any more than the previous commentaries of mine that led to and fed into it) as necessary preliminary reading on the shift from celluloid to postfilmic cinema reviewed in summation here; I'm merely borrowing the gist of its fuller account to license a discussion propelled in this case by a more recent instance of medial disclosure turning up in the digital machinations of the Marvel franchise.

3 Cavell, "Assertions in Technique," ch. 18 of *The World Viewed: Reflections on the Ontology of Film*, Expanded Edition (Cambridge, MA: Harvard University Press, 1979), 133–45.

4 David Bordwell, *Narration in the Fiction Film* (Madison, WI: University of Wisconsin Press, 1985), 53.

5 These metabrandings—these above-and-beyonds of the logo—are variants of the small-scale corporate allegories detected by J.D. Connor in *The Studios after the Studios: Neoclassical Hollywood (1970–2010)* (Stanford, CA: Stanford University Press, 2015) and closely related to the exploration of studio (rather than *authorial*) intentionality in Jerome Christensen, *America's Corporate Art: The Studio Authorship of Hollywood Motion Pictures* (Stanford, CA: Stanford University Press, 2011). For more recent work on the filmic *meta* see David LaRocca, ed., *Metacinema: The Form and Content of Cinematic Reference and Reflexivity* (New York: Oxford University Press, 2021).

6 Christian Metz, "*Trucage* and the Film," trans. Françoise Meltzer, *Critical Inquiry* 3, no. 4 (Summer 1977): 657–75, his work revisited and marginally revised in *Cinemachines* (above, n. 2).

7 In exploring such meta-for(ens)ic "beyonds" of the image system, one notes as well that the teen conviction dramatized in default by this Marvel installment would extend to a courted willingness to "play along" in the franchise's interactive gamer tie-ins. In that context—along that corporate spectrum from computerized screen action to digital interactivity—the desire to inhabit the virtual, versus the will to expose it, is the organizing tension of Spielberg's *Ready Player One* (2018).

2

Cross-Fade to Prose

Reflex action... Reflexion. Not just in bouncing back the thrown light of image from a reflective screen surface, but in ways more modular and serial, even granular, moving pictures can yield up to view their own movement, not just as, but of, pictures. What results is a recursive turn within the course of narrative viewing—understood as its own kind of *reading*. Operating in this way, the everyday "picture show" can help to show how it is, by analogy, that some deep medial reflex—in verbal format as much as in image system—may also work to structure attention in prose reading, from the increment up. The last chapter came again, as in the Preview, to call one aspect of this ingrown linguistic faceting, by comparison with screen machination, the verbal reflexicon: the knowingly word-worked build-up of syntactic impact, where stylistic recognition seems part of the faceted picture. Which is to say that reflex action has its own medial traction in the act of literary as well as visual reading.

Already knotted up in the title of Chapter 1, in its prospective segue to a range of self-flagged verbal energies in contemporary literary fiction, emphasis was directed at just those moments, both in celluloid and in digital cinema, when the picture *shows through* the plane of narration: as story's technical picturing. Even when a marked excrescence or malfunction of technique is quickly assimilated to plot, such scrutinized effects can point us, from here out, to the way literary wording too, in its aspect as verbal mediation, can be at once extruded at the technical level as a linguistic function, whether by felicity or default, and recuperated, as a rhetorical one, in the course of narrative momentum. Both require notice, from theater seat or desk chair, so that it is important to stress again that the true ground of comparison in this study is less a matter of medial constitution, to whatever degree perceived and ruminated, than of our reflex action in response: a matter of viewing or reading at similar levels or attention—or, more to the common point, of participation.

And the narrative prose with which this study is predominantly concerned—that of the restlessly and wittily "bookish" Richard Powers in his diffracted narrative plotlines—has been instructive from the start, not just in that opening epigraph but in his own brilliantly jump-started career. Inserted, so it happens, as a telling part of his unabashedly expository debut novel, *Three Farmers on the Way to a Dance* (1985), there is a meditation on precisely the relation of the cinematic image system to its constitutive audience involvement. To that passage, in its suggestive fallout for the cognitive activations of literary reading as well, we'll turn after some additional cinematic reflexivity as context. Backdated to the period setting of Powers's own First World War novel, his is again an emphasis on the *meta* of the given image, the (near) beyond of viewer contribution in the securing of sequence. In the case of filmic or digital cinema, what may be further induced at such a medium-heightened moment (medium lifted to view from within scene) is not just the reactive affect necessary to sustain narrative investment, even coherence. Emphasis falls as well, in mild aftershock, on some explicit second thoughts: reflections, that is, concerning the apparatus and its service on the technique\text/context model advanced in Chapter 1. It's not often, of course, that a shot like Xanadu's hall of mirrors in *Citizen Kane* (with the further exception of the later extravagant climax of Welles's *The Lady from Shanghai* [1947]) goes so far as to tease attention by risking a glimpse of the camera in our (almost literally) reflected place. More common by far are medial reflexes, optical rather than ocular, in which the edited machinations of motion picturing—or its dysfunction—seem coming under the camera's own lens, as if a reflexive second time, in coming forth to screen view. By analogy with which, in any number of revealing parallels, linguistic mediation is made available—from within the operations of plotting itself—in various contourings of worded narrative. The very fact that all this may sound, as exposition, too woefully abstract for (actual narrative) words is only the proof that, if indeed activated in fictional reading, the effects must be achieved in more concrete and material *terms*, lexical even before syntactic—and therefore in more palpable reflexive *turns*. Etymologically again: tropes, turns of phrase.

In resistance once more to a slack sense of some independent narrative "metalevel" of isolated investigation—and favoring again, instead, a tacit (or "prefixed") orientation toward an inherent (rather that detached) *beyond* or *behind*—response shapes itself from the ground up. And out. Again: determined by certain frames of (self-)reference expanding the text/context interface back toward technique. One may, in this sense, review the categories offered so far (with, for instance, the classic celluloid test case of *Citizen Kane*, in and before its mirror scene) as, in sum: metafilmic, metanarrative, and metacinematic all at once. In the case of Welles's titular potentate: newsreel journalism (1) worrying once how even to photograph him, then (2) faced after his death with the challenge of rendering biographical, hence narrative, his power plays even while (3) projecting in all this the hollow icon of his self-image. The prefixes of such intelinked *metas* may become tedious as vocabulary, but the tendencies fixed on are pertinent—and thriving, with that third aspect of industrial display scarcely outmoded by the eclipse of celluloid. Long before debates over whether, as category, the terminological hegemony of "cinema" could absorb either digital imaging or remote viewing, the term referred to the whole industrial (not just technological) process of motion picturing—together with its commercial distribution—from funded production through reeling apparatus (in both recording and projection) to brick-and-mortar exhibition. To say so is only another way to spotlight at once technique, text, and context—and to do so along the outer, oblique edge of those beveled margins that conjure, just "beyond" the scenic field of a given screen storyline, the machinated seriality of its motion in both the projected sight and the machinic site of its viewed pictures, once plastic and cellular, now post-celluloid.

To be sure, such deep medial reveals need no actual reflective planes for manifestation. *Kane*'s hall of mirrors at Xanadu offers a memorable, but not a necessary, condition in this mode. Inflected by lateral camerawork, it is a nonpareil case of mise-en-scène as mise en abyme. But, even so, any sensed evocation of photogrammatic duplication in the shot's multiple optical regress is more or less incidental—or say thematically optional. Other movies may return us more directly to the film strip in disclosure. To pause further then—in response to its own radical stoppage—over another confirming example of cinema's entrenched reflex action, consider a technique that straddles celluloid and digital production in definitively different ways, the latter including the remote-control functions of "home theater." I refer to the freeze-frame—medium-specificity degree zero, we might say, cinema essentialized in arrest—and bearing only distant equivalents in certain syntactic stoppages of prose fix(a)tion. Classically, the *meta* dimension of the freeze is the radical aftertext—and thus extratext—of cinematic display, the inferential fallout from its summary cancellation: the increment exposed in curtailment of the whole. In short, coming entirely up short in the picture of motion, the freeze-frame results from a single photogram repeated on the strip, with a slight extra granularity and flicker imparted—by visual impaction—in its rapid repetition. This freeze on action is, one might say, even optically purer when manifested in digital imaging. It results simply, there, from a rapidly renewed bitmap scan that seems to betray no underlying process in its arrest: pure fixity (by lightning-fast refreshings) rather than mechanized nondifferentiation. But the difference is minor, easy for the eye to miss or dismiss, and either mode is immediately taken up as metacinematic (if not lately metafilmic) on the halted screen.

In the freeze's definitive celluloid phase, with its function electric rather than electronic, the stop-action jolt serves to call up film's motorized two-dimensional plasticity in the midst of its projection of seemingly inhabited space. It amounts to the disclosure of motion picturing, frame after frame, from the very clutch—or teeth and sprocket holes—of negated movement. And is, yes, always latently metanarrative in operation. Besides textbook examples in such European modernist films by François Truffaut as *The 400 Blows* (1959) or *Jules and Jim* (1962), there is an unexpected deployment of the freeze in a very different auteurist aesthetic—hence even more instructive by its anomaly. Amid the staid and patient long takes (and blunt surgical cuts) in the torpidly populated social ambience of Stanley Kubrick's literary adaptation of William Makepeace Thackeray's novel under the shortened title *Barry Lyndon* (1975), a narrative halt is called—and optically called out. Following long after early battlefield footage, with the lockstep rank and file of dated slaughter answered by the stark implacability of the fixed-frame camera, comes a surprise freeze that pries wide the jammed flow of photograms into a kind of gaping narrative wound to match the hero's own amputation after a gun duel. To whose optical impact, in practice, we come—after a thumbnail sketch of its theory: the most immediate film-historical context for its textual deployment as technique.

Such a freeze-frame is loosely comparable to a syntactic trope in verbal style, a piece of iterative or stalled grammar—as, for instance, a pileup of appositive noun phrases going nowhere, an impasse, stalemate, deadlock, lockdown. But, on screen, its interest is entirely cinematic at base. In his philosophical treatise, *The World Viewed: Reflections on the Ontology of Film*, written early in the 1970s on the cusp between two decades of celluloid modernism, this stop-action image is the most prominent—and markedly ontological—of Stanley Cavell's "assertions in technique" for acknowledging "the fact of film": assertions not just in or through, but *in regard to*, technique, and thus openly metafilmic.[1] What is asserted by such devices is inseparable from the narrative text they serve. For classic cinema as an imprint mode of projection, one may say that a stylistic "assertion in" the materiality of film—on such a technique\text cusp—edges directly into the *meta* by its assertion *of* the filmic. In the very rupture of its temporal asseveration, the freeze is a canonical effect of reflex-action paralysis during a technological era of cinemachination when this device (faded in aesthetic prominence with the digital) felt directly geared to the fundament of the medial process: one picture showing through after another, though in this case each the same in iteration.

It seems fair to say that the effect is seldom more assertive or serviceable than in its lone instance, rare anyway in Kubrick's oeuvre, at the studied anticlimax of his one historical drama, *Barry Lyndon*.[2] As follows—with nothing then following in the account of Barry's personal adventures. Even though all stretches of exposition in the director's own script for this adaptation of the Thackeray novel have been dispatched in mordant flat voice-over, its dismissive tone works with particular blunt emphasis in the last we see (or hear) of the protagonist, one leg surgically amputated after a duel with his brutally mistreated and vengeful stepson Lord Bullingdon, leaving Barry now grappling his way on crutches up to the door of a coach that will take him into bribed exile on a modest stipend if he never returns to England. The acoustic overlay pulls plot itself up short, just before the optic freeze: "Sometime later he returned to the Continent. His life there we have not the means of following accurately"—with these last words ironically concluding a tracking shot that has already been "following," from behind, his one-legged progress toward the waiting coach. A servant, taking his crutches from behind to ease him into the carriage, thus sees him out of the plot altogether. In the last moment of his cinematic "appearance," narrative disclaimer indulges in this useful loophole: "But he appears to have resumed his former profession as a gambler without his former success." Dead end. Begun with the words "He never saw Lady Lyndon again," all motion *in* or *of* the image is just then suspended, the film going into sudden seize-up—with the maimed body still stationed (and stationed still) on the carriage threshold— in a momentarily fixed tableau of abjection, dependency, exile, and truncation: a biographical and ultimately narrative amputation.

In a variant once again of our threefold template from the opening chapter, technique passes all the more directly into text if we know the context, in this case the literary-historical intertext. The coda of the Thackeray novel, describing Barry dying in debtor's prison, is summarily chopped off by Kubrick's script (its "means" of report supposedly foreclosed) with an effacing freeze-frame (faceless, shot from behind) at just the point-of-no-return in deportation: a fictional screen "biopic" pretending to be choked off by its own self-imposed epistemological limit. This snag in optical progression is the abrupt mo(ve)ment that stops cold the film's already slowed progress even as the camera breaks away again, in a jump cut, to a long shot of Lady Lyndon's ancestral mansion—its monumentality distanced spatially as well as emotionally through windswept reeds and trees on the estate. It is there, as we cut to a long-held interior shot, that we see the bereft wife mired in paperwork over the debts left by the excommunicated Barry.

The difference between the six-second freeze-frame just before and a last dilated fixed-frame shot of her Ladyship's cavernous opulent desolation, twenty seconds in duration as Shubert dies out on the soundtrack, is that between a summary eviction from plot and its dreary aftermath, expulsion and non-narrative residue. By dichotomous recourse to its own cinematic functions in remediating a nineteenth-century fictional satire (Thackeray's) of an eighteenth-century wasteland of wanton privilege (England's), the contrastive technical reflexes of pure fixed image abutted by pure camera placement divide up the irony—the cinematic stasis—between them. They do so, of course, by first nipping the biographic arc of plot in the bud, nailing the protagonist with his own ethical dead end. All is charged with the weight of judgment, punitive, decisive, excisional. Narrative satire drives home its own truncation, rather than undermining an entire plot with ontological irony. Nothing, then, could be farther in spirit than such a classic literary adaptation, with its inexorable narrative teleology (even when meeting the optical cul-de-sac of the freeze-frame), than the frequency two decades later of films that contravene their own narrative premises by sabotaging plot itself through paradoxes or involutions. These are disruptions that may be said to *play the viewer* in what we saw identified in the Preview as the "mind-game" film.

Novels of the same period are more likely to *test*, rather than game, the reader in a more active co-construction of the narrative premise. Yet the cross-medial contrast remains instructive. Increasingly blatant, the relation of these sleight-of-sight films to the digital revolution in screen technology, often obliquely entailed in their premise-upending revelation scenes, is what brings their screen frequency into a shared discursive field here with the fiction of Richard Powers: not so much with any overt plot twists as with the disparate plot strands—and the wager, or game, of reader synthesis—in his reflexive technique. And along a different axis of hyperfocalization—or, rather, at a different pole of the same axis of lexical intensity—with the novels of Nicholson Baker, especially in their displacement of pornographic interaction by the gameplay of phrasal reaction.

The fact that, in contrast, the Hollywood mind-game subgenre of the traditional thriller, so prominent at the turn of the millennium, has rapidly lost any real narrative edge since—partly under the continual escalation of so-called VFX (visual special effects) in the now ubiquitous form of CGI environments—is a fact not to be minimized. This is precisely what makes the reductive convergence of mind-game or puzzle film with such reflexive high-tech cinema, as in *Spider-Man: Far From Home* (no trick trickier than the look of the thing all told), so useful in comparison with the more probing textual intricacies and infolds of contemporaneous writing. For the deceptive play of these latest movies, the game they can't help but lose for winning, derives from the fact that they're reflecting on nothing but their own technique—and its technology—from the start. No mind-bending disclosure can compete with the bent, warped, and decimated display frames of these widescreen optical hat tricks, with no paradoxical climax more shattering than the vulnerable glass towers so often sacrificed to this effects-driven aesthetic. By contrast, prose fiction's reflex action—in its passage through prose rather than pixel—tends, so we'll see, to have a good deal more on its mind.

Smoke and Mirrors: Mind Games / Gamer Minds

The cycle of tricked screen narratives loosely grouped under the mind-game or puzzle-film label, though they are inclined to defer any pertinent revelation, are not exclusively exercises in trick endings. Their revel in paradox, their swiveling on contradiction, is the main common denominator. One famous comic example on the roster of plots that paradoxically game the narrative system actually exploits what amounts to a trick beginning, divulging more than we can possibly yet realize, rather than pulling the rug out from under us after we've settled in. The softly piled cloudscape behind the end-titles of Harold Ramis's 1993 *Groundhog Day* would signal a better day begun in the most banal sense for the TV weatherman hero—stupid indeed if the effect hadn't been bookended in the title sequence by a time-lapse rush of similar billows, one of the touchstone cinematic devices in Jean Epstein's sense of film as a thinking machine: an analytic of time itself.[3] In this case the emblematic time-lapse anticipates the temporal distortion by which the hero is forced to turn back, speaking anachronistically, the very hands of time by a now digital clock that wakes him at dawn to the same day over and over again, what dialogue calls "the same old same old.")

The result has a way of rendering each truncated version of a given recursive episode not just like a gameplay reboot but, more intriguingly, like an out-take on Hollywood's cutting-room floor—so that watching the film may feel like sequencing through a file of deleted scenes retrieved in a DVD menu. The net effect, that is, appears more like staged duration on a movie set than like the insane routinization of daily life, each episode the claustrophobic prequel of its own momentaneous remake. With the hero at one point recognizing yet again a particular mise-en-scène and its blocking that entraps him, and halting before an anticipated risk, he quips under his breath: "Cue the truck"—anticipating, as it happens, that climactic use in *Spider-Man: Far From Home* of just this Hollywood backlot lingo ("Cue the lightning"). Existence is entirely subsumed to scenario, persona to the trick of a merely manipulated "protagonist" (to borrow the supposedly loaded terminology from the big reveal of Christopher Nolan's 2020 *Tenet*—to which we'll soon, in the normative chronology the film itself flouts, come round). But first, a couple of dropped threads in the web of *Spider-Man*'s reflexivity that the first chapter, caught up otherwise in more central ironies, chose to defer.

Separately embedded in the film, almost by conceptual default, is not just a seemingly irrelevant mirror sequence but a quite unexpected set of freeze-frames, each commenting on the medium—and anticipating in this way not just the surprise twist but the full-scale paradoxical choreography of Nolan's *Tenet*. In the collapse of London under the trumped-up manipulations of Mysterio at the climax of that latest *Spider-Man*, the Renzo Piano glass-sheathed landmark, nicknamed The Shard, features prominently—along with the thousands of panes of shattered glass that cascade around the hero elsewhere—as if in an unlikely Hollywood allusion to the academic account of such effects in Evan Calder Williams's *Shard Cinema*.[4] What results is a more likely allusion to that second great hall of mirrors in Welles, in *The Lady from Shanghai* (1947). In the hallucinatory maelstrom of his London attack, Mysterio at one unlikely point—playing on Spider-Man's double identity (as Peter Parker) and his insecurity alike—badgers him with the question "Who are you, Spider-Man?" At just this point he hurtles the hero—along with an exploding glass tower, all literal smoke and mirrors—into a reflective looking-glass abyss. When the quizzical outreach of Spider-Man's hand meets that of its nearest mirror double, the screen explodes in an internecine melee of suicidal self-combat. This is an effect of fracturing self-scrutiny that turns comic at the end, when our "hormonal" hero has literally taken up with his heartthrob, joy-riding with her through the caverns of

Manhattan. When soon sailing forth alone again, he presses once more with an index finger at his own glassed image, as in the cavernous shattered depths of an embattled London, only this time to click a final proud airborne selfie.

But the mirror maze in which Spider-Man earlier finds himself—and from which, symbolically, the vanity of controlled self-image must later lift him in restored free flight—has a precedent nearer than Welles's postwar *Lady From Shanghai*. For, according to our hall of mirrors model for all such in-frame repositionings of the visual field, this showy passing shot in *Spider-Man* also takes us back from the phenomenology of rampant digital illusion to a headier ontology of presence. The last is a conceptual aura that certain postmodern film blockbusters, not least Kubrick's *2001: A Space Odyssey* (1968), shared for a while with the metafictional tradition in literary narrative that followed on from, as discussed at the start, the earlier epistemological pressures of Modernism (say Faulkner through Welles). The intertext in question here is thus more nearly a measure of *Spider-Man*'s casual departure from the more undermining mind-game mystifications to which Christopher Nolan's *Tenet* (2020) tries reverting with its own motion-inverting mirror/"window" scene, coming into view ahead. Under the sign of a high-postmodernist simulacrum, that is, rather than film history's subsequent flurry of electronic mirage in the three-ring circus of escalating CGI, the intertext I have in mind is the notorious liquid mirror of 1999's *The Matrix*: a malleable and porous border that drops its mask as a mere visual plane when touched by the hero Neo as a metaphysical interface. What results is an unstable, gelatinous transition between the virtual reality matrix he thinks of as his lived world and the true hibernation pods of humanity's stored biopower, from which the chance of escape requires a kind of repeated neonate transit through the ontological looking glass.

Any such pungent sci-fi crux, however threadbare even by then, has been toppled into parody by GGI manipulation in the Marvel films. In the case of *Spider-Man: Far From Home*, any existential dilemma of being is reduced to that of self-image and public cover story. More telling, however, than the light-hearted and weightless digital narcissism of Spider-Man's selfie, in repair of his shattered glass image—at the level of psychology under the probe of technology—is an earlier moment of what we might call free indirect optics, invading the mind of a character by subjective insert. This occurs when Beck's burst of livid resentment against former boss Tony Stark's dismissal of his holographic technology triggers a quick pair of traumatic zoom-in flashbacks to b&w freeze-frames. The effect does more than recall a Hollywood optic dispensation of the sort mobilized (in visual demobilization) by Kubrick—well before home DVDs and their finger-tip freeze-frames. It also taps back into the gray-scale origin of the medium itself in single photo frames. That's the real traumatic threat of all this mind-game *trucage* in *Spider-Man*: a lapse to the vision of kinetic spectacle itself under arrest, regurgitating only nostalgic traces of its own prehistory.

In a related way, Nolan's later film toys, or say again games, with what one might call cinematic primitivism. It reverts in this way to the medium's basic motor functions within its own fictional reach—far beyond cellular technology per se—into a pervasive futurist mumbo jumbo regarding algorithmic time inversion. The frail veneer of ecocritique in the materializations of tsunamis and firestorms in *Spider-Man: Far From Home* is even more thinly motivated, and entirely unpictured, in the late-emerging mind-game explanation for time-warp in Nolan's version of a re-traversable but not reversible Anthropocene. So atrophied as narrative is *Tenet* that the gamer instinct is directed outside the film altogether by the spawned blogs about the cabalistic Latin Sator square. This is the five-word symmetrical palindrome for which the Russian oligarch villain is named, and within which the reversible lettering of "tenet" is the central "invert," all of which goes symptomatically unmentioned in the film. It isn't a movie you play along with; if there is any to be had, the fun lies after and elsewhere, in its ludic provocations on the web.

Tenere: from the Latin hold, hold tight. In English, though, the title stands, as none of the bloggers seems to notice, as the noun for premise, credo, founding assumption. In Nolan's contorted narrative, less a through-line than a noose, that premise is a "temporal cold war" with the future, the pending enemy empowered somehow by "inverse radiation triggered by nuclear fission." The result is that "entropy" can be "reversed"—so that an event can be experienced, still inexorably, but backward. Here the mind-game disclosure is short-circuited by its own premise, the latter needing to be surfaced soon enough to explain the film's otherwise gimmicky reverse footage—and thus leaving for a trick ending only what amounts to a further leveling explanation for the hero's awkward dialogue early on about grappling with two "antagonists." For he himself is ultimately revealed, no personal name ever given, to be the "protagonist of the operation," having recruited himself in the past for the lead player in the present defense against the future. In this knowing metatextual vocabulary, he is not a character in a story but only a reversible function in a plot structure, always dependent, according to narratologist Peter Brooks, on the "anticipation of retrospection."[5] Or vice versa.

Early on, every effort is made to normalize, or say "naturalize," the film's improbable tenet of inverted action. First there is the extreme sport of bungy jumping in reverse, the hero and his comrade mechanically catapulted into the luxury high-rise lair of an arms dealer. Later in this same scene emerge certain knee-jerk topical anxieties typical of the genre as well, when data privacy and surveillance are slipped in as touchstones to answer our protagonist's surprise that Sator, the arch-villain, can communicate with the future. Electronic data, the hero is reminded, from email to credit card info to text messages, all speak to the future via storage and latent retrieval; the question is only, as his informant cryptically puts it, whether the future can speak back. Not much to go on there. Or is the nameless protagonist himself, we're perhaps finally to guess, the victim of identity theft? In any case, acclimated by these present-tense normalizing analogs and phobias, the plot thinks itself prepared for its wondrous conundra: four-dimensional car chases and the like, one car tailing another backwards, including de-ploding bomb bursts, imploding rather than exploding targets, and the oddly unimpressive rest.

Even the bipolar, two-directional military operation at the end, with its so-called "temporal pincer movement"—is a cluttered montage that has been anticipated earlier by a physical pincher operation, squeezing and then crushing two of the villain's getaway cars between converging trucks and a fire engine. This frequent literalization of the film's supposedly heady metaphysics is immediately followed by the inverted chase stunt in which (with shades of Tony Scott's more enthralling *Déjà Vu*), Nolan's past and future track each other along the routes of their differential vectors. But all this only prepares for the ecocritical revelation in the mouth of the villain, who explains that the future is out to get us for our devastation of its globe. The underlying green allegory is hardly enough to save the plot, let alone the planet, and it is never of course spelled out. But it's hard not to read this flaccid mind-game twist as enacting how the inherent revenge for our brutal stewardship of the earth will be, in fact, nothing more nor less than the future itself.

The convergence of paradox and global apocalypse in *Tenet* recalls the film's inevitable intertext in Denis Villeneuve's *Arrival* (2014) half a decade before. Whereas the circular syntax of the alien language in that film—every reversible sentence its own palindrome—was an intriguing idea that brought together two time-based media, film and language, Nolan's plot delivers no such engaging tenet. Reversing the logic of *Arrival*, where agents from the future make contact with the present to deflect its collision course with nuclear annihilation, and so to save that future for immigrant relocation, Nolan's strained twist on this, by some inexplicable fissile dispensation, requires both past and present to maintain themselves against a vindictive future eager for revenge against what has been left to it, been done to history. Where *Arrival* is about moving forward in time to make that very arrow possible, *Tenet* is about sabotaging the past to prevent it, to truncate world duration itself. The fuller mind-game dimension of the former and far more compelling film turns on presumed flashbacks of the translator heroine regarding her dying child. As if she has been infected by osmosis with the circular syntax of the alien language she's struggling to translate, these intermittent temporal irruptions turn out, instead, to be predictive rather than elegiac: ominous flash forwards, as the reader only belatedly discovers along with the pre-grieving heroine. They invade her consciousness as forebodings of the child she will ultimately decide to have anyway, even knowing its fate. In our threefold model of medial thematics, the "text" of sci-fi plotting hereby works to deflect narrative toward an existential "context" in temporal acceptance precisely by a deceptive turn on flashback "technique." The default in *Tenet*, by contrast, is to fall back on the motorization of reverse-action screen technology as a narrowly motivated visual trope for paradox rather than any deeper game-plan surprise in the puzzle-film mode.

And yet again the naturalizing scientific analogs for all this in Nolan's riff on the *Arrival* logic. The future has devised the algorithm that makes time travel and its ultimate revenge possible, but has broken up its coded script into several metallic lockboxes that must be reassembled as the algorithm with a capital A, resembling some abstract and lumbering grenade launcher, the instrument of Armageddon when triggered. As in the more obvious irony of *Spider-Man* as well, all screen force resides in the workings of an algorithmic CGI weaponized. Here, though, the point is displaced by the two most reflexive twists of Nolan's deliberately abyssal mise-en-scène. The notion of inversion (rather than reversal), as most naturally associated with a visual field rather than an inertial momentum, comes closest to the surface—the surface as an actual transparent framed plane—in the scene where the so-called "proving window" is explained to the protagonist. This disclosure takes place in one of the parallel chambers on either side of a two-ply glass partition (metallically cross-meshed and thus, as it were, doubly screened) through which we've previously seen bullets come and go, fired or "caught," with traces of blood etched in its cracks or sucked back from the closing hole into the barrel of assault. Now we're told that at least the third and last of these giant glass windows offers the test of success when entering the clumsy cement turnstile of inversion at the end of the chamber. If, through this outsize framed pane, you don't see yourself reverse-exiting the machine, as the protagonist is told by a new member of his cohort, then the mission is doomed. With an accompanying gesture, the vernacular call to "See for yourself" all but implies, beyond the idiomatic preposition "for," the need to "see yourself" in mirror inversion. As of course he does, our nominal and only so-named protagonist. (One failure of the film might be diagnosed as coming to a head with this shotgun wedding of epistemology and ontology in a post-postmodern mélange; in any case, in its tortuous version of the "puzzle film," lots of pieces go frustratingly missing or are too silly to fit.) However the inset reverse-action framing is actually filmed (or digitally tricked) for this instantaneous screening of the immediate future, a double sense of rear and of rearward—or invert—projection is implied: the oldest trick in cinema's book, predating the advent of the algorithm in any form.

Long before this climactic "window" into the logic of Nolan's film, a similar abyssal twist is flagged by the uniquely dated term "tape" for the tripod video taken, for no good reason that we learn of, at the protagonist's first introduction to reverse motion in the laboratory shooting gallery. Fitted with the proper electronic gloves (as if in allusion to a necessary *digital* prosthetic), he is shown how he can make a bullet fall up. Knowing that holding should precede dropping, he objects succinctly that "cause comes before effect." But the female scientist insists on his agency either way, showing yet again—this time on a makeshift screen-within-the-screen, no less—exactly the reverse motion that is an intrinsic feature of time-based recording. This is the very innovation maximized in the earliest trick films at the dawn of cinema and later theorized (as well as practiced) by Epstein, among other technical ingenuities, as the true analytic "intelligence of the machine." Even the reversion in *Spider-Man*'s metafilmic flashback to the cinematic rudiments of the single b&w imprint couldn't seem more openly a reflex action of the medium in reversion to its recognized constitution and prehistory both.

And the local point in *Tenet* will later be extrapolated to the encompassing mind-game swivel, where the hero, as a retrofitted and reverse-engineered protagonist, becomes the cause to his own future effects. Quoting from that early scene of embedded screening and its flagrant anachronism regarding the bullet's reverse fall preceding its release: "Either way we run the tape, you made it happen." Spool, tape, disk: each, under the sign of apparatus reading, a reversible, an invertible, trope for a potentially manipulated temporality in the celluloid, then analog video, then digital phase of the cinemachine. Our recurrent three-way configuration of reflexive structure—here technique (sequential recording)\text (entropic plotting)/context (the genre of "time-travel" rejiggered)—will, in sum, have later found the triptych mirror of such metafictional recognition reframed, in the form of a single transparent rectangle, as the metal-screened proving ground (the ground-glass "proving window") of paradoxical machination. Yet again, a roundabout reminder that the film's only algorithmic marvel is the image science—or in the teen idiom from *Spider-Man*, the "illusion tech"—that its fiction shares with the kind of games its audience might otherwise pay a mind to. Or to put it in Nolan's hypothetical terms: say that the lifetime feared wasted on games in *Spider-Man* is here the fantasy of time itself made interactive, if only in limited doses and for those suitably equipped. In any event, here and in so many recent blockbusters, an allegory of the algorithm seems to be the main reflex of VFX, just as, in literature, more richly, an allegory of grammar and its contributory wording may serve to replay the time-based experience of reading.

Escalation / Relativity / Reflexivity

But film experiment aside for a moment, before the promised return to Richard Powers's thoughts about specular reflexivity in the construction of silent melodrama's narrative sequencing, we can stand back from that first (also historical) novel of his to appreciate its broader *meta* orientation. Epochal, epistemological, self-conscious—the gists of three orbiting paradigms subtly intersect from separate pockets of seemingly tangential contemplation in *Three Farmers on the Way to a Dance*. At issue in this spin of association: (1) geometric rates of technological and cultural change in the then-elapsing modernist century (following the cited thought of Charles Peguy); (2) decisive "triggers" of auto-acknowledgment in the recognition of these transformations, aesthetic included (following the Heisenberg principle of relativistic measurement, where perception—and hence representation—redefines, indeed actually remakes, the object under study); and (3) reflexive estimates of performed (or self-biographized) identity within the private arc of behavior, where even individuated personhood is an act of auto-inspection and willed narrative shaping (so that, in Nolan's vocabulary, we become our own "protagonist"). History, representation, agency: all turned inward, each manifested by being about itself. To parse the book's theoretical touchstones in this tripartite fashion is not to falsify their casually meditative inclusion in the explorative course of *Three Farmers* but, quite the contrary, to respect the center of gravity around which they so obviously, if intermittently, collect.

So run them past again this way: the accelerating juggernaut of twentieth-century cultural upheaval as (1) exponential and reflexive at once, with (2) the recognition of such transformations being already a factor in the flux that human comprehension is thereby maneuvering to get a fix on, so that even (3) the private case of biographical self-awareness, not unlike the recursive dimension of modern history and aesthetic genealogy at large, remains reflexively engaged in its own deliberately looped, cumulative understanding. The narrative underway in *Three Farmers* proceeds under these linked allusive rubrics as an unavoidably tacit instance of their governing principles. Escalation, relativity, reflexivity—in short, progress(ion) and its always implicated gauges. Even while this novel's selective and eccentric cross section of human events takes shape, these broader parametric orientations come at the reader out of left, right, and center field all at once, with the result that we don't at first quite know what has hit us in their collision—until, aptly enough, *reflecting* on them further, subscribing to their metanarrative postulates within the book's own open system of inference. Framed by convergent truisms historical, aesthetic, and psychological, the superstructures of self-adjustment are thus modeled from within on the self-mirrored reading of a text that retunes itself in precisely their terms as we go.

On one flank, then, and extrapolating from the thought of Peguy, Powers evokes the unsaid idea of "precipitous" change, comparable to the calculus of falling bodies, in respect to self-accelerating advances in both technology and aesthetic production. But the speed-up isn't infinite, can't remain unchecked. Limits impose themselves as transformation gets maxed out, then renewed again in revised terms. Hence his concept of the "trigger point." By example: "call the terminal velocity a trigger point, where the rate of change of the system reaches such a level that the system's underpinning, its ability to change, is changed" (81). Such triggers mark the point-of-no-return where a system "thrusts awareness of itself onto itself and reaches the terminal velocity of self-reflection" (81). Unavoidably, as this one novel proceeds, and thus the longer such extra-narrative considerations hover in the gap of action, the harder it is to avoid their direct conceptual bearing on the mounting pace of normal—here suspended—fictional plotting. But Powers's most explicit macro example of this first principle kicks in at the transhistorical level: "A billion years of evolution eventually produces a species capable of comprehending evolution" (82). Such is the case in cultural formation as well as in primate brain anatomy, with civilization "no longer just a changing culture, but a culture of change" (82): the chiasm as millennial watershed.

Same, too, with aesthetic genealogy across the vanishing century. Process becomes part of the newly delivered result, and twice over, in a kind of boomerang: "Art that was once a product of psychological mechanisms is now about those mechanisms and—the ultimate trigger point—about being about them" (82). Same as well with the double helix of identity construction. So far, at the metahistorical level, Powers has identified a kind of paradox levitated in a play on words. The sheer momentum of syntax rehearses his claim. Escalation, that is, has a way of stalling in its own overdrive: "Hyperprogress transmutes, paradoxically, into stillness. After postmodernism, we are *still* changing faster than ever" (82). Think of that text-italicized slant—and you have to think *about* it, in contrast to the preceding "stillness"—as a beveled adverbial pun at the very threshold of reflex action in reader alert. In the process, then and "still" too, "Art takes itself as both subject and content: postmodernism about painting, serialism about musical composition, constructivist novels about fiction" (82). The last certainly not least.

Fictive "constructivism," in this specialized sense, is Powers's legacy from the postmodern: the intrinsic formativism of narrative shape—operating full-tilt in the present "novel," which reads in certain stretches more like a treatise on the contours of its own possibility than a fiction per se. That's the main thing to notice in this quick overview of the cultural benchmarks brought so disparately by Powers, if by subterranean connection, to the interrupted surface of event. These pockets of historiographic theory, aesthetic genealogy, and ruminated identity-formation are so wholly detached from immediate plot needs, frail though these may in themselves seem at times, that the associated disquisitions inevitably congregate, magnetized to each other, in a conceptual metatext— but one which, by its own lights, skews the layered narrative we're otherwise reading, distorts it simply by standing back to report on it. These counterpoised reflections—sometimes mere pages apart, sometimes separated by many chapters—are thus, in context, reflexive on the face of it: always bent back upon the narrative whose hiatus they constitute. And motivated by intermedia deflections in their own right.

Developed out of an extended ekphrasis of the titular 1913 photograph by August Sander, those three farmers are ominously snared in moving forward, along a radically forked historical path, toward festivity and First World War alike. They are thus captured, only momentarily spared, on their way "to that unmitigated act of violence called the twentieth century" (212). From which Powers's more recent post-millennial novels have struggled to work, and worked by formally struggling, free. We'll be attending to some of these later plots far more closely, for the tightly geared and stylistically synchromeshed coordination of narrative axioms and their execution. *Three Farmers* comes up first mainly to highlight the broad spread of the *meta* in his fictional thinking, the scope of its resonance across coordinated philosophical registers. Along with extensive citations from Walter Benjamin on photography, *Three Farmers* move(s) danceward on the immediate heels of the three theses just sampled. In the later novels on which we'll be concentrating, such premises are buried at least long enough to emit the signals of a more independent fictional narrative. Yet there's hardly a major plot twist, even in those matured and more novelistic works, that isn't, to some extent, found turning—or turning on—all three of these screws at once: technological history, reflexive aesthetics, and the scripted self.

The coordination of these perspectives in *Three Farmers* is as uneven as it is inevitable. Linked to the geometric rate of scientific, cultural, and aesthetic change (as contemplated seven chapters in), but launched more specifically from a meditation (nine chapters later) regarding the questionable investments of any biographer in bringing pattern to bear on a recorded life, we shift from that latter emphasis on selective narrative investment—that inevitable tendentiousness in the molding of a life story meant to be made representative—over to the widely accepted modern principle that the observer changes the observed, that measurement is never free from such distorting relativity. "These are the recognizable bywords and clichés of our times. Casual talk abounds with the knowledge that there is no understanding a system without interfering with it" (205–6). Implied further here: a sense that epistemological relativity crosses paths with reflexivity at no less than a putative "trigger point" where the system's own comments on itself are themselves part of the "interference" it can't fend off. As, for example, in the metafictive riffs of this one novel.

Including, as *Three Farmers* contemplates it, the social psychology of self-consciousness per se—in its obvious, if unspoken, impact on the construction of a fictive protagonist. For when the system in question is the intrinsic character system of fiction, both modeled on and a model for our sense of social being in a community of action and reaction, then these three excursive templates of cultural recognition have suggestively converged. It has come about this way in Powers's cumulative digressions. An exponential speed in the evolution, not just of technology, but of human self-understanding, has met with the epistemological problematic involved in all observation as a kind of witness tampering in reverse, a skewing of observation by report. What this brings out is the *non*disinterested biographer as prototype for the very work of auto-awareness. In this sense of cognitive development, one might say that there are few rudimentary instinctual reflexes left to *homo narrativus*, mostly just self-reflective ones. In Powers's simpler and unequivocal terms: "With every action, we write our own biographies." Laid down there is a loose metaphor ("write" for make) that will, at the climax of one later novel (*Generosity: An Enhancement*, the focus of Chapter 5), be drawn oddly taut and transfiguring. In *Three Farmers*, though, the idea is couched mostly in supposed common sense and its colloquial rhythms: "I make each decision not just for its own sake but also to suggest to myself and others just what choices a fellow like me is likely to make" (206)—with the very phrase "a fellow like me" spoken in the free indirect discourse of communal notice and its patronage, a kind of choric frame. Inside a book, of course, rather than just in the normal walk and talk of life, any such manifested reflexivity of decision is enrolled as a plot turn—and thus encroached upon by an omniscient scriptor as observer/narrator. The resulting character*ization* shadows, as plot thickens, every potentially accelerated change of private mind with the imprint of design: the character's own or its author's, either one, if there remains a difference.

The idiomatic caliber of language—as in the vernacular relaxation that helps make the above claim by Powers's narrator, about auto-narration, ring true—has been built toward by a quite different style of nomenclature and its hyphenation. First time out as an arresting contemporary narrator in the field of prose fiction, Powers's digression digs in its heels. A passing reflection on the twentieth-century's socio-aesthetic juggernaut becomes a position paper on the novelist's own fictional ambitions. The force of this has gathered as follows. Beginning with the last century's launching view of its own initiatives in the early 1900s, all of this mounting relativity of notice has already been spelled out, in the first of Powers's aggregated digressions, with a grammatically mandated (but nonetheless authorially loaded) hyphen: denominated, that is, as a node of "metaself-conscious" force. Requisite, if distracting, syllabification enhances the point, diagnostic and ironic alike, that auto-reflexion is preceded by an already *meta* sense of human narrative to begin with: the "metaself(-)" as essential plot agent in one's own life(story). In this autobiographical framework, as in the historical and aesthetic registers as well, it is therefore the novel as genre that offers an immanent training ground for just such narrative *recognition squared*—and thus delivers the format of definitive transitions, with their triggering instigators, as the flipped switches of its own structural regress and recursion. In the case of fictional characterization, this involves not just a formal narrative artifice about psychological artifice and its self-fabrications, but, one notch beyond, a storytelling that openly probes reading's own capacities for exactly the kind of participatory response through which inspection inflects the observed. Synthesizing Powers's threefold terms for a multivalent reflexivity, then, we can see how the accelerating press of technological history, the curve of aesthetic evolution, and the channeled course of a manipulated subjectivity—flagging the very ingredients of prose fiction as he variously wields them—may well take each other's collateral temperature. They do so whenever, at a given text's own mounting "trigger points," discourse has gotten out ahead of itself, has gone more than ordinarily *meta*. And has, from that *beyond*, turned round on itself, from one phased sequence to the next, in reflecting on the elapsed at a new level of apprehension and afterthought (as with the reflexive italic skew given to the adverb *still* in that earlier passage about exponential change).

At which "trigger points" of afterthought, time and again, questions regarding the pleasures of the metatext, the extratext, which Powers's fiction sophisticates with distinctive contemporary verve, become less about pleasure alone than about its existential measures at the far edge of conception in a posthumanist moment. With Powers's writing, any grieved death of the novel is survived in the crossbreed of infused philosophical materials, rooted in science, technology, musicology, and so forth, that draw out the premises of narrative invention with new grip and specificity. In this respect, well before the metanomination of 2018's *The Overstory* over three decades after *Three Farmers on the Way to a Dance*, two of the novelist's intervening texts, *Plowing the Dark* (2000) and *Generosity: An Enhancement* (2008), will have thrown into unique relief—around questions of reading and writing respectively, and of course reciprocally—the way "trigger points" might operate within fiction to leverage the self-revised specs of narrative prose.

But back to the broader medial picture, with a cross-cut to the film screen—and to the reflexive logic of its own cross-cutting, as analyzed by Powers. Those foregrounded cognitive orientations, historical and epistemological alike, mobilized by his first novel in the situating of its reflexive variances—technocultural accelerations, their inbuilt recognition in aesthetic forms, and a comparable sense of the "metaself" in patterned accumulation—have certain clear cinematic parallels: in media history, in narrative's montage form, and in the typologies of screen characterization. It is in this sense, too, as the opening discussion has canvassed it, that one broad set of "trigger points" for cinema, in its mutation from celluloid to digital—and in a fashion similar to Powers's stress on escalated change and its reflex awareness—can be sorted out in our now-familiar triad. The triggering recognitions are contextual (historical; cultural; medial), textual (narratival; psychological), and technical (electric; electronic), though such categories often emerge, of course, in reverse order of inductive response—where the perturbations of technique or style tilt plot beyond itself toward the cultural symptoms it only implicitly manifests.

In contrast, *Three Farmers* front-loads the philosophical parameters of its comprehension in an almost essayist fashion, even while taking film into its peripheral field of vision. This novel's historiographic reflexivity in relation to technological media makes use of marked extrapolations from Walter Benjamin, by which Powers is bent on recognizing (in presumed connection with his own writing in uptake) a leading quality of cinematic response: namely, the synthesizing role of the spectator in the split-second rescues (via split-scene rather than split-screen montage) of silent melodrama. This excursus derives from a sense of "movies," or more to the point of pictures in motion, having moved even beyond what Powers follows Benjamin in stressing as the democratization of image resulting from automatic, handheld photography. For Powers's narrator film has "arrived at a gratifying hybrid of the expository and the participatory," where "we and the director" (251) collaborate in the editorial finesse of montage. Powers goes farther than Benjamin in this regard, however, with that explicitly narrative stress: imagining each viewer's necessitated proud activation, for instance, of the last-minute heroic rescue in a silent serial. This can happen only through the spectator's cognitive stitching together of intercut fragments so as to lend them perceptual continuity, first as coherent motor images, then as suspense-building correlations in a scene-bridging episode. Whose dramatic outcome the viewer has thus effected. Certainly not *above* the fray in this metafilmic reflex—just *beyond*, again, in override of the merely given by the inbuilt supplement—lies this structural prod to viewer contribution. Tacitly departing here from the psychoanalytics of suture theory, in which the viewer's gaze intermediates between the exchanged looks of intercut actors as the "absent one" of a disavowed reciprocal identification, Powers wants to suggest instead the openly and knowingly reflexive heroics of our collaborative story-making in early cinema. Yet I stress the point at this stage less as a segue from the self-referenced mechanics of screen montage in Chapter 1 than for the way it anticipates Powers's own assumptions for reader- (rather than viewer-) response in pulling together the disparate musings of his own present fiction—and then, later, for the tacit structuring role of reading across the separate contrapuntal story lines of his typical mature method. Less centripetal in their freewheeling swirl of associations, these later works operate instead by the episodic narrative pulsations of an alternating thematic current. And like the viewer of silent film, it is the reader whose synthesizing investment must pull things together in order to save the day.

That's part of it, certainly, for Powers: the cinematic *model* as well as mode. The narrative force of montage must be *read*, not just watched: made in reception rather than given. On this view of viewer collusion in the fusing of screen shots into film sequence at the very basis of montage, spectators participate in the changes they think merely to observe, complete (rather than just receive) the junctures that editing delivers up in fragmentary forms. More is modeled here than just the perceptual regime of alternating montage. The spectators theorized by Powers are like Heisenbergian observers not just noting but making, as it were, plot's definitive difference. In cutting to its own medial quick in this way, a reflexive sense of cinema projects that of narrative response *tout court*, at least in Power's typical deployment. The spiraling logic of all this will be coming in for closer investigation in the next three chapters. But first here it should be useful to consider—as part of the reason for this focus on Powers—how a somewhat different historical curvature than the one digressively outlined in *Three Farmers* can put his pursued interrelation between advancing technological history and aesthetic form into a more sharply delineated literary arc. Quite apart, then, from Powers's own swift metahistory of the last century (though overlapping implicitly with it at its first postwar turning point in high Modernism) is another line of development. Shadowing, that is to say, the historiographic sweep running down through the type of postmodernist *assemblage* he is bringing near to a close with the kaleidoscopic cross-references of his own first novel, and awaiting a last-ditch apotheosis of this "constructivist" mode in his thirty-part next book, *The Gold Bug Variations*, there is another rough-hewn evolutionary paradigm to contemplate. On this view, Powers's work since the early 1990s fits in with a yet longer-span literary-historical trajectory whose recent tendencies, in the residual use of textual reflexion, the present commentary wants to explore.

One tracing of that trajectory might go like this, absorbing in the process its own Victorian backstory. In any cursory overview of the last literary century, from 1910 on the way to the 2000s, it is likely that nothing more vividly measures a move from the metaformal ethics of modernism to the paranoid totalities of late postmodernism than the gap between E.M. Forster's *Howards End* (1910), with its motto "Only Connect," and the (unwitting?) conflation of that canonical title with the no-longer optative desideratum of recognized interdependencies in Don DeLillo's globally enmeshed 1997 warning "Everything is connected in the end."[6] And from this climactic postulate in his epic of a fiber-optic nether realm, the titular *Underworld* of infrastructure itself, there is a subsequent move to an alternate totalizing impulse in Powers's 2018 *The Overstory*, an ecological trope answering as much to the biospheric umbrella of his theme as did DeLillo's to the technological girding of the globally wired socius. Again the longer view, both aesthetic and generic: from the humanist dream of imaginative and moral connection, in Forster's abiding attachment to "the green world," through a leveling impersonal connectivity to the ecocritical panoptic that might reunite us with the life of our planet. Such is a progress that has led from inherent counterplots of class privilege and exclusion in Forster, with its frail pastoral antidote, through DeLillo's dizzying historical and topographic disjunctures in narrative foci, to the tendency in Powers toward those more symmetrical, rhythmic, eventually dialectical linkages that characterize the contrapuntal storylines of many of his later novels even before *The Overstory*, with their eventual dramas (rather than lurking "underworld" traumas) of convergence and mutual recognition.

Generically, then, as well as aesthetically, the Victorian multi-plot novel, mutated into the epistemological collage narratives of Modernism and the anxious webworked pastiche of its successor metaplots—and seen comparatively in the span from Eliot's provincial *Middlemarch* (1871–2), say, down through DeLillo's *Cosmopolis* (2003)—has returned with a certain abstract polyphony in later Powers. There diverse locales of event needn't be tethered, let alone tightly braided, by realist communal filiations—but are left instead to articulate a novel's sustained open circuits of mostly tacit dependencies and incursions. To whose reflexive cues the onward act of reading is, as much as was silent screen viewing, situated to respond in engaged collaboration. It is into such fictive circuits, more closely traced, that the coming chapters will plug.

Scope versus Focus: Verbalism's Sliding Scale

Rewrite, if you will, technique\text\context as phrasing\fiction\inference (or, where there is a real plot, as style\plot\theme) and you approach the lexical torsion exerted on prose discourse in the two different writers we'll be concentrating on—in their own very different modes of verbal as well as descriptive concentration. And in the different ways, whether with trick endings or not, that they set about gaming the mind. So a word more on method. My stress on "apparatus reading" in the case of such literary writing involves the parsing of diction and syntax as they are together propelled toward a coordinating grammar of narration. Thrown back on such linguistic means from the midst of description, this involves a reading of medium in its build toward message. It is here that the social or cultural context infiltrates narration as its premise, so that the triadic association relating stylistic execution through text to context can be otherwise adjusted for prose fiction, yet again, as prose\ plot/premise. This formatting of the system is meant to suggest that the normal slant of story forward toward its gathering import is only slanted back on itself in reflex when language is weighted more toward linguistic determination than narrative designation—or at least the latter as inextricable from the former. At which point language becomes not just part of the story but a sensed model for its fulfilled assumptions.

This is as true for Baker as for Powers, even when flesh seems—if only nominally, and by many a name—more obsessed over in the former than phrasing. In the compulsive focus demonstrated by Baker's first-person personae across the wider range of his work—their attention always riveted to things in the world, isolated objects, as well as the objectification of bodies and their material functions—words themselves come into unsaid focus as prominent, even at times dominant, among just those functional things. Words are the concretized medium of reading in each writer, of course, the resourceful stylistic signature: technical, esoteric, intriguing, often hypertrophic in such diction's specialist precision. In Baker, however, words are the verbal correlate of his observational obsession, often too exacting by half in their distancing lingual comedy—both in his porno fictions and elsewhere. In Powers, flourished but motivated, similarly stringent wording leads beyond itself into potent terminological subtexts. The reflex action induced by Baker is the vocabular spasm of a one-off: the result either of seemingly obscure book learning or of sheer erotic concoction. Stylistic reflexion in Powers marks more often a linked increment in a meshwork of further conceptual resonance within the broadest possible net of historical and cultural associations.

Minimalist vs. maximalist: that's one way to think of it. But Baker is more extreme than that, Powers more nuanced—hence the latter's revisionist take, in his first book, on the previous generation of postmodern metafiction and its megaforms, in contrast to Baker's near abandonment of narrative scale and its plotting altogether for a resolute fiction of intensively phrased observation. With Baker being something more like a minusculist of studious comic obsession, all cumulative events, let alone plot, are regularly sent into time out—as stressed by the very title of 1994's *The Fermata*, where narrative is mostly kept on hold by a rampant exercise in verbal depiction. Baker's stylistic furor and narrative reductionism lead naturally enough (if natural could be the word)—four years after his debut book, *The Mezzanine* (itself only three years after Powers's similarly para-novelistic first fiction)—to the deadpan removal, beginning in 1992 with *Vox*, of the desiring subject from the erogenous topography of his pornographic mapwork: texts more like anatomical atlases than narratives. Abiding tendencies were discernible from the start in both writers. Hardly traditional novels at all, the first books of each, as we've seen so far with Powers, and in a tendency Baker's 1986 *Mezzanine* also exhibits, tell a tale beyond their own—telegraphed at the level of stylistic signals apart from story.

In this respect, perhaps the most obvious contrast between Baker and Powers is that one writer fetishizes the dictionary, the other monopolizes the encyclopedia. And with a different descriptive focus as a result: percept versus concept, object versus system, the concretization of impression versus the articulation of design, pattern, and interplay. Both require, and so educe in process, the tutoring of reading as what one might call a *learned profession of interest*. One writer does so in the name of notice alone, in novels without narrative, the other in the name of a cross-referenced plotting whose work it is partly the reader's to sort, index, and coordinate. Hard words are their own reward in Baker; in Powers they are spliced in quite markedly to intelligible networks organic, scientific, technological, or aesthetic—botanic, genomic, cybernetic, musicological, what have you. Ferried on vocabulary but differently wedded to it, the descriptive observations are equally keen in each writer, but piecemeal and ironically distracted in Baker, philosophically interlinked in Powers. The same sprinkling of specialist diction—risible in its exactitude in Baker whenever its preciosity bursts on the colloquial turf of a given paragraph—might instead seed entire narrative preoccupations in Powers, often involving a satire of jingoism along with invested technical vocabularies of all sorts, from musical notation to laboratory patois. At issue here is the difference between a wickedly meticulous vocabulary in Baker, exhausted ad hoc on the objects or orifices it serves to italicize, and its ratcheting up to one kind of narrative paradigm or another in Powers: a shift from the contingent logistics of diction (or say *erudiction*) to the exigent structure of fiction in an information-based thematic.

One measure of the antipodal perspective opened up by this contrast is, to repeat, that the throwaway showy lexeme in Baker could, as vocabular matrix, spawn an entire Powers novel when submitted to the MacArthur-celebrated "genius" of the latter's polymath aesthetic. What adroit counterpoint is to Powers, sheer digression is to Baker, who emerges in his acclaimed first text (if not novel), *The Mezzanine*, as a mannerist of transfixed detail in whose prose all hierarchy and subordination is thrown over by a structure of ancillary footnotes every bit as grounded and "central"—as focalized—as anything upstairs in the text. All is a marginal gloss on the persona's conscious (but not subjective) interaction with the objective reality of the made modern universe. Preoccupied at several turns, for instance, with the plastic bags he uses to collect his snacks, incidental purchases, and reading matter on lunch break (a hiatus that subsumes the entire story, such as it is), the narrator, at the climax and closure of his report, gets untold (and certainly non-narrative) satisfaction from the once-bagged milk carton by making it the new disposable packaging for a crumpled pizza bag: "I took an obscure satisfaction in the inside-outness of this achievement."[7] Not so obscure that we on the outside don't get the form/content in-joke of the container contained, *reductio ad absurdum* of the attentively expanded and entirely (as narrative) expendable content of the book's whole dilated prose form. And so, with many such observations logged by Baker before this, it's back up the escalator, at book's end, to the eponymous site of his unnamed office work: "mezzanine" from the Latin *medianus*, "of the middle": dare we say medial? In any case, as titular site somewhere halfway between attenuated temporal narrative and sheer literary description, this is where the narrator's—or say persona's—every verbally couched aperçu can, in only the most oblique and delimited ways, tap into the kind of social and scientific infrastructure on which Powers's fiction more ambitiously builds, not just in its intellectual gridwork but in its frequent media archaeologies.

A deft but straightforward plain style in Baker, mostly vernacular, talky, unrhetorical, never pompous, with even quirky complaints moderated, explodes every few pages with some obtrusive doosey of diction, a little firecracker of overloaded lexical expertise. In Powers, a supple but demanding mastery of phrasing and terminology acclimate readers to entire realms of expertise. In Baker, instead, they snap us alert, diverted from one level of perception to another, from the world to the word. Though this might seem inimical to the author's observational project, it is the opposite. His is an effort to mark the inclusion of language within the negotiable things of the world, where they can do their textured rendering in an aptly concrete fashion. To give just three of the vaunted, daunting, one-off terms I myself had to look up in the first score of pages in *The Mezzanine*—just for fun in this case, but which in a novel by Powers I would have needed to befriend in context as the learned core of some multifarious plot-length extrapolation—Baker's digressive fascination is drawn, with piecemeal precision, to the argot of geometry ("radians," 3), physics ("vibratiuncles," 8), and botany ("cotyledonary," 17). All the while his narrator—or more like enunciator—indulges in the heaving of adjectives into either heavier nouns or syllabically burdened adverbs ("pervasion," 11; "pilferage," 79; "periodicities," 131; "binarily," 81)—or in substituting a hard for a common term, as when the "memory" of shoelace-tying is filed as privileged "engram"(16) or when his antiperspirated armpit gets referred to as the "pleural cavity" (51). This isn't festive so much as obsessive in its obvious comedy, but sometimes an adjectival telescoping like "reminiscential" (40) verges on the blatant wordsplay of a portmanteau unpacking like "reminiscent + essential."

Readers are so inundated and amused by this vocabular bravado that we may more than once turn to the dictionary to see whether seemingly bottomless lexical retention might be instead its own mode of invention, its own kind of lexical or etymological mind game. We check to see, that is, if there could possibly be such a momentous adverb (no, a goofy coinage this time!) as the one spun out in describing how our narrator—or at least authorial mouthpiece—forces the giant industrial toilet-paper roll prevalent in the new institutional bathroom stall "to trundle momentumulously around the spindle" (75). The real spin here is Baker's subpunning thrust of words. In Powers, any such lingo, held to stricter precedent, would join forces—and force—with an active undertext in the prosecution of plot. In Baker, the extruded verbalism is its own relief. And while still with Baker in the men's room, it's worth noting, in view of our pending final chapter on the lechemes (rather than dictionary lexemes) of his invented porno diction, how he chooses to describe his self-conscious difficulty in public mincturation at corporate urinals. Instead of the more technical "tubules" of a nervously inhibited inner anatomy, the gerund in his disappointment over his own "uriniferous tubing" carries an extra heft of phallic synecdoche—parts for the whole part, the tubular member itself—and can thus seem to anticipate the pornolinguistics to follow in the next decade of his literary production.

In Baker's first book, the besetting impulse to descriptive overkill seems to locate by title, in the architectonics of the "mezzanine," some middle ground between digression and its gloss, so that the variable bulk of the book's lower-font footnotes are, as noted, indistinguishable from paragraphs elsewhere mounted on these bases of pure digression. This foregrounding of the text/paratext dyad at degree zero—everything, as it were, *on the same page*, however arbitrarily disposed in typographic format—can only encourage the reader's related sense that the object ontology of things so ludically pursued in the text is linked to the black-on-white thing called print, through which those things called words imprint on consciousness what they foreground against their own neutral support. In this version of a micro-meta stratum, such is the book's graphic as well as linguistic emblem of its own objecthood. This is because anything, as the narrator has discovered in early childhood, any object, however humble, "looked good" if "you set it down on a piece of white cloth, or any other kind of clean background" (38). Note how the preposition "down" (as in the writerly "set it down on a piece of paper") flips in idiom to a kind of visual uppercasing at the end of the paragraph, with the speaker's repeated insistence (and my added emphasis) that "anytime you set some detail of the world *off* that way, it was able"—in another prepositional twist—"to take *on* its true stature as an object of attention" (38). Such, then, taken under consideration by us in turn, is the reflexive paradigm for all instigated reading: whatever it is, write it up in black-on-white, its stature upped in the process, and over it goes from mere material form to font (both senses) of information, set down and off to be taken on, in, and up.

On the track of data more scientifically and politically ramified by literary plotting, we look elsewhere now—across three chapters on the restless narrative experiments of Richard Powers—before returning to the pornographic escalation of terminology in Baker, where "attention" to the female body is most fully indulged when its features are laid down and brought out (more prepositions yet) in the methodical itemizations offered up on the "white cloth" of codex pages rather than in any episodes of bedsheet sex. And where a self-conscious textuality undermines any voyeuristic immediacy. Anticipating all of the chapters ahead, we might return, beyond Baker's "white piece of cloth" as fabric backdrop to the "proving window" in *Tenet*, despite its own shallow artifice (as well as hypothesis) in context: return, that is, for our own further emblem—or tenet—of reflex structure. This would involve an auto-confirmation not of reverse entropy in backward motion, as in the plot of Nolan's film, but instead a stress on reading's unique onward, even while recursive, course. In the quite various fictional test cases that await, the framed narrative page does often become a unique kind of two-way mirror that, as fictive window, lets attention see through to narrated event. But it does so even while looking on at its own share in textual production across the bidirectional course—the "proving" field—of diction, syntax, and their frequently retraced inference. What was that exactly? "See for yourself." Look again. Run it back by you.

By the end of the remaining four chapters, divided three to one on their now literary front, we should have chalked up many further reasons, beyond those anticipated here, for the inclusion of Baker along with Powers—even while apprehending more fully what the study of the latter alone would have succeeded in delimiting about the main topic at hand. If so, we will thus have come to appreciate how this commentary is not primarily about films compared to books, or about maximalist writer compared to minimalist. Rather, it is about the text-adjusted attention spans of an audience when understood as "reading" in either mode: a process visualized as such in the cognitive mirrors thrown up for us by each medial system. And so, as should also be clear in this chapter's transitional fade from visual to verbal form, the true license for such a book is not that there hasn't been one in decades (since Stam's) to compare film and literature directly on the score of fictional reflexivity and its derivations. Motivation comes instead from there having been as little attention paid in the meantime to the analytic yield—for that (or any other) narrative dimension of these separate media—from a close comparison of visual and verbal style. And of their reflexive "trigger points"—as sampled by the schematic discriminations offered so far regarding the tradition of self-enactive cinematics. With or without the two-way optics of Nolan's trick "proving window" either in view or in mind, then, what follows in the scrutiny of literary writing will offer its own implicit series of triptych mirrors: __/. Reframed thereby, as we'll continue to find, a plotted text is seen flanked by technique on the one side, contextual inference on the other, in a coordinated metannarrative reflex of our own readerly attention.

Notes

1 Stanley Cavell, *The World Viewed: Reflections on the Ontology of Film*, Expanded Edition (Cambridge, MA: Harvard University Press, 1979), ch. 18, 133–45.
2 The anomaly of the freeze for Kubrick—apogee of abruptness in contrast to his dominant long-take aesthetic, a kind of editing in extremis—is perhaps clearest of all in the lone climactic appearance of four such time-bending freezes (warp-speed close-ups on the spaceman protagonist in the time tunnel of apocalyptic

transformation) at the conclusion of *2001: A Space Odyssey*, as discussed and illustrated in my *Between Film and Screen: Modernism's Photo Synthesis* (Chicago, IL: University of Chicago Press, 1999), 109–10.

3   For a discussion of Epstein's far-reaching theory of cinematic "thought" in his 1946 *The Intelligence of a Machine*, see Stewart, *Cinemachines: An Essay on Medium and Method* (Chicago, IL: University of Chicago Press, 2020).
4   Evan Calder Williams, *Shard Cinema* (London: Repeater, 2017).
5   Peter Brooks, *Reading for the Plot: Design and Intention in Narrative* (Cambridge, MA: Harvard University Press, 1992; orig. publ. 1984).
6   Don DeLillo, *Underworld* (New York: Scribner, 1997), 826, climactically—after many variant refrains of this idea in passive as well as intransitive grammar (e.g., "everything's connected" [289]; "everything connected" [408]).
7   Nicholson Baker, *The Mezzanine* (New York: Grove Press, 1986), 132–3.

3

Understories

The woods were unfathomably complex, but they didn't know it.
—Jonathan Franzen, *Purity* (2015)

Her maples are signaling. *Life is talking to itself, and she has listened in… If she dies tomorrow she'll still have added this one small thing to what life has come to know about itself.*
—Richard Powers, *The Overstory* (2018)

After the punning metalingual epigraph from Powers that opened this book, our return to his capacious narrative invention deserves another from him: this time about nonhuman semantics—placed in contrast, here, with a quite different thought about the world's organic systems from a contemporary peer in American fiction. But Franzen's is a passing remark about cognitive hierarchies, whereas Powers builds an entire stylistic network out of the premise articulated by his botanist heroine about bioorganic signage: a verbal *undertext* of sorts, literally rooted in forest energy. All is intertwined. An organizing principle of harmonic recurrence in the textual substrate, triangulated with reading as a reflex of recognition, becomes in its *meta* function the true overstory—or encompassing extratext—of this novel's multi-branch structure. And becomes in the process, in accordance with that proposed triadic model in the Preview (in its debt to Brian McHale), the key not so much to an *epistemology* of narrative interconnection, in a modernist vein. Nor to a (preter)natural *ontology* of shared human and tree life in a latter-day greening of the postmodern metatext. What emerges more prominently, from the verbal turf up, is a *phenomenology* of mimetic perception regarding arboreal life's global signaletic reticulation in an indecipherably articulate poetry of nature. Under Powers's scansion, and the reader's in turn, this is a poetry whose prose manifestation in the reflexes of novel reading is certainly not allowed to miss the forest for the trees, but which nonetheless, if not stylistically energized, leaves unregistered untold thickets of inference in the carpeting shrub brush—plot's fertile "understory"—whose phrasal recurrences bind and uphold all broader patterning.

With the novel as much as any genre, literary intensity is often a function of verbal density, generated under the shaping force of style or form. And density is partly a matter of harmonic intervals, whether narrow or many pages wide. To keep order, remain true to form, poetry may decide to rhyme; to keep house, long prose must at least repeat. Beyond and including end rhyme and meter, close recurrence is the spine and flexion of lyric verse; motif the normal engine of narrative. Lyric recurs to its own phonetic beat and measure; the novel returns at less regular intervals to its themes—and sometimes to the wordings that work them up in the first place. Poems may rhyme; novels must redouble—and so may verbally chime in service to this texturing of recognition. Any novelist who titles a book *The Echo Maker* would in part be naming his own procedures at one level or another. And none more obviously than Powers in 2006, whose sense of phrasal patterning—not just within sentences, but among them, chapters apart—amounts to the very poetry of his fiction. With sound play in mercurial ripple across his sentences, a broader-gauge framework of schematic echo is regularly the most notable mark of his intricately linked storylines. Attending to such a scalar balance between narrow syllabic bandwidths and widely looped wording—each advanced with new exigency in 2018's *The Overstory*, the most multi-pronged and disparately character-driven of his books yet—is only to recognize something abidingly novelistic about this tandem work of language. As a philosophical thinker who is also a luminous writer, Powers sees and pursues new connections that, beyond strict formulation, he makes us *hear* in precisely the novel form and play of his words.

Though on fire with ideas, it is true that Powers leaves certain readers cold. Detractors can find his fictions somewhat bloodless in their intellectual sinews; coiled by logical tension rather than credible human suspense; speculatively motored rather than immediately moving; his habitually contrapuntal storylines more propositional than plotted—diagrammatic treatises rather than dramatic treatments; often more brainiac than heart-breaking in their inhabited crises, their rarefied abstract peripeties, their QEDs rather than satisfying narrative closure; and through it all, that unique dictionary recourse so often required of his exacting locutions—and then likely to redirect attention toward more aggressive glosses in the encyclopedias of cybernetics, genetics, musicology, and so on. The verbal ingenuity—the technical wording transfigured by technique—can itself appear leveling. His invented people may all seem to breathe out, as well as in, the same articulate wry air, with spiritual crises bared by internal monologues suspiciously similar in the grip and twist of their informed idiomatic lucidity. The books may thus read, at times, like fictional outings not so much of style versus substance as of vocabulary versus event.

But there's perhaps the crux right there: in the confrontation of inner life and its phrasing, psychology and expression. For what we saw in the chunky punctuation, as well as deliberately awkward formulation, of "metaself-conscious" in the last chapter's glance at his first book—where human agents are always taking dictation from their own scripts for themselves, trying to act like, act out, the kind of people they are—can help explain the inextricable link between personality and discourse in Powers's fiction. As written up in his plots, the human subject may seem verging on its own textual invention. Be that as it may, the novel by Powers most crowded with people, whether or not personalities, plays its hand differently. If 2018's Pulitzer Prized *The Overstory* follows suit in coming across as another novel of tightly phrased ideas from the churning "genius"—and laser-hewn diction—of this deserved MacArthur winner, it may no longer feels so cool-headed in the rigor of its cultural diagnoses. In its ecological fervor, it is by turns rhapsodic and despairing in the face of nature's threatened regenerative potential. And characterization is entirely subordinated—this time by the full weight of its transhuman canvas—to the thematic concerns registered by these narrational mood swings.

Whereas Pirandello once thrust onto the surrealist stage six unfinished dramatic characters in search of an author, a century later, in *The Overstory*, Powers sends out a third again as many fictional characters in search of a plot. If that sounds like a reviewer's barb, it isn't. Because this time they find it, the plot they're looking for—and themselves in the process, with some bitter consequences. This happens when they converge, mostly by happenstance, and in one case only via Midwest TV coverage, in an anti-logging activism, amid the West Coast redwoods, that escalates to the point of violence. Not just personified ideas, the characters jostle and suffer, hurt and purge, with a novelistic impact that remains inextricable, as always, from the linkages, tight and broad, of Powers's language—but this in a context, as never so insistently before, that exceeds these characters by definition. And for which, at revelatory nodes of connection, the reader's reflex reaction to the wording of their world is often the most immediate latch among their lived trajectories: the lone phenomenological voucher of a true articulated overstory.

The novel's conceptual threading and intermesh, it must be said, are certainly easier to track than the lives actually entwined. Each interknit subplot extends backwards into the childhoods of the divergent characters, then forward into their improbable overlap. If all this seems too much to hold in mind at once, it is. Such is the multistory in build-up, even as this dispersedly communal focus becomes instead global in the end; reading is the effort to educe just that ultimate overstory. Part of the idea, no doubt, is that all walks of life may lay themselves open to unexpected onsets of ecological passion—even while the frailty of characterization remains hard to deny. The heavily loaded roster of plot agents, both predictable and implausible at once in their environmental convictions, seems engineered primarily to grid—and gird—the intersections and echoes, not of personal animus, but of language itself in the poetics of Powers's typical scientific vocabulary.

Funneled together by plot, the tracked actors cede much of their credible vitality to quasi-personified tree forms that take up their own choral speaking parts, animated, communicative, medial, bearing witness to the world from the heights and depths of an arboreal sensitivity on a par—though not a level playing field—with human motive. As distinguished from the attitude toward insentient nature in the first epigraph from Jonathan Franzen, in Powers's novel trees not only liaise with each other and their adjacent vegetation, but they are in themselves messages. All antennae out, the novel stages the realized urge to listen up. Its pages figure that urge in the elicited terms—and wrought attentions—of a hypertuned vocabulary, botanic lingo and otherwise, puns, echoes, and harmonic overtones included, that taps directly—often by metaphoric filaments strung across long stretches of text—into the author's familiar linguistic predilections. But with new urgency and leverage. At this pitch of fictional stylistics, to talk trees requires a borrowed and replenished discourse all its own, in the face of which the dated aesthetic shibboleth of "organic form" takes on, however contorted or arcane at times, a fresh tensile application—as part of an unabashedly reformative ethic.

Yet in launching the first of three chapters on phrasal reflexivity in Powers's structuring of fiction, we can best start slow. We begin by noting how the manner by which cross-episode echoism in the phonetics of wording—becoming as much a patterning impulse as any ensemble characterization in this late novel—only serves in this way to disperse, at the broadest scope, the inherent wordwork of the single Powers sentence: in its admitted priority as language act, hence as fictive construct, over typical novelistic characterization. Or if not priority, attempted parity. Powers has in fact scaled down, more than back, the legacy of metafiction that is his 1980s birthright. His work still hews to the reflexivity he was as a novice writer nurtured by, but he has gradually weaned his prose from its most overt mimetic deficits in undermined realist representation. Increasingly, the skeletal anatomy of "constructivist" fiction writ large, to which he was heir apparent, is probed more narrowly in regard to the cellular structure of the sentence. Instead of books laid open to their own "trigger points" as mere books, they engage us more locally as writing tacitly about the challenge of their own writing, their own linguistic mandate, or in other words about the impact of a storyworld not forgone by fiction but under articulation by it. *The Overstory* is unmistakable in this regard, its title a kind of metafictional false lead. This is a book where a global botanic saga is interpreted by human language in a way that surrenders all privilege of invention in the face of the organic real. As in the other two books by Powers we'll be examining at length, beginning with *Plowing the Dark* at the start of the new century, language is honed to the point where, when invigorating mimesis rather than depleting it, the word aspires, not just to materiality as a thing in itself, but to the thing, the idea, it is working to render. It is only in this way that narrative art could begin to claim kin with nonhuman intentional functions in the semiotic ecology of the vegetal system.

These last two decades of Powers's prose have been in a sense presaged and clarified by his 2002–3 interview with Kevin Berger in the *Paris Review*.[1] Noting how much has been "written about the architecture and the large-scale of my work," and granting just how "important" this certainly is to him, Powers nonetheless stresses instead how "it's really the individual sentence that I work at again and again until it becomes the thing it's trying to describe." He generalizes next in a more familiar vein, but it is this emphasized *fusion* rather than just fitness of wording with fictive world that is so striking. Many writers, as he next puts it otherwise in generalization, might well agree here: "To me, that sense of complete commensurability between form and content at the level of the individual sentence is really what writing is all about." But the extra sense that writing should become its own content—*become* in both senses, suit and subsume it—is the distinguishing point in all this. And the way Powers phrases this aspiration suggests, for our purposes in the evolution of American literary reflexivity, a crucial difference from Don DeLillo, whose prose music is continuous across topics, rather than honed ad hoc as in Powers's case. That's what makes the former—and forebear—so manifest a *stylist*, rather than the gifted yet tactical *wordsmith* we find in Powers, the latter having no phonic signature to count on, but avowedly changing manner with every change in matter. As DeLillo, instead, happily admitted a decade before in the same *Paris*

Review, and as we've "previewed" this metalinguistic gesture in its modeling of reflex attention—the author of a book called *White Noise* is ready at any turn (of phrase) to "let language" and its inner noise "press meaning upon me," with syllable and sound in effect dictating sense. In contrast, for Powers language is the weight-bearing armature under pressure from mimetic intent. Explained in his own *Paris Review* interview: "I love to see how much load a sentence can bear." And the engineering is always site-specific, thematically leveraged, as he stresses in his further remarks: part of the structuring of sense rather than its independent spur to phrasal rhythm. Differently overlain from novel to novel as these soundscapes naturally are, Powers calls the typical effect a "double-voicing," where the sentence, beyond depiction, can "reflect the virtuosity of the human mind," not as "set piece" but as a cognitive apparatus.[2] He aspires, in short, to "build sentences that are equal to mental states." Only appreciable, that is, in the coils of the reading mind. Reflective, if you insist.

And when the interviewer shifts gears to ask him about the frequent critique of his characterization, his fictional people often thought not to be quite "palpable," the answer is already implicit: that his words are too palpable, too fully materialized, to let other bodied forms come through convincingly. Powers does allow that this results from the risky split motive of wanting to write books that are both "realistic and metafictional." It is perhaps this tandem ambition that is indeed the most "palpable," the most immanent and tangible, sign of his "double-voicing" in the "build" of a very much made—then intensively remade—prose, where his self-acknowledged status as "a completely compulsive sentence-level rewriter" is felt in the contoured propulsion of the finished products, one notable intensity after another. Aside from the way such phonic and syllabic as well as syntactic obsession, repetitive, insatiable, will be prodded into travesty by the sexed lexemes of Nicholson Baker's word-diddling, I dwell on this level of self-awareness in Powers because it is precisely in such a densening of phrasal momentum on the ground—rather than in the more familiar metafictional "architecture" that may tacitly license and contain its experiments—where this study locates narrative's most immediate, and medial, reflex action. Here rests (hardly the best word) the registered verbal assertion of metanarrative event from sentence to sentence in the adventure of read writing and its restlessly triggered recognitions. These are recognitions in the coming examples, from *Plowing the Dark* to *The Overstory*, that can span whole clustered chapters at a time to institute a reader's curious collusion in the self-generated rules of pattern recognition. And when we catch ourselves being caught up in such exactions of phrase, attention is mirrored askew in the exceeded mimesis. Unlike the full-scale "hall-of-mirrors avant-garde novel" we will find Powers tacitly distancing his work from a decade later in *Generosity: An Enhancement*, still each load-bearing sentence bends outward under its own weight, from amid description, to reflect on its own processed inscription.

So down to cases. Bundling its aggressively separate plotlines and character streams, the overall fourfold structure of the *The Overstory* suggests, at a glance, its emphasis on a metaphoric bond between plant life and human maturation. Written gradually into a bigger picture than the plaited strands of their human backstories in the first eponymous eight chapters—picaresques in search of an epic—the divergent characters sprout there under the section-title "Roots" until their shared masterplot figuratively *thickens*, as if ring by ring, in "Trunk," only then to spread out—by ever-widening circles, and by resulting upward thrust—into its overarching "Crown," from which to propagate again in "Seeds." Matching nature's cyclicity, the tacit circularity is unmistakable, as if a familiar four-volume structure from the English fictional canon (think Dickens's *Our Mutual Friend*) has been turned involute and self-renewing—unrolled like a continuous looped scroll rather than an eventually closed book: from seeds to the roots of full fruition and back again in dissemination. Such titular divisions of narrative labor give away no plot, but instead give way immediately to archetype. They are tropes—but tropes all but literalized in narrative, as with the novel's first of countless plays on words: "Roots" for the separate *routes* that will carry many of the tracked characters west, along various personal paths and paved roadways, to the redwood forest, or merely forward in place to associated revelations at a geographic distance—as in the case of Ray, the property lawyer, wrestling at one point with a brief punningly called "Should Trees have Standing?"[3] The ecological torque of this novel turns repeatedly on such subterranean turns of phrase and their tacit off rhymes. And if we are still left asking, in generic terms, what kind of novel this could really constitute, the answer is precisely a *prose* fiction.

Routings, Branchings: The Echological Turn

In zeroing in on the western stands of redwoods, each vector of story may be thought to minimize the personal in deference to the conceptual—the Powers trademark—here in particular emphasis on the eco-political. En route, language allegorizes, as prose, the same *re*formations it instigates, bioethical and stylistic alike, regarding any paradigm of organic form. Powers isn't just a hard read, but a hard reader. Through the continually readjusted lens of his verbal attention, we learn how to decipher the world anew through the test of reading itself. And in-jokes, like "standing," only bolster the inferential sympathy between vegetal nature and verbal invention. A passing dead metaphor, "thicket of words" (249), has already achieved full metatextual troping when Professor Patricia Westerford, known as Tree-Patty, puts the finishing touches on her botanical masterwork: "She types up the draft. She prunes a few words and pollards a few phrases" (223). As Powers well knows, such is the topiary work of prose—cut to the measure, in his every effort this time out, of botany's organic system—and primed for the reflexes of our systemic recognition.

In a novel balancing prose against plot in this way, the thinness of character psychology is framed to invoke more than it forfeits. The emphasis is to make characters learn for themselves to devalue the clench of personality in favor of collective being and purpose—and so to merge, if not entirely submerge, troubled personal stories in the vicissitudes of longer-span natural histories. These are histories that the characters must not just brush up against, but learn to decipher, in the world around them. To which end the vocation of prose fiction offers its own direct homologies. Even if one were to assume an ethic of reciprocal impersonality, in this particular naturalist saga, as converting defect to virtue in regard to what some critics lament as the author's slack "people skills," still the insistent theme of *The Overstory* plugs directly into Powers's eccentric strengths as well—including perhaps their signal feature: the fertile thesaurus of his verbal imagination, exercised to the full in the encyclopedias of botanic lore. True, a serious novelist, let alone a gifted one, engaged in any such unapologetic act of consciousness-raising about global deforestation and the sacred life of trees, has only his writing first of all, moral fervor and political stamina aside, to build on— whether in celebration or polemic. More to the point in *The Overstory*, when the purpose is manifestly to elicit not just the venerable organic system of forest renewal but, more intimately, the very *medium* of tree life, the writing has only its own medium (the tactical channeling of its language) to draw on, and out, for exemplary cross-reference: its rhetorical medium as such, lexical, syntactic, figural—always verbal before representational, transmissive before mimetic.

More than evocative, the novelistic medium must here become programmatic in its cognate disclosure of arboreality's own elusive communicative system. In this respect, the forest colloquy joins forces with Powers's inveterate dictionary prose, driven by a confluence of specialist lexicons rather than any cultivated stylistic fluency. Beyond mere "windy" effusions in the rush of leaves, the summons to any true organic music—requiring close lexical transposition into human prose—is bound up in the conjured internal soundscape of the trees' own pulsing biorhythms. One result is that, for the novel as a whole, quite apart from the recorded botanist audiobook (Tree-Patty's big hit) featured at more than one point within it, reading is listening. It's too early to prove this, but none too soon to pose it as this chapter's leading hunch—and heuristic. Here trees' legal *standing* in court is associated with implied vertical *stance* in their native habitat. Etymology bears covert witness in many such phrasings, including Ray the lawyer's own last name, Brinkman, an irony borne in on us when the suspended animation of his post-stroke paralysis holds at the border of death for pages on end. The novelist who, in *Orfeo* (2014), speaking of music, and by analogy of prose's own notation, approximates a phonetic anagram in locating the "islands of silence" between sounds—and does so with that haunting silent *s* floated amid the sibilance of the phrase itself[4]—arranges in *The Overstory*, we'll find, for phonetic language to ferry across just such churning words between insular (yet sometimes not quite insulated) silences. This happens most tellingly, as we are to hear (without seeing), in the cross-currents of a climactic homophonic wordplay: a verbal reveal only to be apprehended under pressure from the long build-up behind it. Suffice it to say for now that *The Overstory* has no way to transliterate sylvan tongues, the forest's cellulose signaling, but through its own linguistic grid: not a loosely woven trellis of suggestion but a tight lexigraphic and etymological schema whose most striking nodes are alive with auditory stress (in every sense of that noun)—as focused at one point on the punning clues of an actual crossword puzzle playing on a sound pun for the syllable "leaf." In advance of the settings required for full exemplification, we may characterize the gathering rhetorical effect of such volatile phrasing as serving to familiarize the otherwise uncanny notion of arboreal messaging with a sense, somewhat less foreign to normal reading, that alphabetic language may often slip out from under strict authorial coherence into a seemingly independent agency of its own, kindred in this way to the sometimes audited natural—or preternatural—signage of the forest.

To this end, as a reading lesson, no novel's title could be more instructively (if abstractly) metanarrative. The very coinage, in its tacit synonym for masterplot, is typical of Powers's associational diction in that it springs, unspoken, from the botanical argot of "understory" (think underbrush) for the blanketing of a forest's floor. This is a curious term that comes underfoot over half a dozen times in a novel whose opposite coinage, never in fact let loose into the narrative discourse, has its penultimate appearance, just before the title page itself, when copyright information assures us that the novel so-named, and if only pro forma, is "printed" with tacit ecological commitment "on 100% recyclable paper." Whatever the "Overstory" may be, it goes unnoted as such throughout, a pure extrapolation as we read. By recognizing this in overview, we are closing in—by what might be called reverse zoom—on what makes Powers's trope of the closed terrestrial biocircuit and its looming metaplot so different from the preceding generation of his postmodernist forbears in American fiction. The overarching is not in this case overweaning. The unmastered mysteries of a capital-S System in which human energies have found themselves embedded—that anxious horizoning frame that constitutes the stock-in-trade of the paranoia novel (Thomas Pynchon to Don DeLillo)—is a trope turned inside out by Powers so as to limn (ultimately limb) the intricate workings of a vulnerable botanic superstructure and its tongueless signage.

In all facets of their vitality, trees (as italicized) *"pour out messages in media of their own invention"* (355). It is this overheard interplay of arboreal signals and receptors that is both manifested in, and modeled by, the audited *echology* of Powers's prose. Across its eight parallel storylines—its "Roots" or (again, in one pronunciation) self-echoed "Routes," together with the whole array of verbal recursions that brace and interlace them—the interpretive work of what we might call *echocriticism* is a first line of response. Only by tracing the spores and seedlings, the tubers and sudden shoots, of vocabular outcroppings, all in the linked lingo of organic interdependency, does one sense the pattern before—and beneath—its tangled ground cover and towering foliate canopy. I speak in further metaphor, of course, responding in kind to the novel's loam and efflorescence of tropes, its figurative title included—hovering, above it all, somewhere between global abstraction and tethered emblem in its crowning bloom: a never-named or specified tale to be told only on the pulse of readerly recognition. One thinks by contrast of Powers's academic satire in *Galatea 2.2* (1995), about the learning curve of artificial intelligence, with the hero's half-hearted effort to teach a phonorobotic computer enough language to render it an independently functioning literary critic. Robots must be programmed with our own language; trees predate us with theirs. The organic story they tell, never over, isn't easy to translate.

In contrast to the novel's supposedly entitled overview, the received (if not widely used) term "understory" takes its lexical exit with this, its eighth, appearance: "A distant branch snaps, and the crack shoots through the understory" (492)—from which new "shoots," in the other, botanical sense, will soon protrude. The subsequent prose of causal explanation is immediately elided into a mere chiming declarative, playing with two odd plural singulars: "There are mink nearby, in these same woods, and lynx." And links—the kind figured in this case by echoic troping in its own right: a music of interfusion between a curious singular plural ("mink") and the falsely audited *s* of the equally double-duty "lynx." Such are the frequent chiming byways of echology in Powers's novel, instanced late in the day by an allegory of echo's dying fall itself. On the verge of cabin fever in the mountain wilds of Montana, outlawed by his previous violence against the lumber industry, the character nicknamed Doug-fir is in despair about a logged-out wilderness: "This place is *dead*" (386). The italics are not just for emphasis. Doug's is the bleated word *as word*, a spectral phonetic palindrome, about to be parsed and parlayed at once, spit back and spun round, by indifferent nature: "The *ed* bangs around the Garnet Range two or three times before giving up" (386). Even just twice, and the knell would be fully renewed in its own dying away: dead e*d ed*. Conservation of energy, diminishing returns, the larger system writ small in writing per se: a sly syllabic economy thereby at work even in this re-sounding dentalized stutter from the realm of inanimate— yet still accusatory—nature. So the prose of reflex action often goes in this novel, leaving us, leaving reading, to sense detected patterns less than explicit—and regarding the organic intricacies and recursive systems of the plant realm rather than the sounding-boards of cliff faces.

In repeatedly moving from any minuscule textual detail, down in the weeds of syllabification and syntax, to the broad sweep of the overstory, however, Powers is often doing more than extrapolating from the technical idiom of his botanical topic. In all this we are kept in mind, as readers, of our own work in decrypting a set of language acts tacitly shared, in vitalist translation, across echelons of sentience between humans and the forest primeval. Verbal echoes come to sound like the reverberation of deeper bonds. Beyond all paranoia in such *über*plotting, entanglement turns restorative. Yet how could any calculated stylistic ecosystem—or echosystem—plausibly carry conviction as a cross-species articulation of shared vital signs? The question isn't rhetorical, but neither is there a ready answer. Except from—and through—the lexical texture of exemplification.

So the nagging query remains. In the face of society's most pressing global concerns, what in the world—this world of animal and vegetal rather than digital life—would such a nonelectronic ethics of *connectivity* between plant and human biology, tree being and human being, have to gain from (however ingenious) a web—or say scrub—of ground-level wordplay, even in anomalous technical forms of oblique verbal herbage? From one perspective, at least, the gain, the yield, would amount to no more, but decidedly no less, than the promotion of a certain reading posture, often just slightly askew to expectation—and, as such, an exploratory mode of analytic notice. Reading would open in this way to a deciphered semiotics of nonhuman systems, raising the stakes of attention in the will to linger, look harder, discern otherwise. *Deep reading*, then, versus anything conceived as surface reading, would stand revealed not as its own unfeeling and predatory mode of extraction, the self-interested dredging of interpretive symptoms, but as a flexible way forward, leaving clearly in place, and further contextualized by examination, the interdependencies that style's own pressure excavates, explicates, and sometimes mimics.

Nothing in this commentary is meant to, nor could, detract from the persuasive agenda of Powers's book as a genuine ecocritical text: a landmark one (to speak in its own kind of topographical dead metaphor)—and this, as might be expected, from the most important contemporary novelist operating at the cross-mapped intersections of science and human desire. No question what the story *means*, politically, ecologically, for all its mysteries of organic linkage between linguistics and the loquacious "chemical semaphores" (499) of tree life, that delectable phrase for the forest's nonlinguistic communiqués: sublingual semiotics channeled by a minimal internal rhyme. Any interpretive emphasis on the literary, the letteral, in assessing the linguistic scientism of the book's prose, evinced by the whole phonetic and etymological sedimentation of its lexical complexity, is only meant in turn to highlight, while always in the closest league with meaning, the revisionary stylistic organicism of his *echological means*. This is the system whose lateral resoundings serve to delineate the fugue-like structure of Powers's never more than tacit, nor less than immanent, overstory, unrolled in harmonic process across his orchestrated octet of storylines.

Which first come together around the next-to-last of them, concerning the introvert tree-loving girl—and eventual botanical guru of print and audio culture—Patty Westerford, introduced in the penultimate chapter of the "Roots" sequence in a way that anchors and codifies most of the disparate backstories so far. She thus takes her late but centering place—located as a kind of ideological clearing house—in the through-lines of motival developments so far, her presence weaving them together around her governing passion for the otherworld of trees. Daughter of an "ag extension agent" who took her with him, from a young age, as he traveled the Midwest landscape, "Tree-Patty" eventually finds herself, along with the majority of Powers's cast, drifting inquisitively—Westerfording, as it were—toward the Redwood coast. Trees have always, in the figurative sense, spoken to her, even before she could write back with her science. As a young child, she was distressingly slow in learning to articulate words in her inherited human tongue: a malfunction eventually diagnosed as resulting from a deformed inner ear. In this virtual muteness, she consoled herself with a "secret language" in her devotion to an arboreal dollhouse world of "woody citizens" (114) made by her of "pine-cone bodies" and "acorn shell" helmets, demurely housed together in the "burls of trees" (114). All this compensatory play—braced by its "minuscule architecture of imagination" (114)—generates the seedbed of a lifelong mission, with her "acorn animism" (114) eventually nurtured into a botany doctorate, scholarly renown, and even a popular print (and audiobook) audience. Literature and science cohabit, as in the novel we're reading—especially when its spokeswoman sets out to read the trees in an apperception cued to the nuances of prose form.

Undertext: The Thick of Diction

Beyond her tree-foraged dollhouse community, the young Patty also seeks out the messaging of "booklike bark" (119): the very phrase a layering of consonants, on prose's own part, that sends unmentioned roots into the deep etymology of *book* in the *beech* (or *birch*) on which runes were once carved. When eventually finding her words, she finds they aren't ready for social circulation. They are as ingrown as her forest sensibility. It is "her father alone" who, as prose captures it in the oscillation of internal echo, "understands her woodlands world, as he always understands her every thickened word" (113). Years later, her degree credentials eventually in hand, she nevertheless returns as soon as possible to a committed fieldwork, "the green negation of all careers" (129). It is there that she loves to hear the wind *through*—in both senses—the trees: not just sounding its way *between* branches but *via* those appendages, a breeze strumming those limbs to help the latter breathe forth their Aeolian messages. In another micro-echology, the mention of leaves that "turn" in the wind are what "turn" that wind ("on") to its associated whisperings: "The oracle leaves turn the wind audible" (130). Why not an adjective ("oracular") rather than a noun used as modifier?

Too predictable? Too portentous? In any case, whenever the nonverbal linguistics of trees is evoked, the prose of the narrative is likely to thicken or buckle its own English contours, as with the implicit surplus (and junctural elision) of "oracleaves." And the next sentence follows suit in the self-adjustment of its own internal echo: "They *filter* the day light and *fill it* with expectation." Such is the association of a forest's macro-process with the minims of prose's own reflective echosystem, as made explicit when Patty comes upon trees, in her research, "etched with knowledge encoded in native arborglyphs" (113). Beach, birch, book: medium in reflex.

Whenever the motif of language occurs in this way, whether as trope or epistemological datum, it tends to entail some degree of lexical kink—or, better, knottiness—in Powers's own prose. Tree-Patty's story sets the mold—and does so in the familiar drag on grammatical momentum induced by minor surprises or aberrations in diction. Speech impedance is not a malady in such writing, but a tactic. Reading Powers is the act of slowing over idea through the medium of words. Later in the biographic track of this seventh (recapitulative) chapter, when Patty contemplates a forest "sprouted from a rhizome mass too old to date even to the nearest hundred millennia" (131), its primal source is immediately restated—in a tongue-twisting syllabic node—as "this great, joined, sin*gle cl*onal creature that looks like a forest" (131). The very shadow of oxymoron (single/clonal) sets in as a kind of fractalized lexical node, pars pro toto for the entire overgrowth of botanical entanglements.

So it is that the "every thickened word" of Patty's incipient speech seems to have authorized in advance the novel's own most intimate summons of vegetal density: not just via a passing mimesis, in some broached phrasal performativity (of integrated glottal and velar cloning), but in a more deeply probed metalinguistics linked to tree "signals"—again, an arboreal semiosis. And precisely as figured, so we're soon to note, both in—and as—the pulped wood of a book: the one we've been reading for many seemingly disparate chapters, and to whose spine the corded rhizome is now tacitly analogized—as a "kinship" fostered "deep underground" (132). Out of nowhere but narrative's own backlog, five brief paragraphs are suddenly devoted to previous characters we've met, locating them now on compass points, spatial and temporal, in regard to Tree-Patty's present professional life of sophisticated botanical expertise. Convergence is for the first time explicit in the Over(t)story—asserted almost by the sentence-level equivalent (albeit in the negative) of that *parallel montage* equilibrating the separate spans of the novel's uneven microplots as they have shifted until now explicitly from one character's moral arc to another. Yet: "These people are nothing to Plant-Patty" (132). Not to say mean nothing; they would be meaningful to her if she knew of them, given their various conservationist passions. Instead, they simply "aren't": they don't exist for her at the plane of narrative manifestation, never will. "And yet," as figured here, "their lives have long been connected, deep underground" (132). Regarding the assembled characters in such "underground" filiation (a political twist as well in that adjective): "Their kinship will work like an unfolding book" (132), for which a photographic folio in the first chapter is the establishing paradigm as arborist chronicle.

Nature's Flip-Book

Few novels, intent on giving us a long-term overview of planetary dependencies and endurance, could begin more promisingly. In the multi-generational chronicle of the first chapter, named for the present-day inheritor of the family legacy, "Nicholas Hoel," history is serially sketched in—almost at the elliptical pace of its own embedded technical emblem in a pre-Victorian optical toy. Generations back, the head of the immigrant Iowa household—and farmstead—was inspired by the zoopraxiscope in launching a family hobbyhorse. With its spinning images in a glass drum offering the flicker effect of protocinematic motion, a related idea dawned. Since then, decade after decade, the men of the Hoel tribe have sustained the documentary "ritual" of photographing—from a fixed tripod in front of their house—one shot per month of a still-growing chestnut tree planted by the original settler. When the progenitor of this technological tradition had first assembled a year's worth of b&w images in a stack, he "riffles through them with his thumb" (11)—in the manner of that other precinematic optical toy, the flip-book: in this case, the predecessor as well of time-lapse effects, each split second overleaping, by eliding, a month's growth. As if true to the family name, intermittence becomes holistic. And does so as an explicit model for the narrative's own ellipses. "Three-quarters of a century dances by in a five-second flip" (17), writes the narrator by metonymy in his own elision of any unfolded sequence—until, with the cinematic prototype now historically in place and specified, "one more flip through the magic movie, and faster than it takes for the black-and-white broccoli to turn again into a sky-probing giant, the nine-year-old cuffed by his grandfather turns into a teen" (19).

And so it is, by association, in his own arboreal picturings and scripts alike, that Nick Hoel becomes, by novel's end, the representative of the forests themselves, always haunted by "the time-lapse pictures of the chestnut his gypsy-Norwegian great-great-great-grandfather planted, one hundred and twenty years before" (20). Recalling on our part the cinematographic emphasis in this commentary's first chapters, what Nick remembers are picture shows of change per se, figured as growth. It is in this way that the flip-book has miniaturized the time-lapses of the plot so far, though not so much the irregular, shifting tempos of its anything but staccato prose—not at least, until almost five hundred pages later, when Nick is assigned the closing passage of the novel to bookend his place in the first. By now any remaining "magic movie" is freeze-framed by aerial photograph. Nick has had the inspiration, less as draftsman than as installation site artist, to use whole fallen trees to translate their own abiding message into English, trees given quite literally the novel's last word, as word, in their own anglicized witness. For they are dragged into place to spell out "STILL" (502), a cross-hatch of vegetal legibility ultimately available only from a stratospheric vantage point. Set in place at the end of *The Overstory*, whatever they are here made to be suggest, it is clearly in resistance to the temporal rather than the spatial sense of "over." *Still* present after all these years—but with the extra twist of an ambivalent adverb (both *fixedly in place* and *even yet*) as well as the adjectival double of the former (*immobile*). What we are stationed to "close read" in that lone word "STILL," even from an aerial "distance"—and in the subdivided split seconds, as we will see, of its passage's incremental momentum—is, with its surprise vegetal resurgence, prose's nearest echo of nature's text. Nick's "articulated" trees compose no book, only a message, but one already taken up, as we are to discover, in time-lapse registration even as the tree artist has just completed their scriptive pictogram. Immobile, yes, but not unchanging at that, nor removed from cycles of decay and new growth.

Partly determining the power of this closing episode is its immediate convergence with what had seemed for a long time two other quite disparate lines of plot. We might by now have intuited some deep connection between Nick's tree painting, including his foliate graffiti scripts, and the pre-codex and tree-themed calligraphic scroll willed by her suicided immigrant father to Mimi Ma, second of the introduced characters in the eightfold cast. Yet it is her own last rather than first scene, her mind awash in arboreal messaging, that abuts most closely, as we will see, upon Nick's own final act of woodstock "graphology." Farther afield yet until then—though suddenly operating in immediate counterpoint to, almost superimposition upon, Nick's final tree-built wordwork—is the previously marginalized story of the computer genius Neelay Mehta. Miserably injured in a childhood fall from a tree, he goes on from his wheelchair to orchestrate a Silicon Valley computer-game empire under the corporate name Sempervirens ("always flourishing," "evergreen"), dubbed for the designer's Redwood City studio. After his brand's floppy-disk launch with *The Sylvan Prophecies* (191), Neelay's genius takes the company product through one hi-def iteration after another, down to cutting-edge 3D, in its signature *Mastery* series—where exponential expertise can lead its players to revel in control over whole virtual continents of their own devising, fantasies of terraforming and wealth extraction uncramped by reality. But Neelay eventually suffers an epiphany, realizing the hollowness of this model. He decides instead to equip his gamers with the data-searching finesse needed to become "learners" rather than mere players, "mastering" the life of our actual planet (not some escapist world of their own optical concoction)—and not from participatory virtualized POVs but from actual satcam overviews. The empty eschatology of total mastery over a fictive universe becomes instead the eponymous overstory of documentary narrative, open-eyed and investigative. Sempervirens has become globally environing, with the epistemic urge replacing the ludic as monetized adrenaline rush. And with the "branchings" of the internet in new sync with the actualities of organic life. One doesn't have to dwell for long over this conversion experience to find it figuring the intellectual voracity, rather than sheer esoteric gamesmanship, of Powers's own polymath style.

    It is precisely the last "chapter" of this evolved corporate story, realized from satellite vantage, that converges (via overview) with the final phase of Nick's scribal endeavor. Instead of reducing cellulose to the tabula rasa of inscription, the unexpected symbolic reversal, on which the novel closes in and down, is to have Nick write *with* (not upon) the dead trees themselves. And on their behalf as well. So that, in an unspoken wordplay, their inert logs are arrayed to log in their own message for upload to Sempervirens's orbiting camera hook-ups—of which we're not even sure Nick, the word artist in wood, is aware. When Nick as a boy first embarks on his pencil drawings of trees, based on his fascination with the photographic flip-book, he doubts he can do them justice. Yet such is the structural pivot, the cryptic metanarrative chiasmus, involved in his eventual writing of nature's ongoing will and testament, its message immemorial, that the character once daunted by a vitality of tree forms beyond "his *powers as an artist to reveal*" (19; emphasis added) now exits the novel in figuring, by proxy, the *artistry of a Powers* in just such a materially paraphrased revelation.

Time-Lapse Syntax: Between Arborglyph and Hyperscript

This emblazoned word of razed nature, "STILL," is the novel's true coup de grâce, and its tacit metatextual gambit bears more speculation than satellite photos directly bestow. What if the tired metaphor of "organic form"—in the internal feedback system of a literary text—could in its own right, as scriptive form, do more than blandly shadow a living ecosystem, but offer instead a cogent parable of a global terratext? What if the fallen trunks of trees, as well as their cross sections, could be read, in the way Nick's labor attempts, as fashioning their own messages? And what if these messages were transmissible at the right angle and distance of vision? Terra firma would become in that case no longer just a tabula rasa for predatory human imprints but a silent arboreal outcry from the forest floor.

That is what Nick's version of terrestrial installation art, his implanted earthwork sculpture, accomplishes. As transcribed on the page, rather than reproduced, the word "STILL" appears in vertically elongated sans serif caps, stripped bare—even though we know that Nick's usual ecological inscriptions have been graced with tendril filigrees like the florid margins of an illuminated "medieval manuscript" (231). This time the medium is bark and leaves, pith and parasites, rather than pigment, the felled trees fringed, if at all, by their own withering leafy flourishes. "The learners"—again Neelay's gamer addicts and fantasists turned planetary students of biodiversity—"will puzzle over the message that springs up there, so near to the methane-belching tundra" in what we have heard alluded to as the "boreal north" (355), as frigid, by etymological coincidence, as it is arboreal. On the novel's last page: "Satellites high up above this work already take pictures from orbit" (502)—and that adverb "already" soon becomes a threefold spatiotemporal refrain, extending well beyond the momentary "blink of a human eye" (502). At the data-mined pace of a global algorithmic archive, "the learners will grow connections" (502)—with that dead metaphoric cliché ("grow" for 'develop') given a freshly rooted context in the organic focus of this aerial photography. Then, too, the "giant word" spelled out in the sights of satellite telemetry by Nick's bulking calligraphic monosyllable—as if in evoked counterpoint to the imprisonment, by now, of the other tree-terrorists, Adam and Doug—is a "shape" that at first "arrests" the learners. And in an upended trope "reads them their rights" (501)—where we might expect, instead, 'reads them the riot act.' In any case, it would seem that the tree-fashioned curt adjective/adverb for fixity and endurance alike (dead "STILL"/ "STILL" changing)—almost a synonym for sempervirens—is therefore a word that reads its mortal readers in the throes of their own curiosity.

Yet again the lexical understory contours the literalized optic overview. For here is a vegetal "still life" of earth art that names at once its own severed condition of possibility, as text, and the transcendence of that finality: stillness and staying power respectively. Inaugurating its own time-lapse momentum, the prose now moves us through closely magnified adverbial snapshots of the dead wood's escalating new fruition. This is to say that, after all, the aerial satellite frame of downed trees turns cinematic as we look, at least if we watch—and listen—closely. The parallel impetus is clocked by three repetitions of "Already" that exceed any fixed view. "Already, this word is greening" (502): again, that word "STILL," by metonymy with the wood that fashions it. Change is still manifest in the mode of figurative inscription, as made explicit in syntax's close convergence of "wood" and "word": "Soon new trunks will form the word in their growing wood, following the cursive of these decaying mounds" (502)—and "cursive," yes, despite their block cap treatment on the page. The second adverbial impetus: "*Already* the mosses surge over": an odd freestanding intransitive, rather than surging over *something* in particular—as if the pure *urge* of vitality itself is at one with "the beetles and lichen and fungi turning the logs to soil" (502). Imposed lexical composition lapses to compost. In cinematographic terms, the severed death of nature, begun as an aerial freeze-frame of downed limbs, has been as if pixelated into a newly time-based erosive moldering.

Soon too, in syntactic pacing, we come upon the fulcral time-lapse of the third adverbial downbeat accompanying that lone wooden monosyllable in its narrative rendering. Even within time present, the eventual is once more flashed past: "*Already*, seedlings root in the nurse logs' crevices, nourished by the rot." Again that clumping of adjectival and possessive form that so often marks a thematic, not just a syntactic, flashpoint in Powers. The unsaid "nursery" of the world guides us through the densely ridged awkwardness of "nurse logs' crevices" to the immediate payoff in an internal phonetic rhythm of cause and outcome across the chiastic bracket "root / nurse / nourished / rot." In this syllabic span, the phonetic closed circuit mimes the energy of recirculation in the vegetal ecology under report. Compulsively rewritten, we can presume, the sentence has been obsessed over until it "becomes" its own systemic interdependency, its nourishing interface complete in the reflex of reading.

As if in liturgical solemnity, Nick has said "Amen" at the completion of his bulking—his lumbering?—cellulose script: for "verily," since he "remembers that he read once, back in Iowa… that the word *tree* and the word *truth* came from the same"—wait for it—"root" (501). It's up to us to look it up: "sturdy, firm." Etymology carries its usual weight in Powers's prose. But the pun itself on "root," hardly incidental, is in fact definitive. Everywhere in the depicted world of this fictional work, words turn woodwards—and vice versa. The diegetic system is one in which—no stray analogy this—there are "trees older than moveable type" (254). And, at any age, potentially as eloquent in their own defense—and even as fungible in their mobility. So we've just seen with those trees "photographed" from above in closure, their message under telekinetic overview in a time-lapse video that is nevertheless all prose's own—and where the trace of typeset can itself be more movable than meets the eye. I repeat: "Already the word is greening." But repeat not exactly, more like simultaneously: "Already the word is screening."

Speaking the Book

I began by suggesting that the novel's summons to the *medium*—rather than just the organic manifold—of tree life needed the conduit of a taut prose medium in its own fibrous right: alert to its own grain, resonance, subterranean filaments; not just phrases audible in the crosswinds of enunciation but words with their underground feelers out, probing, improbable, uncanny. Operating here is a conservation of linguistic energy that remains dependent on the circulatory system of a lexicon and syntax fully enmeshed—every bit as much as the sylvan undergrowth of its championed ambience—in webs of connection and interlace. Along the inner linings of its effect, prose is an entwined capillary action not so much allegorizing the pulse of tree life from the top down, but schooling cognitive recognition from the lexical ground up, seeding its own underlay with strange depths of phonic porosity in the turf of wording.

Where inference may lie fallow until unearthed by second thoughts. Few authors dependent on the force of linguistic facility telegraph their effects so delicately—or at least with such deadpan neutrality. Powers can be wry, satiric, enigmatic, but in his language, the intricacies of his diction, he is usually the least showy of wordsmiths, the least blunt of punsters—with the rare reflexive exception, of course, of our Preview's "What's a meta for?" Ordinarily the lexical warp is made to pass uncommented upon. "Boreal" and "arboreal" play against each other, as noted, many pages apart—without further ado. And when typography is specially enlisted to flag an effect, it is a device cited rather than imposed—as when a website time-lapse video called, in cutesy branding fashion, "ArBoReal" (483) is downloaded by Mimi Ma under her new alias Judith (in the continuing evasion of police capture). Without any such chance of typographic intervention in the play of flagging caps, the novel leaves it for us to note that the tree-lover, Doug, who went to prison (for arson and accidental manslaughter) instead of Mimi, to spare her, alleviates the claustrophobia in his viewless cell by listening—innocently amazed that people with "speech impediments" are now recruited for such recording chores—to none other than Tree-Patty's audiobook through the solacing "buds" (479) in his ears. This is the same author who bestows on his hero in *Orfeo* the surname Els, and abuts it more than once with "else"—as if to suggest the split psyche of the man repeatedly other to his own motives in his self-inflicted solitude.

This is also, after all, the same Richard Powers who once authored a kind of self-help guide for "writers," encouraging them to leave keypads behind for the triggering of voice-recognition digital code. His brief *New York Times Book Review* essay on "How to Speak a Book," despite its title, offers no advice to audiobook reciters. It details instead his devotion to writing through voice-dictation on a tablet PC, involving the feedback system of decipherment itself.[5] He is quick to historicize. Over the evolution of human literacy, "most reading was done out loud. Augustine remarks with surprise that Bishop Ambrose could read without moving his tongue." Subvocalization was long in coming: "Our passage into silent text came late and slow, and poets have resisted it all the way." Powers explains further: "Speech and writing share some major neural circuitry, much of it auditory. All readers, even the fast ones, subvocalize." In none of this is Powers directly issuing instructions, in the role of literary critic, for that silent reading which would elicit the "phonemes" he mentions as so crucial to the shape of phrase. So Powers's claim is finally a suitably modest, if infinitely suggestive, one: "Mostly," when dictating, "I'm just a little closer to what my cadences might mean, when replayed in the subvocal voices of some other auditioner." Not auditor, note, but a literate agent trying out for the role of attentive reader.

Two discrete instances of such audition near the end of the novel are found to arc within or between single words in sparking verbal microplots that immediately scale up into alignment with the whole curve of the Overplot. First, there is a punning flashpoint in the story of Ray Brinkman, the Minneapolis lawyer (horrified at one point by broadcast images of police brutality against the West Coast tree activists), now a movingly bedridden stroke victim who can barely grunt out his desire to play "Crss... wds" (371) with his wife, as in their former marital routine. He is convulsed in frustration by not being able to articulate his solution to their attempted puzzle except in scrawling out the alphabetic tendrils of a barely legible—but relieving—cross-syllabic "Releaf" (represented graphically rather than typographically on Powers's own page) in response to the original newspaper prompt: "starts with an R. *Bud's comforting comeback*" (374). Yet again, the pun can be laid at other than our author's door. Yet Ray's twisted, snagged script bears immediate comparison with a distant motif in the novel—and with the climax coming: namely, Nick's habitual way of "writing nature." The hard-edged san serif caps that always represent, on the page, the content rather than form of Nick's arboreal word art, even long before the climactic "STILL," force us to imagine for ourselves—in contrast, again, to the illuminated decoration with which they are compared—the leafy untrimmed look of his lettering, whose "borders teem," as mentioned, "with fronds and flowers form the margins of a medieval manuscript" (231). In Ray's case, however, the impaired, pained venting in letters of the homophonic pun on "Releaf" has recruited modern digital reproduction to simulate the spastic scribal flourish of the damaged hand's involuntary squiggles and volutes: a paralytic scrawl more leafy than readily legible. In this way the filigrees and flourishes we associate with Nick's ecological calligrams, his scraggly fronds of script, have been deflected, with hypertrophic visibility, onto the more cryptic, crippled scrawl of a never explicitly parsed (and indeed crossworded) pun awaiting Ray's recognition, dug deep from the undersoil of the novel: a novel where the only *relief* for arboreal devastation is precisely its *re-leafing*, "already" inchoate in those recuperative iterative lap dissolves we've noted on the "greening" of the novel's last page.

The second and far more covert node of epiphany, or echological *epiphony*, is associated with a last venture of tree art that precedes the closing "STILL" life. Years after his arboreal heroics, with Nick also now on the run from the law for his eco-terrorism, we find him reduced, by way of gainful employment, to "scanning bar codes" (397) on boxed books—the doubly pulped fate (unsaid) of the arboreal—at the "enormous Fulfillment Center" of an (equally unsaid) Amazon of deforestation. The "product" there is "not so much books" as—so the sentence lisps out lazily in its own *crss-wrd* hiss—"convenien*ce. Ease* is the di*sease* and Nick is its vector" (397). A vector, a thrust or trajectory, syllabic before sociological. Worlds apart from the "booklike bark" and "arborglyphs" of botanical inscription and its devoted legibilities early in the plot, phonetic diagnosis names at this point an opposite syndrome, as national ailment, even before the noun of malady, the restless "disease," fully arrives in syntactic delivery. But that is an incidental slippage—a minor ironic sabotage by lexical contagion—compared to what we discover on the next page. In secret provocations apart from his day job, Nick's polemic vandalism is still bent on defacing public as well as private property with outsize tree paintings, whose "furrows of bark"—when *read*, as it were, up close—are said in this most recent case, with their dark irregular striations, to resemble a "two-foot wide UPC bar code" (380). With a pun neither explicit nor funny, opening only between and across lexical ridges, it's the inward turned, blurred "furrow" of this phrasing that claims attention: the double decryption of this *bark code* as an undersong culmination to a novel-long *bark ode*. Lexical ridges, yes—scraped past in this ultimate "reflex action" of understoried registration.

Crucially, too, Nick's final messaging, "legible from space" as a stratospheric upload on the learners' monitors, is matched on the ground by a visceral download in the closing pages. Immediately preceding the aerial recognition of "STILL," Mimi Ma, alias Judith, having refused to sell off her own inherited, tree-dedicated calligraphic scroll, a priceless relic of her suicided father's Chinese heritage, is flooded by tree speech, where "messages hum *from out of* the bark she leans against" (499). Depth is itself measured (almost in metrical spondee) by an excess prepositional uprush (with the arguably tautological "from" echoing more than directing the "hum"). Immediately reverbed from this already onomatopoetic *hum* ("origin probably imitative," say the dictionaries), the transcendental buzz surfaces, escalates, across the vector of another prepositional doublet—and then four more such thrusts along the infrastructure of a third encompassing sentence: "Chemical semaphores home *in over* the air. Currents rise *from* the soil-gripping roots, relayed *over* great distances *though* fungal synapses linked *up to* a network the size of the planet" (499). That "network" is no dead metaphor where the learners, our wired surrogates, are concerned.

An "echological" reading of Powers's novel will, of course, not only pick up the rebound of phrases across the text, articulating its own subsystem in answer to that of the secret forest's. It will attune itself as well, in reflexive notice, to re-soundings that reach beyond—back into the literary "network"—for a new interplay with its previous "actors," near and far. Tree-Patty is at first mocked among academic botanists for the very claim that later makes for her scholarly and popular renown: exactly the confidence that trees communicate, sign themselves, as above, in "semaphores" rather than just in the trace(d) presence of spores and seeds. Short of an intuitive uprush of audition like Mimi's in the park, the work of discerning the trees' secret code is, in effect, that of a fine-tuned disciplinary stethoscope, as if eavesdropping on the leaves themselves. Their impulses are transferred to our ears by a phonically keyed (indeed, as we know from Powers's advice to writers, voice-activated) prose set in train, at times, even by more or less esoteric crossword effects. And, as part of the literary system, by implicit intertexts. Famously in *Middlemarch*, George Eliot analogizes an impossibly totalized human sympathy to the aberration of "hearing the grass grow," whose preternatural overload would mean that "we should die of that roar which lives on the other side of silence"—a sonic fate quite minimally approached, as it happens, on the keyboard of her own chiastically launched assonance (*die/side/si*). Powers's gambit stops short of this contemplated fatality. Rather than risking obliteration by audition, he implies that an ear tuned to the inner hives and havens of a forest vernacular—with its parallels in involute or even recondite lexical play—might instead revitalize our senses. With it we might hear what lies on the *inside* of silence, whether in paged words or in the mute *barchives* that prose, in this novel, so vividly transliterates.

But there is more to note in apprehending that twitch-is-which oscillation of "bar code" as a narratographic reflex rather than just a lexigraphic slippage. That more is the context of narrative as a whole in *The Overstory*. Yet again the echocentric is redoubled upon itself, yet here in a single span of words. As a homophonic crossword pun, the effect of this unbarred crisis of code ('bark ode') is in one sense undoubtedly extreme. We might miss it—or not; or in making it out, think we were making it up. Which is the (reflexive) point, but here in a fiction premised on the mystery of signage itself, of nonhuman messaging, on the signal system of trunk, pith, root, and leaves. The stakes of reading are at a unique premium in this novel, and the codes, bark and otherwise, thrown into dizzying recess by comparison itself. The yoked monosyllabic integers in English that capture—in their own double articulation (c/k)—the double vision of painted cellulose striations and imprinted computerized hash marks encrypt more than they say. They serve to conjure in this occulted way the inaccessible coding of tree life as surely as the commercialized graphic jotting depends on the triggered algorithmic script set in instantaneous laser motion by the pattern's "legible" (optical) differentiations. As a novelistic irony, prose's reflex action at this point is the very recognition of this regress. Or put it that one graphic opacity (in the painted representation of a sheath of wood) translates the other (on cardboard labeling) into a reciprocal cryptic pictogram of silent intent, only to be sounded out by subvocal linguistic equivocation in a fast-scanned pun. Call this crunch of phonetic code, by narrative association, the underwriting of any overstory. Being there, reading, is our way of affirming there being reading—even if never more than latent and always in translation. What more can a novel ask of us in recognition?

Notes

1. Richard Powers, "Interview with Kevin Berger," *Paris Review* 164 (2002–3): 13–23. Paris Review – The Art of Fiction No. 175.
2. And there is no downplaying the vocal, the aural, in this "double-voicing." With his larger project's keen-eared methodology sampled in "The Sonic Neurology of David Foster Wallace's *Infinite Jest*," forthcoming in *Literary Fiction and the Hearing Sciences*, ed. Edward Allen (New York: Routledge, 2021), William Allen's comparative study of Wallace and Powers—in a doctoral thesis nearing completion at the University of Glasgow—approaches the linguistic texture of these writers, framed by their own remarks on prose style, from a post-postmodernist perspective looking back less to literary-historical benchmarks of metafiction than to the tendentious theoretical touchstones for the postmodern condition proposed by Fredric Jameson, Gilles Deleuze, and Jean Baudrillard. There, in rough conflation, the waning of affect and the implosion of interiority under a generalized regime of the simulacrum renders a deadened schizophrenic agency as the supposed model of cognitive enervation in the flatlands of a radical capitalist superficiality. In the ongoing resistant attention of Allen's subtle ear for prose force, however, it is the mark of auralized style in both authors to revoice an embodied rather than emptied affect in the performance of a somatically engaged verbal energy circulated through text and reader—as if, one might say, to restore lungs, throat, and tongue to the reduced (and reductive) "body without organs" of Deleuzian emphasis. One result, for Allen, in his chapter on the weaponizing of aural enunciation in connection with the schizophrenic surgeon Kraft (read: craft) in Powers's 1993 *Operation Wandering Soul*, is to detect onomatopoeia as a synecdoche for the novel's ultimate structuring function in its match of fraught phonics and distraught mentality: sound echoing sense at the broadest stratum of narrative intent.
3. Richard Powers, *The Overstory* (New York: W. W. Norton, 2018), 247; subsequent parenthetical citations refer to this edition.
4. Richard Powers, *Orfeo* (New York: Picador, 2014), 381.
5. From *The New York Times Book Review*, January 7, 2007, unpaginated, https://www.nytimes.com/2007/01/07/books/review/Powers2.t.html (accessed October 4, 2021).

4

Wording Unbound

This chapter's title might seem to apply, in alphabetic terms, to the reflexive lexical detachments of punningly coded text in *The Overstory*—especially in light of that late appearance of painted bark as the barred dupe of barcode in the novel's subtext of decryption. Wording in Powers does sometimes disintegrate into phonetic lettering, loosed to new transfusions. But this chapter actually returns, nearly two decades earlier in his fictional work, to a narrative of textual suppression in which the hero's last shreds of vanishing sanity depend on the eventual release of words for normal reading: words unshackled from their ban long before their suffering reader is unbound. The story of all this, however, must itself be unraveled from the blatant double-plot in which it is, for a long while, obscurely knotted up: a bifurcation so different from the veritable subgenre of Victorian fiction that goes by that term. If *The Overstory* suggests that it is in the nature of the world when fully and openly encountered that there are always transhuman mysteries waiting to be read, *Plowing the Dark* (2000)—across one half of its stridently divided plot—puts its stress instead on the need for book reading (bound text) in a more traditional sense: the very thing that is reflexively vexed, for us, by the binary format of this one novel in its strained antiphonal progress. But in just this respect *Plowing* cuts to the quick of a common pattern in Powers's fiction, offering his most unhedged example of radical scenic disparity. As usual, even in novels that repeatedly mount such an elusive set (here a raw and largely inscrutable dyad) of separately self-propelled events, we find the phenomenological cast of the fiction asking of us, in reflex, to elicit their overstory as reading's resonant extratext.

When E.M. Forster issues his famous moral imperative in the epigraph to *Howards End*, "Only Connect," as discussed in contrast with unchecked global connectivity in DeLillo in Chapter 2, the need to answer that imperative is borne first of all by the reader of his carefully interlaced novel of manners under social critique. This comes easy to us with guidance from the novel's polished formal design. For a certain shifting segment of the characters, instead, the sponsoring edict names a defeating struggle, its failures those of spiritual and imaginative illiteracy, ethical retreat, and denied communal sympathy. Reading is the very scene of cohesion, of invested connection, in Forster's epistemological Modernism. Connection isn't so easy in the post-postmodern reversals engineered and enjoined by Powers's fiction—where connectivity is often under a continually tested duress. Characters may go for the length of whole novels oblivious to the urgent correlations, across space or time or both, that the reader is meant to apprehend—but by no means effortlessly—in a parallel montage of narrative sectors that's mostly a matter of jump cuts rather than lap dissolves or sustained superimpositions.

If we look a couple of decades ahead from Forster into a comparable realist Modernism for a nearer precedent in American fiction, we might think that Powers has engineered a massive repurposing of a classic counterpoint between the micro and the macro—the biographic and the sociological—in a text like John Steinbeck's 1939 *The Grapes of Wrath*. In its Great Depression exodus plot, a focalized itinerant abjection on the part of the long-suffering Joad family is interspersed with bursts of depersonalized context that make no bones about how the family's plight is to be situated in the broader American epoch. The third-person but intimate account of the family's grueling migration from Oklahoma to California alternates in this way with an innovative third-person collectivity in those rhetorically driven interchapters. Call these, by cinematic analogy, the operation of a reverse telephoto lens. Every specific setback and official brutality incurred by the Joads is, intermittently, referred away to generalization in an overarching politics of a bitter case in point. Though quite different from Faulkner's relativistic but convergent storylines in *The Sound and the Fury*, still Steinbeck's metanarrative lift-off from a bleak family saga to a national symptomatology of power differentials in a relentless class critique does operate its own version of a modernist scalar epistemology in demoralized epic form. On the brink of the next American century, what Powers's 2000 counterpoint achieves, instead, is no such lucid exercise in synecdochic form. Too late for that, in the invisible circuitries of a new global geopolitics. Rather, in its greater demands on a synthesizing attention, *Plowing the Dark* develops a narrower metatext in exerted if tacit reflection on its own narrative's inclusive—and for a long time elusive—compass. As with Steinbeck in his own very different syntactic and lexical cadences, the technique\text/context template from Chapter 1 can yet again be found modeling the reflex of reading. It does so by registering the technical maneuvers of style, inflected from within plot, as the quickest link to context.[1] But with the question at first, in Powers, not how is this part of a bigger story, but how is this even one story to begin with? Answers are pried from discrepancy itself, as typical of Powers's style, by the weight-bearing leverage of the heavily worked sentence.

In this novel quintessentially—but in most of his others as well, including, as we've seen, *The Overstory*—neither the discourse nor the story spells out the connections that reading is meant to achieve in order for separately situated plotlines to enter into functional counterpoint. Leaving his narrative agents struggling on their own adjacent or remote tracks, Powers typically dials down any internal shock of recognition on the part of the characters for a pattern recognition mostly reading's own to achieve. This is never more stringently the case—this deference of character purview to reader overview—than in the cryptically named *Plowing the Dark*. Certainly the title's faint agricultural trope offers little clue to the possible thematic transit across the reversibly obscured thresholds of its plot's bicameral precincts—in the etymological sense, a story of two rooms: virtual reality cubicle and makeshift prison cell. Nor is there any direct verbal guidance on what doors of correlation might communicate between them.

Bifocal Loci

As we've traced them out in the last chapter, the far-flung narrative filaments of *The Overstory* do finally entwine. Even for characters who never meet, let alone become co-conspirators, the vectors of narrative at least run along gradually closer lines of event or ecological investment as correlated actions plow to their conclusion. In contrast, long before the segregated protagonists of *Plowing the Dark* meet (with sci-fi implausibility) only in a spectral netherworld of electromagnetic hypotext crossed with postmortem mirage, mutual exclusion has been the modus operandi. We realize we are being asked to negotiate—and by our own attention, in fact, to transact—a very different kind of structure, one equally characteristic of Powers's writing: coerced polarity rather than educed commonality. This mode of reading is very far from the social realism of the Victorian mutli-plot novel that Steinbeck's structural innovation grew out of, where lifelines are mimetically lived out in varieties of contingent (if narratively destined) overlap. By a kind of intramural tension instead, Powers tends to wall in disparities in a structure of pressurized disjunction, scaffolded by ironies of mismatched scale and locale. In these deceptively open rather than closed systems, reading may be said to encounter—and asked to span—the intricacies of the *intraplot*, where the very terms of reading, reflexive as such, are internal to the countervailing forces set in play.

The pattern is recurrent. One part of a Powers novel may comment indirectly on another, by analogy or contrast, without asserting interpretive priority. Updating realism's fondness for the multiple plotline as its own kind of shortcut to a more broadly representative social canvas, and turning it instead to a technocultural diagnostic of global interdependence, Powers's typical plotting is entirely strategic. It oscillates in its own diffused play between micro and macro, where precarious human events are reframed (from within) by the broader systems through which their energies and options are networked and enmeshed. From within—with no ongoing superstructure mounted to correlate or resolve the disparate lines of action. Yet even though suppressing the logic of such interplay for as long as possible, narrowing it to a sheer antithesis of scale and location, *Plowing the Dark* is the exception that proves the rule. The long downplayed is a force that here blows up in an uncharacteristic melodrama of ignited recognition. The plot's reflex hints of counterpoint as secret correspondence are thus ultimately fulfilled, though belatedly, with a figurative as well as narrative vengeance. In the preceding novel, *Gain* (1998), building on a discursive pattern evident since Powers's first book, *Three Farmers on their Way to a Dance*, each sector of narrative gains on the other as it goes: a two-and-a-half-century chronicle of an American soap company, in the case of *Gain*, tracked in its increasing agro-chemical diversification while pitched in incriminating alternation with the grueling decline of an ovarian cancer sufferer from the neighborhood of corporate headquarters—and a mounting class action suit against its toxic contamination. For most of their length, the superficial indifference of one plot sector to the other—the narrative fissure between corporate expansion and corporal withering—is, of course, the credibly suspected point of their cause-and-effect alignment all along. Until litigation argues the convergence into the open—with the inertial momentum of the inevitable.

In *Plowing the Dark*, however, the force of severe contrast alone—rather than just juxtaposition and disjunction—would seem to prevail for most of the book, without any pending narrative collision in the offing. Only a blunt polarity: augmented electronic reality over against bare life, technological freeplay alternating with political incarceration thousands of miles distant, escapist invention versus physical and psychological torture, digital mirage versus mental delusion, VR versus psychosis. Halfway around the world—a global setting that keeps wheeling between locales on a seemingly frail thematic axis—stand the electronically expansive confines of a Seattle "Realization Lab," its digital phantoms escaping their own six-sided projection booth, and, in bald negation of this space, by optical as well as material antithesis, the fetid cell of a blindfolded American "spy" under terrorist capture. Against the fiber-optic liberations of VR is thus abutted, time and again across a mid-page "chapter" number, the punitive brutality of solitary confinement in Iraq. Rooms with and without a view—and rooms too much of one's own in either case, detached from ambient reality—are sealed off from the world as lived. Yes, we can't fail to recognize, early on, what superficially pastes the episodes together in their flagrant contrast, even if not suspecting their true glue. Yet the sense of a more definitive bonding doesn't have to wait for the "big picture," with its geopolitical reveal, in the final stretch of the novel's plot—when (partial spoiler alert) a digital simulation previously cordoned off in the luxurious exertions of experimental computer graphics is itself mapped onto the anti-American Mideast in the form of electronically targeted killing machines. Well before this, a certain textual reflex all its own has bridged the recurrent gap between sectors of attenuated event (simulated retinal transport versus retributive immobility), where the strain on reading itself, the test of its transfusing force, has come to the fore in a play between computer script in Seattle and withheld text in Iraq, code-driven chromatic phantoms and a refused paper solace for the imprisoned mind.

Moreover, braced against the issue of reading exacerbated in this dichotomous way is a macro history of human writing—with a species-deep narrative instinct developing its representational means in steady build-up toward the latest "trigger point" (to borrow that metahistorical phrase form *Three Farmers*): namely, the algorithmic script of audiovisual simulation. All this evolutionary stress on maximized technological fulfillment is therefore both reviewed and advanced over against the private desperation of an interned subject denied the relief, the virtual phenomenology, of any such written words. This novel is yet again, for Powers, a book about the human desires that meet it halfway: a book about life in quest of the legible. And about the dubious alternatives that may eclipse its own discursive medium as literary fiction. In this respect its immediate complement, arriving most of a decade later, is *Generosity: An Enhancement* (2009): a novel about its own *being written* more than about fiction being read, yet in the process—the author's usual shift of scale and frame—a novel about the variant evolution of writing over the centuries, lately in the code of a "natural" language genomic rather than linguistic, including its computer decryption.

In *Plowing the Dark*, with its sustained contrast between disembodied virtuality and a jailed and all-too-incarnate agony, the shunts between euphoric phenomenal manifestations in digital space and an alternate merciless claustrophobia meet (that modest spoiler alert again) only in their disclosed paramilitary connection—and only at the classic node of closure in (presumed) death. Not just comparable but enigmatically shared, it is a death elusively figurative and literal at once—and disembodied either way. With extreme cortical dematerialization on one side, biological oblivion on the other, the 3D circuit's boundless digital recess in Seattle ends up tangent to the abyss of suicidal escape in a ravaged Mideast—a final convergence that thereby serves, on either side of the enigmatic equation, to leverage a shared redemptive deflection of death by two kinds of release: from techno-complicity in political violence, at one pole, and from its fallout in a vendetta of scapegoating, at the other. When the two plot lines are thus finally and precipitously entangled, all but choking each other off, the intersection has been mysteriously accomplished only around the magic realism of a placeless reach that is meant explicitly to exceed both the excluded worded texts of a captive subject and the undermined computer script of laboratory virtualization. Only a plot that has worked up, if not quite through, a good deal of representational archaeology and techno-metaphysics could linger even momentarily, as *Plowing the Dark* thinks to do, on such a groundless closing plateau: could, perhaps we are to think in turn, have succeeded, by inference of its title, in tilling and harrowing such an obscure topology. If all this sounds hazily abstract, that's only at binocular range, in the attempted (and premature) merger of discrepancies. Up close in each zone of the action, the narrative drive is progressive enough, in the arc of figuration and its phonetic underlay, to motivate collision. To plow our own way quickly through the novel's alternating (more than criss-crossed) storylines can at least take some measure of their distributed tropes on the way to the mysterious cyber update of the book's darkness-before-the-dawn closure. And can help draw out what it might mean to have traced, in this final phase of plot, or at least of text, the very idea of reading driven beyond its limits in two media at once.

Call it a plot, but along the way it may have seemed more like a template of premises. Schematic it certainly is. At loose ends in her own life when contacted by Stevie Spiegel, a former college roommate (now a programmer, though himself once torn between engineering and poetry), the disaffected New York artist Adie Klarpol decides in the early 1990s to come on board a well-funded Seattle-based digital project to help with the cybernetic "drawing"—and advise on the art-historical background—of virtual reality environments in an open-ended experimental enterprise. No sooner do we see her trying to acclimate to this new mode of hi-def technical visualization (and its blurry purposes) in the so-called Realization Lab (RL)—known to its adepts as "the Cavern"—than we are tossed without transition into the Beirut classroom of an Iranian-American man, Taimur Martin, deliberately but painfully split from his stateside girlfriend, and who, as a suspected spy, is suddenly imprisoned by Islamic fundamentalists as a hostage in protest to US aggression. Wonderment escalates on the heroine's end of things, unendurable privation on his—until their defections (from virtuality on her part, from life itself on his) impinge on each other in that transient appeasing moment of disembodied transcendence near the book's end. For most of the novel, however, these alternate centers of simulated motion and rank inaction show no sign of connection other than a stark metaphoric polarity: she releasing her four walls, along with ceiling and floor, into a computerized phantasmagoria; he trapped, blindfolded, by his own four walls in absolute perceptual isolation, chained shivering on the floor to a useless radiator. Back and forth—with seldom even oblique segues—go the storylines, no knotting up or off in sight. As a strictly figurative contrast steadily gathers shape, an alternate link between plot strands—conspiratorial rather than metaphoric, and disclosed to the heroine in the traditional mode of military-industrial paranoia—is borne in belatedly only on her side of the narrative ledger. As the daily feed of the Gulf War's video spectacle, in its ballistically hyper-mediated Desert Storm, comes remediated to American TV screens, and is avidly tracked by her teammates in the Realization Lab, it dawns on Adie that her VR contributions—funded in fact, she only now discovers, by the US Military—have directly abetted the new wired war, in everything from flight simulators to the GPS of smart bombs. "Realization" turns on its duped perpetrator. Not just enabling an enhanced aesthetic register and new bodily prosthetic, the naively remotivated artist has helped materialize a new mode of physical extermination.

Computer-Script Ekphrasis

Long before any such disclosures about the Cavern as lair—or at least larval breeding ground—of ballistic experiment, we know only that in this giddy new endeavor, the former poet Stevie has found renewed faith in the engineered power of script: "Code is everything I thought poetry was, back when we were in school. Clean, expressive, urgent, all encompassing" (7). In this same spirit, Adie, his hesitant recruit, disaffected with the commercialization of the art market, finds a new conviction for visual making in the immersive splendors of VR, one of her first inspirations being to make the famous oil painting of Van Gogh's modest bedroom into an audiovisual enclave of creaking floorboards and changing light though its open window. Ekphrasis—a reputable if niche genre in poetry: the verbal description of a visual object. Think instead, in this mode of Realization, of a process more like ex-phrasis: an algorithmic phrasing exceeding itself, its script, in this externalized reach beyond even image for the thing itself in simulation. What, then, is the way to understand the cybernetic equivalent of ekphrastic art when, under computer dispensation, to describe is to digitize, pixelate, and either to manifest on screen or, in the millennial date of the novel's 2000 publication, to transmit by direct retinal sensors through the goggles or headsets of reception? What to call a cybernetic rendering of a famous painting, quite beyond its mere digital image as such in reproduction, when capable of inhabitation as a mobile perspective and a 3D enclave?

In one quantum art-historical leap, representation's whole telos is achieved: sheer depictions in which the viewer nonetheless becomes a spatial tenant. Beyond electronic ekphrasis, this is code-made space—a cyber realm caught up so completely in its own ontological closed circuit that even the hyphen in such a phrasing is equivocal. Say, equally, *code made space*: binary signage made over into virtual worlds. Its possibilities strike the jaded artist as a transformative act of graphic assertion, of plastic art reborn anew, so that her work in the Cavern carries Adie back in imagination to the "underground grottos of paint's nativity" (10–11). The result, we're helped to see, is that "a few trillion bits of math" have been energized "to fool a few billion years of ocular evolution" (15). Short of this hardwired techno-ekphrasis in the medial conversion from computer script to immersive image—though conditioning it in narrative words to begin with—falls the novel's own verbal conjuring of retinal marvels in transforming a mere room, a box, into an envelope of image where "even the floor and the ceiling were movie screens" (12). And words are there, ironically cross-knit, only to take up the slack when the virtual elation dissipates. Given that it is only a "glorified walk-in closet" (12), the Cavern's power of transport in the vitalization of its image system—in its role, that is, as "Realization" Lab—leaves the participant suddenly depleted when the control buttons are switched off. The ocular subject, the pure POV, is inertly rooted again to place, to immutable space.

Such is the syllabically registered malaise that descends, on exit from such retinal deceptions, when the subject is returned to the solid, stolid ground of reality—as phrased in the contrast of "motion-sickness" to a new kind (itself lexically warped and dilatory) of "still-illness" (14). Readers of the second chapter of the present book, rather than of the book in question by Powers, may be excused for hearing in that phrasing's liquefied alphabetic effect the syllabic equivalent of a step-time image collapsed into a freeze-frame. In any case, cinematographic homologies aside, after the motor illusionism of the RL—in simulated transport from the physical world as we know it—the returned rut of stasis induces is own dis/ease. But it does so as underwritten, we might say, here and throughout, by the tiny dynamisms of alphabetic language itself—long before the human history of writing per se, marked as separate from that of graphic representation, is maneuvered into prominence in spanning an abiding plot divide at the book's climax. In short, it is we, not the characters, who are momentarily joggled, in a reflex of double vision, by the syllabic wooziness of "still-illness." At just this point of contrast between "Realization" and reality, the working over and up of a rewritten phrasing—always, as Powers allows in his *Paris Review* comments, in an urge to approximate the "thing itself" in depiction—is captured here in a mimetic override that may seem deliberately stationed, in these boundary terms, to distinguish prose from the too mechanical similitudes of VR. If so, the effect represents again this author's sense of metafiction ground zero in the written word.

Episode by virtual episode in the Seattle locus of plot, the phrasing of report in Powers's rendering falls into sync with the evoked code behind the Cavern's dissolved borders. Besides coming into foursquare correlation with Van Gogh's bedroom, one of Adie's pet projects, besides toying in pixels with the pointillism of Seurat, is to have the RL also place on file a 3D version of Gauguin's exotic jungle, to be tinkered with at command. So that when she, in a worded directive transmitted by voice-recognition to algorithmic code, calls up "a philodendrum tendril" (33), we see the phonetic intricacies of language itself, diction rather than binary digits, sprouting new shoots: or, say, a lexeme refashioning its pith by syllabic graft in a spirit that anticipates the more overt organic wordplay of vegetal ecosystems in *The Overstory*. In a similar vein of tendriled interwine, when extended metaphors in *Plowing the Dark*, recruited to grasp this cybernetic universe in its transposition from code to "realization," are shifted from optical to audial, assonance holds its own amid sibilance—with the wizardry of the Cavern analogized at one and the same time, and across a palpable phonic cadence more complex than ordinary italic emphasis allows, to "countl*ess* d*ots* in a c*os*mic halftone pr*oces*s, the *ham*mers of a trillion player pia*nos*, the progr*amm*ed n*ubs* on the dr*um* of a gala*xy*-s*ized* music b*ox*" (31). Here and later, prose is out not just to approximate the intricate, clean-edged technics of code, its triggering symmetries and recurrences, but to trace ripples of mutation at any level. And their pulsations in uptake. Another case, as with "still-illness," where verbal enactment operates at a scale all its own: whether in "becoming" the numberless humming drumbeats of pixel accumulations or the vertigo of withdrawal from them. Even while wholesale and inhabitable "graphical worlds" (9) are being uploaded, edited, and vivified, their subliminal discontinuity is carefully stressed: a tissue of micro-trapezoidal fragments, an "ecosystem of polygons... nothing but vertices" (36), sheer pixel increments, self-generated by a "fractal, recursive code that crept forward from out of its own embryo" (37). In a kind of species mission creep from zygote to main frame computation, evolution is merely a metaphor there for gestated possibility, with the "*rep*"/"*emb*" off-rhyme operating in transaction across the tripled emergence of prepositional impetus in "from out of"—as if syntax itself has crept forward in a time-lapse audio all its own.

The RL bears no ontological relation to the Real, but has squeezed it out by simulation. Opposite to a camera obscura, bringing the imaged world in upside down through an optic pinhole, this video chamber, as permutable Cavern, inserts the viewer into its holistic ocular space through a billion pinpricks of aggregated light. Semiotics is afforded its own tacit crash course in these described illusions. Offering no *index* of the real, the purely *iconic* space of the Cavern, we might want to say, is referred away repeatedly to the arbitrary *symbols*, the computer "language," that fuels and festoons it. A house of cards built of six dissembled surfaces. But always within a teleology of pure presence, where a millennial human dream is supposedly fulfilled in what might be termed a *technontology* of palpable immersion. Where all is signal. Where the signified, wired from within, becomes the perceptual thing itself. Where the white polygon of projection dissolves the irreal blank cave into kinetic vista. Where image and material being are one. At the height of prose's effort to evoke such a phenomenon along spatialized facets, vectors, and vanishing points that its writing, its own syllabic matter, cannot fully command, we are all the while kept in mind of the hero's antipodal chambers of horror in serial imprisonment, where the envisioning power of read words, even in their innate limits, is cruelly excluded. In this way, with increasing recognition on the reader's part, the ramp-up in techno-sorcery in the one plot becomes a recurrent catapult to the other. By the jolting contrasts of prose's own jump cuts, we return time after time from encaverned fantasy to those denuded confines through which the captive Taimur, mauled and blindfolded, is hauled. For the author of *The Gold Bug Variations*, in their titular harmonization as a composed narrative format, what remains here of his avowed "metafictional" motive might seem mostly to devolve upon the reader's challenge in imagining the counterplots as part of a single fiction to begin (or end) with. In the process, however, it is the local metanarrative energy incumbent on the sentencing of event that does the intended work of hovering between character and construction.

White Cube, Blank Room

In an early move within one phase of plotting after the hostage is knocked unconscious —a move lateral, rather than contrapuntal—there is this: "Black collapses inward, and you are nowhere" (73). Blank, blackout. Next paragraph: "You come to in a white room. Nothing to make out. A squalid plaster box" (73). The grammar seems at one level, of course, that of a hard-won self-awareness within disorientation, but its second-person (instead of third-) pronoun has a way of entailing the entire textual spectrum from narrator through plot agent to reader. Pitched between, on the one hand, script in apostrophic address to its character ("You come to"—in the dead metaphor of transit as consciousness) and, on the other, script as the solicited participation of the reader in the scene's virtual perimeters, the anxious metanarrative pronoun "you" remains ubiquitous in this alternating phase of the narrative, disquieting at first, even grating. Ultimately, its ruptured expectations could be termed psychosomatic in their iteration. In its strained, almost schizoid, distortion of internal monologue, the subject-as-othered-unto-itself becomes a case study in character under dissociative duress: a human agent *subjected* to—and *by*—a cognition inseparable from self-address in its slipping grip on consciousness amid the anguish of isolation and torture. And it isn't just, in this regard, the fulfillment of that autofiction of reflexive self-biography ironized in Powers's first novel, as we saw in Chapter 2, where one *is* as one is seen. More to the point in *Plowing the Dark*, in the terms of reading's formal or structural "conscription," we may say (or make that you may say) that the equivocated second person of the linguistic shifter—"you" imposed upon "he"—locates by readerly jolt the underlying narratography of the text in a single syllable, a reflex of grammar even before syntactic activation.

At first, at least for an undeniable brief moment, through its unchecked skid into the immanent phenomenology of the *meta*, it is "you," the reader, who *are there*: via an audience address that links the minimalist blank of the character's airless holding pen ("white box")—gradually arrived at ("come to") in recognition—to the unbounded cyber vault, and vaunts, of the antithetical chamber from which you have been wrenched away by discourse. It is *our* second person, then, as readers, as well as Taimur's, that must negotiate plot's temporary move away from the spectacular manifestations anchored in the Cavern's "white closet," complete with its implicit parody of modern art's white-cube display space. With our momentary denomination as "you" in grammatical (and chapter) transit, sharing with the terror victim his return to conscious entrapment and despair, this is what we readers have come to: all the way from engineered pyrotechnics to hand-administered excruciation in the "augmented reality" of narrative prose alone. Differently understood, and in extension from this first tremor of the pronoun: it is, from here on, our own piecing out of Taimur's backstory along with him, chapter by cramped chapter, that is required in the architectonic tabula rasa of his peeling and filthy "plaster box." We, too, must work in pulling his battered memory together in jagged fragments, even as he does, in his own right, simply to maintain his sanity in the absence of any other narrative distraction under the ban of reading matter by his jailors. It is this parallel work of reconstruction that brings us as close to a coherent through-line as he (as "you" yourself in his person) ever manages.

To put it yet otherwise about this pivotal grammatical turn: it is just here that we find ourselves shifting from a narratological to a more tightly reflexive register, well before its inferences can be fully compassed. We are pulled up short by a grammatical torque setting in, as noted, before any stylistic effects of diction or syntax have yet been mobilized in confinement. I dwell on this—as we are slotted to dwell within its straitened focus—as something like the zero degree not just of narratography but of linguistic reflex. Our "you" and his "you" coincide at the outset, yes—a laminate, a superimposition—but what is layered by suggestion in this address is only unfurled on reflection, where the *meta* becomes the extratext. For if "you are there" from the first with a demeaned and molested hero barely there to himself, occupying a white polygon in the form of a blank but waiting text of desperate recollection, you are already—beyond mere identification—being accorded precisely the ballast, orientation, and imaginative solace that the character's jailors will be denying him for so long. You are, in short, reading. This is the old-fashioned prosthesis that, if in a different key, the virtualities of the counterplot have manifested via nonverbal computer code and its captivating apparitions: the generative energy of "script" per se, algorithmic or otherwise—in Taimur's craving case, the very lifeline of writing and reading so pitilessly withheld for so long. Underscoring his deprivation is exactly that narrative variant (or outright inversion) of free indirect discourse we've held under the lens: traumatic inverse, as noted, of that model of selfhood—of self-consciousness per se as an autobiographical inner script—that was broached in Powers's inaugural *Three Farmers* as an epiphenomenon of modern life's inveterate reflexivity. Any sense that the hero in *Plowing* is taking charge of his own actions and reactions under internal dictation is a split-second false lead. Third person doesn't open to interior monologue in this case. Rather, second person seconds the character's demeaned perspective as no better than *yours too* in these blinkered confines. Here, then, is a cognitive slippage operating by induction as we go—and precisely as induced in and upon us under the forward pressure of wording: an effect that may be best understood as a reflex of grammar in the channels of affect.

All that said about the (pro)nomination of person under abasement, and the phenomenology of reading that grammar thereby orients, it remains the roundabout sense—not to be dislodged entirely from first impressions—that Taimur is reduced to talking to himself, narrating himself, in a way wholly consonant with his being starved all but to death for any other mode of narrative. Without this steady emphasis on the withheld mental release afforded by reading—by representation, by the *textual virtual*—there would be no dramatic irony in *Plowing the Dark* sufficient to organize the continued switchback from the conjured vistas of computer wizardry to the foreclosed imaginative landscape of his bitter incarceration. Whereas, for the lapsed writer Stevie, the Realization Lab operates as an apotheosis of "poetry" in its script-based world-making signification, what gets stressed in the novel's alternate hemisphere is the denial of an equivalent release in reading's freedom from the here and now. The phrase "nothing to make out"—in Taimur's first "coming to"—is only the earliest sounding of this dissonant note. If he didn't *narrate himself* into consciousness, there'd be no story at all in this half of the novel.

Even in illicitly removing his blindfold whenever possible, as the prisoner does, there remains little to see—and for the longest time nothing to read. He must, as indicated, set about deliberately textualizing his own emotive data bank, but the effort runs thin over months of scanning, sorting, and collating. The archival trope, however, is explicit from the first. For reading matter, he has only the traces imprinted on his memory. As a US hostage in a high-profile war zone, he has every reason to assume that he has himself "made the world papers" (101). But he's never seen them, any of them, and must look into himself—though in newsprint's own terms—for whatever story might help fill his time. So it is that his whole world is refigured as the textual formats denied him, newsprint their most convenient metaphor. Whatever papers he's "made," his survival effort depends now on *remaking* a more sustained—and sustaining—feature story in his own mind: this, from within (phrased with such metonymic economy) the constriction imposed by "your two column inches of captivity" (101). This redemptive impetus—against the drift of morbid torpor and spatially troped constraint—amounts not just to drafting, but to inscribing, a figurative aide-de-memoir with rescued thoughts that might serve "to materialize on the crazed plaster ceiling" none other than a "microfiche of your own devising" (101). As much as with the fiber-optic images dissolving the walls of the Cavern, this counterplotted agent dreams of *projecting* his thoughts, mind over matter, onto a splintered and webbed—indeed in the double sense a 'crazed' surface: inscribing not evasive screen memories but the grooved synaptic paths themselves in "textualized" manifestation. Yet, given the years of internment, the archive of memory is too soon played out. He begs incessantly for the temporary *parole*—pun unsaid—that would put him in legible contact with the otherworld of writing, rather than merely of privately filed (cached, fiched, ceiling-traced) recollections insufficient, amid the starvation and brutality, for any effort *to pull himself together*. It is just this barricaded desperation that so punctually transpires, in alternating chapter clusters, in stark syncopation with the lavish, code-derived vistas of the Cavern and its permutable computer scripts. And in turn (or more like all the while) with our own reading between these opposed scenographies—and increasingly between their lines.

Second Person Twice Over: The Legible Regress

Only belatedly, and only temporarily, does imprint come to the rescue. Taimur's makeshift jailors have finally given him, without apparent irony on their part, one stray volume in English called *Great Escapes* (255), and they can't imagine what he would need a second book for, even after has he read and reread this one. Prayer is their fundamental(ist) paradigm, not narrative, not words for the word's own referential sake. But he keeps pleading, and some limited further relief is provided—verbal relief itself, even beyond literate comprehension, in their next and final offering. Reading is emancipated, made freely available for a time, and with it wording itself unbound—even without full comprehension. For what his keepers ultimately offer to allay his increasing hysteria, more by default than to proselytize, is the Book of Books, the Qu'ran, in (oddly enough) an illicit translation: a tome whose original cadences are designed for endless worshipful recurrence, for chant rather than narrative captivation.

"You" are taken by surprise along with Taimur. For after continued beatings and repeatedly denied requests, a "forbidden transcript" is "dropped into your lap... Words that can take you out of yourself. A book for those who believe in the unseen. The world-changer. The Reading. The holy Qur'an" (296). What results at last, in retreat from festering abjection, is Taimur's version of the materialized "unseen" enjoyed by digital hallucination in that "world-changing" retinal otherworld of the Cavern, where in fact "translation," beginning with the mention of a "real-time translation algorithm" (29) is a repeated motif in the phenomenology of VR. As emphasized again by the second-person address of Taimur's plot, the very text we are reading, even before the one the prisoner will now take up, is reimagined as an external input no less imported from beyond than the triggered optical synapses induced through the headgear of VR. Here an arresting overlap—synchronic and diachronic at once, across spheres of narrative action and centuries of textual transmission—bonds this counterplotted novel at a new level. Centuries before the manifestations of the Realization Lab's wired white cube as retinal gear box—its encompassing projection chamber flooded with realized (even when not realistic) optical intoxications—the transcendental promise of the Cavern has its fabled prototype disclosed not just, as long suspected, in Plato's famous puppet Cave of epistemological shades and shadows but, as we're now to find, in yet another cavernous grot of epic disclosure, of mediated revelation.

The untoward advent of the Qur'an into Taimur's miserable space has, in short, installed a new primal scene of confinement and cosmic release at once. As "you" are allowed to read on in this transcribed text, reception is translated back to the moment of sacred influx—Mohammad in his cave imbibing Allah's word—even while Taimur is being addressed still in the second person by the novel's own narrator. It should be noted that this device of modified internal monologue, as provisionally unpacked above, will be used by Powers in later fiction for more tactical narrative shifts from third to second person in moments of psychic fracture, as at the frantic climax of *Orfeo* (2014). Yet here in *Plowing*, as we know by contrast, it has traced from the start an entire arc of characterization: from something like mere rhetorical immediacy, with a character at first going through the motions of consciousness in an involute version of free indirect discourse, to his own later plummet into split subjectivity under remorseless torture. And all the while the immediacy of such apostrophized exposition, so you've noticed, puts you, the reader, even more immediately into the character's place.

Nor is this any less the case when he is actually reading, rather than just "read into existence" by you. For then, lost in a book, and just before Taimur's attempted suicidal flight from the actual lived story in which he finds himself, second person marks a remission in the solipsism of "your" misery by revealing an origin story—there in prophecy's dank confines—for the whole primordial model of omniscient address under the god's eye view of cosmic plotting. Such is this novel's definitive regress of identification as textual re-enactment. When reading the sacred transcript even in its profane (and still steadily puzzling) translation, presence is subsumed in transfusion: "You lie in the Prophet's slime-laden cave, taking the complete dictation all over again" (324)—with text doling out to the sounding-board of your own enunciation those rhythmic words that "tame the abyss" (323). Here is a "torrent of words" in their "sense-free cadences" that bring solace (for the prisoner if not ultimately for the novel reader) "even in the absence of story" (322). By grammatical transfer, "you," Taimur, are the receptacle and conduit at once, and less of the words than of their rhythm. It is through your own determined salvation by text that we read on—about you. That's the overarching momentum in any rounding out of this episode. More specifically, the term "dictation" here invokes—in its prophetic mise en abyme—the originary call to prayer, with the holy text its instruction book, a primer of supplication: "Say: I seek refuge… " (324). In stressing this aspect of the Qur'an, where holy "dictation" institutes in fact—as effect to cause—the chant of "recitation," a metatextual moment could scarcely wax more metaphysical. Yet in the double fold of such a dictated "say," the summons to prayer inhabits the same grammar as the rest of the second-person narration. Where any "refuge" thus achieved, spatially imagined as closet or cavern, room or box or transfigured cubicle, is inscription's own reflexive reward.

Regarding the pace of response, however, any such discursive fold, any narrative tendency to bend back on itself, needs a certain downshifting and deceleration in analysis—or else its real metanarrative traction is lost: the grip in backdraft of its aftertext. Much depends on seeing this figurative material get tucked in—and then more tautly unfolded—at just the right distance from the narrative surface and sequence. In the grammatical imperative to prayer, via the sacred scripture, w/he may take instruction (as just delivered) in a self-fulfilling response: "Say" as follows—and so we do, simply by reading. The novel's address to its character as a "you"—however much funneled through (and re-factored by) the battered subject as his own distraught interlocutor—has, in light of this passage, marked a last performative stage in a surrender of sequestered consciousness to the circuit of social call and response. With an inescapable inference for the admitted scripting of all human agency—in submission either to divine fiat or to the fictive model of narrative design, to Allah's prompts or to story's mediating discourse—the hero has all along, as we've closely recognized, been tutored in taking his own secondary dictation. This has transpired through continuous second-person summoning, in situ, by his own narrator in detailing exactly the brutalities he is undergoing. "You come to in a room…" Dozens of such pronouns later: "You lie in the prophet's cave…"—and then one level in, recycled from scripture: "Say [you]: I seek refuge." Metaphysics aside, including the law of Allah, when the protagonist, right from the first, is educed into shifting scenarios by second-person address, he has drifted halfway from personhood, and soon in his own increasingly beset mind as well, toward the being-written of a human placeholder in a plot not his own: anticipating the complementary fate suffered unacknowledged, as the next chapter will show, by the pawns of narrative writing in *Generosity: An Enhancement*. The metatextual spectrum spreads wide when "you" and "he" depend equally, in a highly unstable address, on the worried grammar of predication for your next conscious move.

Short of any cross-novel comparison with *Generosity* in the hierarchies of discursive dominance, in *Plowing the Dark* the peopled world continues to turn, the geopolitical globe to spin. The rotation that has taken us from cybernetic Cavern back to the prophetic cave of transcendental relay now turns from cave to a structure of buttresses and architraves, from divinely redeemed dank squalor to aerated holy mosque, from private sacred dictation to public incantation in the rotunda of group prayer. Such is the escalation from closet to domed apotheosis in the CGI bulk and scope, girth and sweep, of the RL's final showpiece, its virtualized Hagia Sophia, Seattle rather than Istanbul. Such, then, is the novel's final spin back from Taimur's obsessive rhythmic text, conjuring in its own right a vicarious hovel and haven like the prophet's lair, and the Cavern's exfoliation into cathedralized made space: its deliberated move beyond the 2D prototypes of painting and film to an electronically engineered architectonic monumentality. Fulfilled here is a sense, from the start, that the acrostic moniker for the Realization Lab was hinting in its own alphabetic right at an elision of the R(ea)L. By now, the asymptote of such simulation has aspired even beyond 2D templates made habitable in virtual 3D extension (Van Gogh's bedroom, Gauguin's jungle) to the peerless reconstruction—or rather, manifestation—of the world's most sublime enclosure, itself modeling the arc of the cosmos. Yet, as the plot backfires on itself, this soon-suspect digital epiphany—etymologically pro-fane in its secular techno-mirage—is found to model optical trajectories and overlapping vanishing points that convert this temple of temples into an implicit training ground, or workout machine, for nothing less than the pixel-cued destruction of other regional monuments like it in a deconsecrated Arab space under US imperial assault.

Before this "tactical" irony comes clear, however, a larger strategic genealogy has been retraced. Occasioned by this "full-scale" fiber-optic model in the digital reconstitution of St. Sophia, aesthetic history seems swallowing its own tail, since the "mosaic saints" are posited here as "the world's first bitmaps" (343). In ocular fact, those sanctified bodies are only what the quasi-mosaic distribution resembles on detailed inspection: "Up close, their resolutions pixelate into discrete rectangles" (343). But, yet again in this novel, cyber images are leashed to the inscriptions that encode and precipitate them. And here by a new fractal logic of microchip rather than ceramic chip pixilation. In the malleable enclosure of a narrative fiction or in the variable space of the VR caV(e)Rn, all width of vision is referred back to invisible script—again to a "real-time translation algorithm." Yet a script sometimes audible in its linguistic instances. In an alliterative response to the fading of the mosque's fabled "calligraphy," the "*room of holy wisdom is a ruin*" (344), its dome, like the wis/dom it projects, entirely factitious. Say, instead, that the only *writing on the wall*—in default of eroded calligraphy—is the unseen alphanumeric computer script that configures that wall and the domed, doomed grandeur it braces, generating it via a pun on a new mathematized "paint-by-numbers" aesthetic (372) of electronic accretion rather than laid bricks. All this faded glory in an encaverned high-resolution advent (digital fidelity the new mantra of the faithful) sends us, soon enough, back to the vile enclosure (that "slime-laden cave") of the prophet's revelations—as rehearsed in Taimur's foul cell, residual site of participant witness through the timbre and rhythm of read text.

In counterpoint to which, again, the blown cover of a plot-long fable fed passively to Adie about disinterested aesthetic experimentation in the RL protocols. It is her dawning recognition—against the hostage's darkening hopes half a world away—that paces the novel's last phantasmagoric phase. Veering between minimal lexical transmission in Taimur's self-encased "cave" and maximal mediated form in the caverned vastness of the mosque, between holy text and the holistic simulation of a sacred shrine risen in its name, the split plot (along with its reciprocal figuration) now oscillates on a narrower, more frenetic wavelength—until violence has dissolved even the difference between those bifocal narrative loci. Yet the leash is as frail and frayed as it might seem, digitally manifest at the end as a kind of disembodied brain wave. In the meantime, it is not Taimur's hostage video on TV, as he is forced to take part in it, but the 24/7 media relay of Desert Storm footage that finally *makes the connection* for her. The mystified electronic pulse to follow—putting her and Taimur into disembodied sympathetic vibration—is only a metaphor for some visionary circuit risen in cybernetic compensation for her guilt.

With her own liberated artistic expression funded all along by the Pentagon, as she has managed finally to discover, it is clear that her labors of love have been insidiously co-opted—and not just for use in augmented-reality gunnery simulators but for the live-ammo feedback loops of electronically targeted ballistics. The result is a morbid and Gorgon-like distortion of cinema itself, in the mode of slow-motion violence rather than freeze-frame arrest. As broadcast TV is spewing out images of "smart bombs beaming back video to even smarter bombers" in a third-order digital relay, all has become "Kabuki footage: slow-motion replays of skystrewn annihilation" (394). By such image streams the entire cohort of her Realization Lab "tunes in to the course of the war's master narrative," confronting in this way the reverse of the Cavern's deceptive mandate—not aggregating a new world but disintegrating the old: "Babylon became a bitmap. Pilots took its sand grains apart, pixel by pixel" (395). Life imitates art, death replays artifice, in this storming of the desert.

Within that very trope, something remarkable is about to happen at this crisis point in the maintenance of an underlying (and even potentially eponymous) motif. There is more than militarist escalation on display at this turn, bombarding Adie from the TV broadcasts. There is its intertextual equivalent—and a late unveiled clue to the novel's title itself. As if in the unsaid scriptural matrix for the whole double-plotted saga ("They that sow the wind shall reap the whirlwind"), Adie is wised up by a supervisor in a twist of this biblical allusion, normalized by modern grammar, when told impatiently that when *"you sow the Whirlwind"*—exacerbated cause (in caps as well as italics) to further exponential effect—you inevitably "reap" the full storm of weaponized electronics she's horrified to be complicit in (396). Instead of an alternate biblical turning of swords into plowshares, and in perhaps another proverbial idiomatic matrix: when *you plow the dark*, sowing technological prowess in pixel cultivation, you seed modalities of violence previously undreamed.

Vision's "Active Verb": From Childhood Storybooks to VR

In recoil from her recognized place in a communal aesthetic experiment turned surreptitious war game, and then recruited for warfare itself, all Adie can think to do is sabotage her part in their soaring landmark achievement, the Hagia Sophia model. And so she sets about erasing those digital "drawings" of hers that have fed into the construction of that archetypal, calligraphy-etched temple. Given that Adie's devoted labors were just "a rough draft for technology's wider plan" (398), at least she can, if not amend, then pointedly delete her part in that collective work in progress. Yet the "draft" metaphor locates the sticking point, since she soon finds that the webwork of the Cavern is less like an image bank than a seamless and thus elusive text, undifferentiated, hard to edit, its projected facets articulating only one "continuous chasm"—with "chambers" compounded upon each other like unspaced words. The textual reflex could barely be more explicit. Functional segments of the algorithmic code are discovered "run together," we're told, "the way old Greek was written: no spaces, no commas, no periods, just one long flow without dams or rapids, a single subterranean stream that never changes its course. But never the same stream twice" (400). Heraclitus as patron saint of cybernetics. The linear and self-enjambing code that got under the skin of her recruiter Stevie (eventually Adie's perfunctory lover in this suspect mating of the arts) by striking him as a higher poetry—this encrypted script is now an unrhymed recursive verse as difficult to edit by compression, by excision, as an ancient Greek manuscript would be, unrelieved by lexical breathers. Powers's metalinguistic instinct never lets up. As here with the computer-streamed river-of-no-return, all vivid figuration tends to trope its own medial code.

In the process, plot keeps the broader allegorical inferences on edge. At some time well in advance of her military-industrial reality check, it had become clear to Adie that the Cavern was not a "tech novelty"—not "even a tool, really"—but "more of a medium, the universal one" (267). And the medial analogy becomes explicitly linguistic as she mounts her resistance. VR instantiates its own grammar: "However much the Cavern had been built from nouns, it dreams the dreams of the unmediated, active verb" (267). It acts, it activates. As site of predication rather than description, it resembles "the thinnest first parchment, a thing that rivaled even speech in its ability to amplify thought" (267). Yet far beyond the reach of visible inscription in this insinuated media archaeology, electronic script has become a "lucid crucible" (269) for material making. In that very phrasing, the inmixed phonetic rhyme ("ucid"/"ucib") is so far from incidental that it reminds us how pixelated light alone in VR is the pulverized medium—lucidity per se—in the algorithmically churned cauldron of retinal wonders. And so far from lexically accidental that it seems almost to name as well as to exemplify the pressurized alembic of sentence-making in Power's molecular—and heavily stressed—prose aesthetic.

"The Cavern," understood in this way, "threatened the final disappearance of interface" (270)—text included, from parchment to laptop. In this pure self-realizing medium, "augmented" representation is subsumed to presence. And presence subsumed in the bargain—not just literally, but as if by allegory as well, across the counterplot—to death: death in figure and fact. So we return, yet again and finally, from the electronic Cavern to Taimur's blank captivity—and to its displaced cave of remission, where the once-parchment text of the Qu'ran helps the brutalized hero in maintaining his grip on the articulated pulse of consciousness in lived time. And even helps him to calculate that time. In between the cadenced metrics of his Mohammadan reading, keeping him in touch with the pace of duration itself, the imprisoned psyche also has the patience to calculate the years of "your" imprisonment, now going on four. The reader may be as astonished as Taimur by this sum—Taimur, whose (de)graded ordeal has been the *timer* of our counterplot—given the perturbations and elisions of jailed duration that narrative has dipped in and out of while pacing his ordeal. But certainly the grammatical second person indicates primarily, yet again, the character in propria persona: "You clutch to that dead reckoning"—a funereal idiom in this context—"as if to life" (379). The number of incarcerated hours seems itself uncanny, with narrative brought out as a psychobiological instinct, a true libidinal metanarrative as aftertext, recognized only in retrospect: "Some desperately inventive internal storyteller has won you survival through your thousand and one nights" (379). With that inventive desperation further internalized in summation across an expansive verbal rhythm of its own—you/

your; won/one—the lingual reflex yet again miniaturizes the space-making power of narrative dilation in a single shaped phrasing.

At which point, another convoluted metatextual reversion: not to the cave-bound prophet taking dictation from the Holy Word, but to a recitation from Taimur's own biological origin. This flashback arrives in the formative tone and tongue of his Arab American mother, reading to him from a quintessential fictional scripture and its tall tales, all of it intoned in a language closer to the novel genre's own wellsprings. Secular and sacred literary history converge in the ur-scene of orally acquired levitation—and potential flight. The man who has unconsciously become his own Scheherazade, in the absence of external text, rehearses at length—in the wasting hours of his carceral solitude—what was for him the original oral motor, as well as implied maternal nurture, of all such Arabian tales and their heritage. In his remembered bedroom, as for Mohammad in his fabled cave, words had once found their potent breathing space—linked further to the VR Cavern, in this case, by an insinuated metaphor of technological generation in a dialing apparatus. These are words, narrative increments, whose flickering traces—signal and static alike—seem glimpsed yet again in this novel, across that same technological trope, by the phonetic wavers of alliteration and assonance. With maternal orality as the ground of verbal consciousness, here for siblings under the spell of the reading mother's accented English, audited intonation is its own RL, a "realization" in the archetypal form of deliverance: "She *turns* the dials"—with a syllabic torque that communicates itself along the chain of effects—"and the three of you *tear* off, *tour*ing in every direction, past the speed of light" (383), as if the latter were a spatial horizon to be exceeded in the phrasing's own echo of "fast." In a thin bridgework to the pixel lumens of the Cavern, this otherwise anachronistic paradox of a medieval speed faster than light may hint at desire overriding its own lexical underside in escape rather than mere aerial transit. As the passage seems poised to suggest, that is, words as such are doing the work of transport, both as reported and as enacted, in capturing narrative's own magic Arabian carpet in its fleeting "speed of (f)light" (383). Like the RL coding in the counterplot, even narrative reminiscence about reading can recover the undulant compaction of a run-on, pre-junctural wording in a Greek-like stream of discourse. Although Taimur's time with the contraband Qur'an translation is short-lived, the memories of a hybrid *mother tongue* that it has served to recover pull their full psychic weight against the now undermined coded foundations, the deleted computer script, of the Cavern's immersive and delusional mosque. For such is a construct, a group input, erected by a digital collective—rather than a massed faithful in material service—as the temple of technological transcendence; and worse, so it turns out, as the testing ground of the same technology's efficacy in mass military destruction, with drone purview replacing that of magic carpets in the traverse of Arab lands.

Terminal Dis/connect

All this about the pixel-fabricated mosque remains so far, of course, unknown to the battered, captive avatar of his own internal thousand and one nights. Even while a distant disincarnate "she" decides to "turn... dials" of her own, rather than those of his mother's storytelling mechanics long before—Adie adjusting the controls in scrubbing back her contributions to the RL files of the faux Sophia—the hostage plot drags grievously on. And it is only when Adie's hacking merges her consciousness, in effect, with the apparatus itself—disappearing the graphic operator into its disabling revisions along certain cryptic algorithmic streams—that the two zones of narration, surviving their prolonged segregation, are finally, if confusedly, fused. No plot points really explain why his suicidal self-concussions should release his synapses into electronic connection and VR transport. That narrative bridge is reading's weird leap of faith. With Taimur uprooted from cave-associated page to another site of imprisonment once the computerized American bombing begins, and thus separated from all textual solace in the worst throes of his hostage agony, he seems, if only on this verge of annihilation, all of a sudden to intuit just the kind of techno-savvy counterplot that has been intermittently eclipsing him. Self-violence opens him to the remote violations of the real in Seattle. In the panic attending his final narrative crisis—over against a disclosed military implementation of virtuality's coded scripts in an alternate space now closing in on him remotely—it is "you" again who take to pounding your bloodied head against the wall. On it goes, in the imploded third person, this masochism of escape: "'Make it stop,' you hear yourself scream": either the prolonged misery or, more immediately, the homeopathic pain of a bludgeoning suicide. "'Make it stop. Make it...'" (390). The only wished-for action is at this point an unmaking, marked by the violent slamming shut of consciousness—and its closing out of the chapter. The character all along summoned into presence only by a battered laminate of self-address and reader credence is now commanding his/your own role in the cessation of that conscious presence: "Make it stop," yes. "And then it does"—yielding to what we may well assume is a truncated death scene. Certainly phrasing is inflected by a bottomless monosyllabic point-of-no-return: "You look down into the abyss, giving up your grip, and drop" (390). The topple is there, along the phonetic descent from "rip" to "rop," in the slippage of grammar itself, marked by a slant rhyme across the fungible noun/verb dyad—first a grip, then a/you drop—made available to notice only once the damage is done, the phrase made, the tiny reflex actuated.

But what "you" are thus plunged into is now, at least in transit, only another prison chamber, another holding pen—as the whole of the claustrophobic chapter 41, spanning just three blunt sentences, is wedged in to annotate: "This room"—as if to say, to insist, *not that other on*e, the swollen Cavern of usurped domed splendor—"is dark, and without dimension. It has no door. Or any window where you might have entered" (390). And thus no view. It is a virtual crypt—or casket. Yet from the spatial and optical negation of its final (entitling?) "dark," still "you" seem, in your death drop, to have been burrowing ("plowing"?) further down—as if through the center of the earth—to that other virtuality altogether: the monumental rondure of Sophia's shrine in its Seattle bitmap avatar. And in the midst of this hallucinatory shuttle, "you" (reader and character alike) make preternatural contact there with its fugitive artist—as mistaken angel of mercy—trapped in her own act of deleting its architectonic code, on symbolic behalf (as might be implied as part of her sudden penance) of a real Islamic East and its sacred traditions.

That's Adie, last we "see" of her. And what about Taimur? As the longtime captive desperate for reading matter, "you" are ushered instead into a script-driven computer resplendence—compared to whose depictive facility, as we've recently heard, "movable type" was merely a faltering evolutionary link in the capacity for human messaging: "no more than a shadow puppet show" (404). As insinuated by that metaphor, beyond its suggestion of Plato's rather than Mohammad's cave: the shadows of ink on paper have now come off the page as material simulacra. Which, up to a certain phenomenological limit, has been their condition all along for the reader. What Van Gogh's bedroom was to Adie in impasted pixilation, the laboratory of her Cavern has been to us—and his textual "cave" to Taimur as well: evinced as virtual in the automatisms of alphabetic transmission.

But more than analogous flights of alleviating fancy now bring Adie and Taimur into contact—and at considerable risk to narrative persuasion. This final reciprocal encounter of repentant artist-programmer and militancy's featured victim—intersecting at the shared flashpoint of cognitive obliteration, technical and psychic by turns—can seem almost ludicrous: a sheerly ludic twist on the novelist's part, gaming the entire system that the book's structural irony has cautiously bifurcated until now. In this rare moment of magic realism for Powers, it is as if all erasure, all blanking-out, is made to convene at the brink of death as de-realization. Or, more to the point, made to define the void itself as de-scription. Suffice it to say that any conviction this may carry is only as a fantastic, *Arabian Nights*-like remission from a punishing real. But in just this respect, as a scriptive trope risen to a surreal disembodied topology, it has been markedly prepared for—right up until the end. At one abrupt juncture after another—distantly linking the book-starved hero to the algorithmic script of another narrative sphere—the textual analogy for RL has been hard to miss, even before the figurative overlap of Cavern and prophet's cave.

And one episode (or more like passing allusion) of explicitly *textual* reflex late in the novel—braced by a strategic contortion of its prose—seals the gathered implications in the story's plot-long genealogy of human text. As the cross-narrative crisis mounts, compromising the triumph of the St. Sophia simulacrum as a laboratory for VR armament and thus, in turn, indiscriminate racist assault, anything like the idealized techne of manual writing—as homo sapiens' defining tool use—has been quite decisively eclipsed, as we well know, by the virtualities incident to cybernetic script. Referential imprint has been flamboyantly outbid by immanence, real space outplayed by the extrusions generated through code—all in a postlingual apotheosis that nonetheless harkens back, for species benchmark, to the primal impress of letters on parchment. Recalled here is the epoch of literacy when "realization" was still comprised by verbal representation or graphic art, tightly caught up in the mimetic function. This very idea—this emphasis from media archaeology—may seem residually flagged, in a minimal ripple of aftertext, by the convoluted syllabic, and lexigraphic, curve of phrase to follow in recovering not just a pre-digital but a pre-codex urge to traced speech. Aftertext as extratext again: in this case lettering registered not at the onset of meaning but as its secondary (if all but immediate) reflection. For recalled at this point over the mere span of four echoic monosyllables, as if optically screened for us as well, is the historical moment when writing was "trapped" in the "old scroll's closed O" (400). That's so bold a throw of the syllabic dice that the very alphabet seems upping the bet. But the game is also a topography. Into an apt rabbit hole we are tossed by the literalized shape of phrase, a plunge into expressive depths where letters first dreamed of generating their own pictures. In the phrase's own circuit of assonance, that awkwardly taut wording is folded over itself in a reiterated graphic rebus, limning exactly the rolled textual tube, as stored scroll, that antedates, at once, both Taimur's book-bound Qu'ran and Adie's pixelated mosque calligraphy. This happens to be the rare passage I was alluding to in the Preview that can come close, in alphabetic reduction, to the pixel thematizations of digital cinema. Recalling Adie's own passing archaeology of inscribed visual signage, we seem yet again thrown by association, in that outpour of *o*'s, from the procedures of modern literacy back down to the "underground grottos" where drawing and writing were, in "nativity," once one.

In Adie's now fruitless, belated, and entirely symbolic protest against technological co-optation by military engineering—prosecuted through her own version of stealth-bomb detonation in the effacement of relevant symbolic code—the artist of the virtual has finally broken through, via the roundabout magic of paranormal sighting, to her indirect victim. Taimur is already collateral damage from American military aggression in the broadest sense. Beyond this, his latest makeshift cell has now been shaken, Desert Stormed, by the indirect results of Adie's duped imperialist in(ter)vention. By sliding association if not causal implementation, it is through the Cavern's computational prototype for ballistic guidance systems that the haptic plausibility of an augmented real has put all drone-scanned space at weaponry's unmanned reach. At which point the hero, finding (or losing) himself at the end of a rope he himself moves to sever, is finally tethered for the first time to his novel's counterplot.

Here is an irony that sorts through its own dark logic only under further reflection. Situated by unorthodox second-person grammar at Taimur's pole in these vacillating focal points of plot, we yet again cooperate in the direct address. Only when no longer living your story, submitting to your "desperately inventive internal narrator," do you grasp, even in letting go, the encompassing masterplot. Three chapters after Taimur's presumed death (by willed concussion, hemorrhage, and surrendered mental grip), the bottom has dropped further out of his null and viewless room, his limbo, his (and "your") tomb of consciousness. You have by this point disappeared into what we, not you, understand now as a placeless shared mirage, and "dictation" has resumed here not, by proxy, from a replay of Mohammad's pipeline to Allah but from an access to narrative discourse per se, in its familiar second-person assault. Again: "The room that holds you falls away"—given *up*, at the moment of your "drop," into a bottomless recess. "Space opens out in every direction, too big to see across"—like the global distances between previously unbridgeable fictive hemispheres of the book, though now telescoped in unexpected optic disclosure: "A single dome rises so high above you, its shell might as well be the thing it stands for" (407). If the sense is "so high ... that," the subordinate grammar installs its logical claim; if "so high" has, at least at first, more like an exclamatory force, then the comma splice captures otherwise the same coincidence of cause and effect. Then, too, beyond evincing with this subjunctive grammar ("might as well be") the mimetic curve of heaven's arch in gold leaf intricacy, there is another stylistic turn, or curve, as well. For what also gets implicitly spelled out in this wording is the millennial telos of secondary representation in the quest instead for equivalence: the very dream of the simulacrum manifest now in a domed epitome across the scriptive belling of "shell"/"a*s well*." True to the pixel-compressed virtuality that has conjured it, and enforced by a strictly lexical symmetry, the optical signifier is indistinguishable now from the mosaiced thing. Beyond all representation, in the digital transcendence even of foregone interface, image and reality merge. As do physical fact and dematerialized fancy in this closing techno-epiphany.

So back to what's left of plot. Precisely to protest, if not actually curtail, the wired military violence to which VR leads in the realm of weaponized image systems, Adie is last seen, though no longer visible in fact, going through the motions, the sacrificial ritual, of canceling her own aesthetic contributions to the Cavern's voluminous transmutation into Shrine. She knows at least, if only concerning her part in the larger design, that some plugs can, as it were, be pulled. Subsumed to her own version of a missing person as a result, abdicated from the RL team and surreptitiously roving the coils of her coded image bank, she has drifted into ontological parity with Taimur's own out-of-body freefall. In just this uncanny way she emerges for him dimly, glintingly, as a misread angel of annunciation. Her apparition as such impels, in effect, one more unconscious narrative postponement, one more life-saving jolt of eros as a vital force—before it is time, in plot time, for him to be rescued by US diplomacy under longstanding pressure from the real redemptive agency of his devoted girlfriend. When he is hovering instead weightless under the pixeled dome of St. Sophia's sacred mosaic space, what transpires is only some impalpable tacit contact with a salvific female image. When his near-lethal passage over into the virtual is answered by Adie's own eerie sense of some unknown presence in the material void she is scouring, Powers's book-long antithesis of disembodied spectacle—over against physical abjection—has taken a dizzy fix on its own overdue vanishing point. For here the book's prolonged structural dialectic approximates some nebulous third term, unnervingly fatal in its finality, floated in a mortal afterlife quickly figured as renewal, as disinter(n)ment: a mode of all but etymological *restoration* from within the punishing whiplash shifts of story.

In this electronic no-man's-land of their suddenly tangent spheres of consciousness, things happen almost too fast to sum up. The digitally guided artillery that a new algorithmic medium of prosthesis for our "scribal" race has aided in mobilizing has made unforeseen room for another story altogether: of unarmed death survived. Plotlines forcefully divorced until now have been wedded beyond all expectation. Computer machination has so completely outstripped incarnate life that its virtuality can only be credibly penetrated by pending death. No one, least of all its co-participants, could have seen this preternatural ending coming. Yet, for the reader, the labor of summation continues in the mode of comprehension (both senses): coherence and the broadest possible grasp together—the last inducement of the aftertext. Bifocal loci, as noted above. But seen through now to what resolution? The dark hereby plowed has become a black hole. It is hard not to belabor the baroque (or better, the unspoken *byzantine*) complexity of all this in trying to work out its implications. And, to be sure, part of the strain is there in the text itself. But, just as certainly, it is worth resisting a dismissal of its mystery as some passing fillip of techno-spookery. Powers remains more himself here than any such write-off would allow: more covert dialectician than magician, invested reflexively, in abetting just that role, in the *writing out*—verbal realization rather than effacement—of convergent plots. In the closed system of this narrative economy, the false bottom of one narrative zone coincides with the disembodied vandalism (script deletion) of the other in a close encounter of canceled science and canceled fiction: rejected virtuality and forfeited self-narrative. They are lost together in a mental limbo at the overlap of technoscript erasure and bodily self-effacement, with digital architectonics looming now as temple, now as sepulture. The technique\text/context template for narrative on page and screen alike, specified in the verbal sense for prose as style\plot/inference, needs here to be further pluralized at its hinge point. For it has been style alone—phrasal echoes from Cavern to incarceration—that binds the two separate plotlines, those independent textual sequencings, into thematic inference as a unified if open-circuit field.

The reflex in activation at this point is not just passingly metanarrative but more structurally encompassing. Think it through—as its enigmatic twist almost insists you do—and pattern becomes meaning. Recalling from the Preview the breakpoint between Modernism and postmodernism as determined, on Brian McHale's account, as a swerve from reality's epistemic complexity to its ontological dubiety, we can see the latter issue concentrated, functionally as well as thematically, in the simulacral maneuvers of the Realization Lab. Concentrated—or one might say contained. All while the phenomenology engaged in reading across the novel's structural divide—and manifesting each sector of the plot in some mode of credence if not correlation—has, as is typical of Powers's fiction, taken up a variant of the alternate epistemological issue into its own fragmentary system not as divisive social infrastructure but as narrative counterplay. Reading is the act of discerning, from internal evidence, some formal totality for the alternating current of its narrative. For the real phenomenological crux of such overcome disjunction only arrives, even as it is downloaded onto the characters themselves, when computer artist and military-industrial scapegoat meet as spectral emanations in the disembodied zone of sheer figured manifestation, no more real to each other than if they were merely read about. Which for us is all they ever have been.

So the conceptual work at play in these multi-plot novels by Powers, and invited in turn on the reader's part, is to trace the discrepant phases of such narrative in the force of their surprise overlap—and to mark the reflective vantage this entails from one "trigger point" to another. What results from their selective reading in this book is hardly a rigorous taxonomy, let alone an exhaustive inventory. The spot-checks of reflex action entertained in these few chapters do little more than mark off a sliding scale of reflex recognition in fiction—alongside comparable "reframings" on the film screen—that range from a more or less narratival focus to one emphatically linguistic. Edging into and adjusting each other, the representative categories are less rigid than investigative. As in the threefold distinction just reviewed—between a vexed and redirected epistemology, a contestable ontology, and a subtending phenomenology in the reading act—stress falls not on binding divisions but on valences of response in the thick of fictional operation, offering one kind of coefficient or another in the multiplication of meaning from within a given inscription. So that a defining caveat bears repeating. In all this, true to its etymology yet again, the *meta* subsumes nothing; the *beyond* of its intensifying emphasis is extended from within, an over-reach of inference turned back in reflection from meaning to its italicized means. And rethought there in process.

This is where the strategic mirror reversals of cinematic technique return for closer comparison yet. Our next chapter turns to a book, at the end of this century's first decade, that is far more directly concerned with visual narrative, in particular with video filmmaking, but the resonances of recent screen practice have infiltrated the plot of *Plowing the Dark* as well. It isn't just some middle ground of script—between algorithmic notation and scribal recitation—that links the Cavern and the cave of dictation. Nor the fact that the heroine is just as much in the dark about the true optical turf she's been plowing as if she'd been elsewhere, like the hero, the whole time. There is another complementary field inferred, if only at the end. This happens exactly where the suddenly grooved fit between the bifurcated puzzle pieces of Powers's plotting most resemble the trick ending of a mind-game film. For that, we know, is a genre where characters, alive or dead, or both at once, are never so fully rooted in separate realities that they can't, on the plane of fiction itself (film or here novel), be revealed to intersect in some radical fashion.[2] Whether the energies of reading or viewing, once duped, can productively be regrouped into rethinking the whole narrative after the fact, or have actually been moved toward hints of (re)solution as we follow along, analysis operates within the same bandwidth of participation.

And invites there an extra word of methodological clarification. Even in the internet epoch's wholesale computerization of the cultural field, an instinct to compare the frequently laid-bare electronic substrate and its ocular deceptions in recent trick films to the verbal fundament of a contemporary novel and its occulted deep structure—even a novel that takes as its partial topic the *algorhythms* of digitized VR—has its limits. Doing so is hardly to settle in any measure of explanation for some blanket sense of "convergence culture,"[3] as lately understood at the delivery level of commercial production. Certainly films and books can both be downloaded, for streaming or scrolling, on the same cellphone or iPad. Then too, in Powers's case, the particular novel in question was at least partly dictated, as we learned in the previous chapter, through voice-recognition software on his own tablet PC. But the most revealing issue at stake isn't the potentially leveling convergence of *platform* but the local conjuncture of intrinsic *form*—across variant features of these two time-based narrative media, optical and syntactic. It is there that the increments of image find their correlate in the serial texture of patterned diction (whether under phonic dictation or just phonetic decoding at the reader's end). This is where a reflexive default to electronic process in the sequencing of the screen mirage, as occasioned by certain techno-canny plots of fantastic science, bears most illuminating comparison, in any fruitfully delimited media environment for the computer age, with the specialist technical language put into narrative play by what we might characterize as the search-engine aesthetic of a novelist like Powers, whose readers are repeatedly set an informatic task in prosecuting the data-driven reach of his plotting—and its granular *terms* of engagement.

And yet the risks are high in the Powers novel still open before us, not so much in fooling us but in outsmarting itself—and precisely when narration leaves behind its bedrock scientific foundation. What really are we to make of the book's final mutual lurch beyond embodiment, on the part both of a code saboteur aspiring to post-electronic escape and the physical misery of an attempted suicide? If their shared visitation in the disassembled digital semblance of the Hagia Sophia dome is more than an ameliorative onset of the mystical, how might it be conceived as seriously dialectical: establishing a cogent "third space," rather than just the reciprocal eradication of the given two? Only, perhaps, if it means that people long oblivious to each other, one scripting the digital, the other craving the textual, one in the unwitting service of a military superpower, the other settling for an antithetical sacred writ, are now no longer imagined people at all but just characters on an out-of-body page, leaving all further reflection to us in the mirror of our perplexity. As we will see in *Generosity* again, as before in *The Gold Bug Variations*, this is not an unfamiliar move in Powers's closural gestures.

To accomplish such narrative tapering, just as to capture its force in analysis, certain organizing tropes must emerge to synthesize the polarized topographies that collapse into each other in the shutting down of story. *Plowing the Dark* is no exception. Spun back and forth at the end from the Arabian Mideast to the Pacific Northwest, and finally hovering somewhere in a renegade electromagnetic betwixt, the novel's rotating lived centers of structural juxtaposition, geopolitical irony, retinal versus textual investment, and the rest—abutting disjunctively until the end—have finally broken past mere contrast, even beyond open confrontation, mysteriously enough, so as to interpenetrate, undo, and release each other, if only momentarily, from their given terms of technopolitical deadlock. The impossibility of all this is just its mordant point. It would take a miracle. That's what metatextual fictions are sometimes there for, to push beyond, to write life's way out of plot's own dead ends.

As is the case with the reflexive final trope of this one novel, certainly, whose coda unites Taimur not just with his girlfriend, bent for years on his release, but with the daughter he has never before seen: twin living embodiments of the redemptive angelic specter Adie's pixel emanation has otherwise been intercepted to figure. When, in the novel's brief last paragraph, his proud daughter hands Taimur a drawing she's made of "you"—a self-image that "you take in your trembling hands. A crayon man returning to a crayon home" (415)—the naive sketch seems reverting to those pre-Cavern grottos of manual representation alluded to as the deep genealogy of the VR image. And just before this, the child has ratified the other half of the plot in its narrative rather than optic fixation. For the daughter, in her first living hug of her father, "grasps at long last," in his very person and body, and only a paragraph away from our novel's own end, "the fable she's grown up on" (415). Not just with, but *on*: a nourishment in the form of hope. For as long as we've been reading, Taimur has craved narrative for his privation—while for hers he *was* one, a whole life's story. Linked to an explicit metanarrative allusion—the girl as "this Scheherazade" (415)—such a belated "grasp" of a storied origin, when that implanted word is idiomatically dematerialized, recalls the convergent effects that have sparked our own recognition toward the end. These, again, have allowed our own final, if not prehensile, "grasp" as readers—an embrace *comprehending* in the remaining two senses: taking in the novel's encompassing formal logic by finally holding its two halves together in understanding. For here in this returning *Arabian Nights* allusion is one last triggered jolt in Powers's prolonged open-circuit narrative, whose latest phrasal flashpoints have arranged after all, when all is done in its very saying, to throw the switch of programmatic connection and closure. To repeat: that's what metanarrative texts are sometimes there for. As flagged by the novel's title in the next chapter's further test case, that's a kind of *Generosity* for you.

Notes

1   In the last paragraph of chapter 21 in *The Grapes of Wrath*, for instance, climaxing one of those pivotal interchapters: "The great companies did not know that the line between hunger and anger is a thin line." As thin as that defined by an aspirate *h* and a single vowel in the clanging internal rhyme ("hunger"/ "anger") of that particular line: prototype of the contemporary portmanteau "hangry"—and then some. Two sentences later, at the chapter's close, the hunger, as if it were the spoilage of withheld food, has taken on metaphoric overtones of potentially explosive organic rot—"And the anger began to ferment"—as if to confirm one's subliminal sense of the nonphonetic crossworded anagram of threat, the "danger," lurking (invisible to its perpetrators, inaudible to its normative readers) in the

even thinner alphabetic line between "hunger an*d anger.*" In narratographic terms: micro\plot/macro. Even in Steinbeck's mainstream realism, then: the reflex action of style's phonetic compact (both senses) and its graphic distortions.

2   Turn-of-the-millennium films like *The Sixth Sense* (1999) and *The Others* (2001) are "canonical" here. As I write, an extreme case of this narrative gaming at the mortal interface occurs, by an absurd influx of supernatural possession near the close of a psychosexual thriller, in the much touted 2021 Netflix Series *Behind Her Eyes*, where even its link to interactive gaming emerges unspoken in an unexpected twist of supernatural "avatars."

3   Henry Jenkins, *Convergence Culture: Where Old and New Media Collide* (New York: New York University Press, 2006).

5

Writing Unpent

From this master of ratiocinative cross-fire and specialist scientific finesse, Powers's often breezier tone in *Generosity: An Enhancement* comes across as unexpectedly relaxed, if often sardonic, in his return to the genomic coding that made his reputation with the breakout ambition of *The Gold Bug Variations* (1991). The light tone of *Generosity* was mistaken in some quarters, along with the novel's pared down length and reduced plot complexity, for a lightness of weight. On the contrary, with the intricate nomenclature of genomics scaled back from its earlier brandished expertise, and linked explicitly to a quest narrative in the DNA of fictional storytelling (the genetic longevity of plotlines and genres themselves), this one novel glosses the others rather than just simplifying their mechanics.

This time we are not steadily being treated—as otherwise typical of Powers's *infofiction* (higher version of the "edutainment" parodied in the pop-science TV broadcasts of *Generosity*)—to the spectacle of erudition in its coruscating shimmers of vocabulary and its tirelessly variegated factoids, with plot's most crucial sentences offering laboratory clones of their own referents, generative duplicates of the complexity described. More than before, instead, we are on the inside of the writing looking out, a writing tentative and trenchant by turns, tracing the labor of plot (rather than learnedly witty exposition) in making its intermittent progress. In this new "constructivist" reduction, architecture is inchoate, design sidelined by exploration, words feeling their own way toward story. In the compact scope of this metanarrative, the stripped-down process ends up outstripping its own elemental functions in reflecting on the burdens of their exertion, their narrative execution. *Generosity: An Enhancement* becomes in this way the lucid compendium, rather than a worn-thin retread, of Powers's craft, including the familiar pleasures of its extratext in split-second phonetic as well as conceptual recognitions—though in this case held to a tactical minimum by the very motif of writerly inhibition.

To begin appreciating the logical structure of this compressed meditation requires catching the novel's wryly downbeat (because slyly wised up) tone. As seeded in the heroine's eponymous nickname, the book may seem named, once read, for its generous resistance to the stingy, commonplace availings of plot itself: a defiance shored against the narrowly fateful in novelistic design. Certainly the plot as such, any plot, hardly comes easy to either the novel's characters or their narrator. At every level this is a story that barely wants to get written, and knows it, but only finds out why in the process of discovering, after all, how to. How to inscribe itself—and how to want to. The plot's paucity of options is lamented by the narrator at more than one point, and often on behalf of the main character as erstwhile writer—long before that lapsed aspirant storyteller has become the victim, or at least the pawn, of an authorship not his own. And this tension between the pressure of plot and the independent measures of agential being is not just categorical and abstract, strictly narratological, but tense on the ground in the nervous work of phrase as well. Ultimately, the arbitrary and foreordained intransigence of plot can only be resisted by a freedom modeled on the stray attractions of style, in all their fitful allegiance to free play: less roving than in Powers's usual registers, yes, but deploying still the cross-stitches in wording that tuck phrasing back into its own etymologies, thread unexpected seams between semantic registers, snap syllables loose into new permutations—even while doing so, here, against an ongoing stress on the intractable writtenness, the fixedness, of any such writing in its mode of *life story*.

Generosity versus the Lot of Plot

The novel unfolds as a case—ultimately a strenuous case study—of a narrative storyline when story is conceived as always on the make and the move. Uneven but inexorable, plot is clocked in this novel at differing tempos across its variably phrased increments, some of which can be leveraged as a mental respite—or call it a suspended sentence—in the drawn lot of the inevitable. In contemplating this across the narrator's adept plaitings of phrase, we may remember that one independent meaning of *plot* (as of land) shares with another of *lot* a sense of topographic space needing not just to be stepped off for its determining perimeter, but traversed in the form of narrative pace. Hence the temporalized nature of story space, the variable speeds that govern its crossed (or criss-crossed) terrain. On this question especially, *Generosity* is restless, eloquent, and, in its own terms at least, emancipatory. Within an analysis of classic narrative modes and their canonized postmodern departures, it ends up reorienting with rare clarity the entwined *a priori* of time and space in narrative sequence. It does so with a demystifying precision about the merely formal ways in which fiction, unlike life, can effect the "defeat of time"[1] not just, as explicated, by the apparatuses of elision, compression, and prolepsis, but, in a further inference, by a loosening of expectancy altogether—a relaxation into the still possible rather than the endemically destined.

On the score of the more overt *temportations* of plot time, there is an unintended provocation in the Wikipedia entry on *Generosity*, where we are alerted to the "real-time" intrusions of author into plot. Inadvertently, that mention begs the question of the narrator's own interest in the potential for fiction's "defeat" of anything like such a temporal "real." So it is, given the storytelling persona, that his repeated swoops in from the unspecified (but in fact immanent) site of writing are never descents from some external scene thereof: no lamplit desk or, in Powers's widely publicized case, no backlit voice-activated laptop. Writing speaks for itself, speaks up for itself, as if from the page alone. Not just the fact of the written but the act of its production. Such reflex moments are less globally metafictional, in any canonical sense, than they are intrinsic to script in inventive operation. These brief autotelic monologues in search of plot—these reflexive monoscripts, so to speak, of narration itself— are less disruptions of the storyline than they are the priming of writing's own pumps. They don't so much privilege the labor-intensive "real time" of composition (though their thought bubbles are indeed simultaneous with the narrated scene) as they foreground the material torques and warps to which temporal sequence can be submitted on the fictional page, skipping either a private beat or an entire historical upheaval—and coming out the other side of an elided duration. Where, in their habitual approximation of the "thing itself," that thing turns out most often to be the imperative word itself—together with its impedances—in the prosecution of story.

Inferences for anything like the "real time" of writing are thus, at best, contrastive: meant to highlight the irreal leaps, forward and back, that the credited pace of narration, rather than its drafting, can command. But that irreality is in its own way cognate with certain profiles of mentality's own duration, its blockages and flashbacks, syncopes and fugue states. Experienced time can itself be uneven, arrhythmic, elliptical. Writing in Powers answers to this not just when plot is found spinning its wheels, shifted into neutral for an expository intrusion, but when a cinematic prototype of spooled and spliced temporality sets in for an explicit flashback or "jump cut" (85). Such effects are modeled, by analogy with fictional transitions, by the descriptive camera work of a video broadcast studio to which the plot cross-fades at more than one point, including its play between "Establishing shot," "Interior," "Close-up," and "Voice-over" (23), as well as "shot reverses" (25). In this way, when storylines are overlain by a discursive (rather than just a narrowly scriptive) temporality more self-conscious, variable, and invasive than any simple "Once upon a time," it is then that what is "defeated" is not plot but only a plodding clockwork progress untrue in its own way to lived sequence, to its lapses and precipitous revivals. As with the burst of psychic resuscitation that is to save a life at the climax of *Generosity*.

Temporal fallout in this respect awaits a steady thickening, and then sporadic attenuation, of this one novel's own increasingly busy—and literally extravagant (wandering)—"escape plot," prosecuted at the whim of the unidentified storyteller even from within his own distrust of any and all formulated storylines. Any instinct of ours to *read for the plot* has been all along rewarded with little transparency—and much reticent fuss. Early on, we are tasked with excavating the very ground of depicted event from the imposed forms of its narration, assigned to retrieve the kernel of the told from its anxious telling. With obvious autobiographical resonance, Powers's narrator begins by conjuring a part-time writing teacher of creative nonfiction in an alternate Chicago, a virtual and "in vitro" Second City (7) whose loosely mapped topology has been "genetically modified for more flexibility" (7). If world-making can even go to work on a fixed and documented zone of metropolitan real estate, for narrative's own purposes, how much more is an invented character, especially when a failed proxy of the narrator, likely to find himself prey to creative manipulation— biogenetic modification—in his comings and goings?

In momentary rewind, then: "genetically modified for more flexibility." A throwaway mixed metaphor of urban cement and molecular biology? Far from it. The least turn of figurative phrase in Powers tends, as we know, to be structurally loaded. And never more than in this not yet contextualized instance. Though only to be triggered later in its full thematic detonation, with this first sounding of "genetic modification," as secret keynote, we have stumbled upon the earliest cellular or molecular stirring of a major plot development—with the novel's immigrant heroine its lab animal and scapegoat. Unguarded in her good spirits at first, and transcending victimage in her titular generosity, she is gradually co-opted by a media campaign for the in-utero enhancement of personality by gene therapy, a molecular intervention in service of the "gladness thermostat" (256) of mass American perfectionism. As always in the sociology of Powers's fiction, micro goes macro, though tracked in transit by the merest figures of speech. In this way the heroine's story is linked to the separate developments of her writing teacher's life, as well as—across more disruptive scene changes only slowly brought into connection—with the story of the academic child turned glamorous TV journalist and a renowned geneticist turned human biofuturist. Unlike the wholly separate plot strands of *Plowing the Dark*, however, with all connection withheld until the last saving moment, this version of narration by parallel montage more closely resembles the silent-film thrillers we saw Powers's first novel celebrate (in Chapter 2) for their enlisting of the "constructivist" viewer in the narrative's own rescue action: piecing intercut scenes together to achieve in phenomenological terms the deus ex machina as a redemptive event rather than a mere mechanical projection. This is because in *Generosity*, as soon emerges, the principals of the first plot are separately threatened, and know themselves to be, by the media alliance of the other two, the TV host and the longevity guru.

Journalism, Journal, Journey: The Textual Excurse

With none of this multi-plot knot yet in view by the time of that earliest turn of biological phrase regarding urban genetic deviance, that mutated version of an alternate-reality Chicago, still there is a further sardonic anticipation in the way the narrator closes out this same paragraph, stipulating how the very words that so willfully conjure a transfigured metropolitan network—as the dedicated grid of plot—"are not journalism." Period. Followed by a fragmented emphasis on what they are instead— a redirected mode of making detached from the given in departure itself: "Only journey" (6). The venture of this fiction, topographic and otherwise, is a thrust, via the virtual, into the as yet unsaid: the kind of gesture by which one syllabic root alone can generate succession. And another charged anticipation straddles the alliterative lilt of that compound turn of phrase, even in its unmasked courting of cliché. For what might seem like a minor fillip of etymological wordplay around the French stem "jour" is actually the launching gambit of a narrative whose determinate momentum is not just that of writing per se—but, more importantly, is climactically *figured as such*, no pen or paper on hand. Begun here, what slowly unfurls is a tissue of metaphors, threading together other sinuous stylistic maneuvers, whereby all action is the inscription of time present, jour by jour, in a vocabulary not necessarily the subject's own. Moreover, little do we yet know that the phrasal seesaw between "journal and journey" is shortly to offer the academic subtitle—the narrator having gotten credit for it before his writing-teacher protagonist, one Russell Stone—for a college course at a fictitious (i.e., genetically modified) downtown Chicago college: namely, "Creative Nonfiction 14, RS: Journalism and Journey." In which the novel enrolls its own readers, in effect, on a P/NP basis.

As Russell is tracked by narration along his subway route to his first class, this part-time writing mentor—unnerved by self-doubt, and long ago given up on his own creative career—is surveyed by "exposition" (109, as the narrator later calls it, preferring its mode to scene and dialogue) from an imagined seat on the same train. This introductory trope of sheer narrative transit is thick on the run with reflexive tics—or say dense in the static airspace between action and its depiction, where the only real breathing room is that of the fashioned phrase in transcription and uptake. Right from the start, all this is written up—as if drafted in headlong uncertainty—in a sketchy, ad hoc manner. It has seemingly sprung to mind from a mix of thinly veiled pedagogical recollections on Powers's own part and sheer fabrication on that of the writer-narrator—with his protagonist identified indeed, and in more than professional terminology, as "my adjunct" (5, 12). Since the character is underprepared for his first class, "it is up to me to write his assignment for him" (5)—with, again, the split valence of scalar application: the noun (given the double genitive of its "his") covering not just, in a narrow plot turn, the pending class outline, but instead, globally, the whole narrative plan of action *assigned to* him (as narrative object) from here out. The tone of the authorial persona thus wavers between identification and invention, even across the comma of a single simile: "I know this story, like I wrote it myself" (5). Not merely the colloquial "as if" in that phrasal linkage, but hints, perhaps, of the more demotic and substandard "like": an empty filler in the mode of "I know it because, like, it's all written by me." In sensing a whiff of that everyday colloquial "like"—eliding all force of analogy in a redundant hiccup of equivalence—we may note there another early microcosm of the novel's architectonic form, where the flourishes of execution are superimposed, in putatively real scriptive time, upon the floorplan of event. Early, though, the narrator admits of his character (like an older self trying to focus on memories of a younger and unformed one): "I can't see him well, at first. But that's my fault, not his. I'm years away, in another country… " (3). Seeing is under the burden of looking back—even while the reader is only trying to look in and on. And onward. But no matter, the mix of memory and invention has time on its side: "The blank page is patient, and meaning can wait" (3). With this turn from cognitive distance to scriptive practice, an autobiographic aura seems to have surfaced only to be purged. With other autonomous storylines still in abeyance, the contrast with *Plowing the Dark* is stark, archetypal. What no realist ploy can heal or even alleviate in the one novel without a turn to magic (or mystic) realism—that breach between polarized storylines broached by no plausible rapprochement—contrasts in its successor, *Generosity*, with the latency of any and all plot: the tentative over against the once antipodal, narrative still incipient rather than aggressively segregated.

The air thus cleared for the unwritten in *Genero*sity, the hero goes forth under a potentially liberating dispensation: "He'd be pleased to know that in my mind, he's still mostly white space" (13). Life's best hope: a vista of the unwritten, the unallotted. Further, what instructor Stone, on the first night of his writing class, is at least being spared (as the narrator's "adjunct" and proxy) is the confessional trend emerging from the coming classroom satire as the world's "runaway first person," where "Memoir is the new history. Tell-alls are the new news" (13). We need, implicitly, the *novel* per se as stopgap. The epistemological edge of make-believe is truer to the potential news of life's flux than the imposed self-knowledge of the packaged memoir. White space is the tabula rasa of potentiality itself, but the way is not reliably smooth or flat. Although the narrator briefly asserts that "I know this story," a sudden lurch of the subway car disrupts all confidence. It is a derailing moment for the machinery of narration: "The train wags, he pitches in his seat, and I don't know anything. I stop deciding and return to looking" (5)—as if, such is the twist, we are to presume some recourse in any of this to a visible world beyond the survey of discourse. Instead, of course, all is confessed inscription—so that an arrest in the hero's notetaking, the furious work of his pen, suspends (by figurative association) the narrator's attention as well. Stone's "pen freezes in midair; he looks up. I glance away, caught spying" (4; John le Carré: "All novelists are spies"). Never again, this potential eyeing of the executive writer by his failed in-plot double, but the risk has been summoned—as if to clear the way for effects of textual self-reference just below the threshold of such an unabashed leap of focus from scene to its setting forth (technical term: metalepsis).

Once the poor adjunct RS reaches his recalcitrant class huddled grudgingly under the teacher-initialed limp rubric "RS: Journalism and Journey"—thereby surreptitiously consolidating the narrator's own earlier slant rhyme on the shared etymological stem—the turf of lexical byplay is fertilized for much to follow. Russell quickly discovers that the students would want, at best, to blog their "journals"—or make videologs of their daily encounters—with little interest in crafted prose on the page. They aspire only to whatever expressive gestures it takes to "perform themselves," each of them "a work in progress" (9) in their own right—even while we recall that Russell, too, exists so far mostly as performed by his narrator. In his cornered role now as creative mentor, however, he has begun by asking the students to introduce themselves via their "life philosophy," and feels that turnabout is fair play. But the narrator gets there first. Introducing his own voice into this exchange—as if eavesdropping upon his character from behind the curtain of the drafted page itself, and coming to his rescue in this "assignment" as well—the narrator diverts all instructional wisdom through the pipeline of projective identification. Life-philosophy? "For convenience I give him mine" (8). Funny, and a funny word for it, "convenience," with the so-called "philosophy" following in a clipped paragraph all its own—one that doesn't surprise us, given that earlier moment on the train where "I stop deciding and return to looking." Put categorically now: "When you're sure of what you're looking at, look harder" (7). Close writing, by any name. "Convenience": the shortcut afforded by intersecting levels in the foisting off of authorial energy onto invented character. Call it the short-circuit between portrayed life and its merely performed writing: exactly, in short, the "nonfiction" part of creative narrative that may, as in the novel we're reading, register etymologically as the metatextual *con-vening* of author and avatar. As so often in Powers (already, for instance, with the "adjunctive" relation of character to his older narrator, as well in the delegated phrasal drift of *jour/nal/ney*), word roots are found to trace unspoken links in the connective tissue of all things fictive. This latest moment of "convenience" is more than emblematic; it's again programmatic: when you're sure of a word, read harder.

As such, the levels of recognition convened by this etymological moment are part of a carefully wrought template we're watching (reading) set in place early on. The sense that Russell's students don't have stories to tell, but only to embody, that they are in their own persons creative nonfictions, does of course—when matched with the being-writtenhood of Russell himself at the hands, and under the prying eye, of his own narrative superego—inscribe the very logic of this metaplot in embryo. But one of those students stands out from this background of self-invention as an authenticity already personified: namely, and by nickname, the book's eponymous heroine, née Thassadit Amzwar, called Thassa, "a Berger Algerian, from *Kabylie*, via Algiers, via Paris, via Montreal" (10). For her spirited genial outlook she is dubbed by one of the students, after Russell gets christened Teacherman, none other than "Miss Generosity." It's a name that will itself soon be etymologized to a fare-thee-well in connection with the "happiness gene" she is presumed to harbor, even before her being punningly anonymized as "Jen" on edutainment TV—and then collared for a guest spot on the wildly popular Chicago-based *Oona* talk show. This is the household word short for O'Donough, "the richest Irish American woman in the world" (228)—and thus, as the idolized O-word, via pseudonym for Oprah, the ultimate "genetic," indeed racial, modification of the novel's setting in a "virtual Chicago." The rest of the conundrum seems real enough. What in the world, especially the diasporic world—we are led to wonder even from Thassa's first appearance in the nonfiction class—can possibly explain her unstinted relishing of the real? What but a freak of nature, of the sort only science can now parse and extrapolate from—and then only popular media can fully capitalize on? Unlike her warmly embraced fellow students in the opening scenes, this young woman doesn't struggle to write her life; she seems simply to live it from moment to moment, video camera on hand to celebrate and archive its variety, a miracle worker in the field of affect. The whole gamut of personal journalism to which the writing course gravitates is displaced, in her ambitions, onto the receptive impersonality of a video POV in documentary wonder at the world as it is.

Yet reading, if not writing, eventually surfaces as part of the explanation for her openness to the world, since it turns out that it is the literary word that had originally, under Algerian ethnic crackdowns, turned oppressive constraint into secret exploration. As part of the backstory that emerges about a troubled upbringing that throws her pleasure principle into even more striking relief, the tribalist eruptions that led to the Algerian civil war had once so curtailed free speech that its very capacity had been more like anatomically excised than just legally forbidden. Here the narrator borrows (and respells) the medical term for tongue removal to mark fundamentalism's surgical strikes against the politics of language use itself, let alone individual free speech. "A generation into the country's third major linguectomy [rather than lingualectomy], words are again a capital offense" (29). Against this backdrop, nonetheless, in Thassa's surreptitious forays "the world of books opens to her, without borders" (31). For this liberating transport, as we learn in our own reading of her backstory, she brings her mother, otherwise a "document translator," as well as her brother, along for the ride. Reading is expedition, *journey* after all, familial, communal, so that, in an otherwise proscribed French, "She, her brother, and her mother travel together to various foreign parts," including "even Duras's Saigon" (31). Such are her visa-free, interdict-defiant, and altogether redemptive verbal excurses: escap(ad)es not in release from a literal prison, as in *Plowing the Dark*, but from the factionalist prison-house of mandated language.

Everything, in short, has prepared Thassa for a course (including a college class) that would help in charting for herself such turns, such *tours* of verbal force, such self-birthing *journées*—even while rerouting them, in her case, into the yet more documentary immediacy of video essays. These are travelogues not of exotic destinations now, but of an unfolding present, wherever she finds herself, deciphering the given, looking again. Very much as in *Plowing the Dark*, the committed "look harder" of reading, in honor of its originary flight from privation in both Taimur's and Thassa's different cases, is elevated to theme—not in some hermetic metatext of sequestered and circumscribed mental energy, but instead: reading as metaphor for attention per se. When at times in *Generosity*, by filmic or video analogy, the Powers narrator tampers with the lives he is story-boarding, when he edits them by openly spliced retrofits or apologetic flash forwards ("Forgive one more massive jump cut" [85]), he is not mutilating lived time but refiguring its inconsistencies in the lacunae and stray ligatures of writing's own disjunctive contours.

As Thassa's rapt concentration on the world around her is contextualized by the post-literary agendas of her fellow students, the novel's matrix episode—its own seminar in life writing, as it were—grapples with the clash of epithet and negative noun in the very idea "Creative Nonfiction." It does so in mounting a comic send-up, without dismissive put-down, that installs an opening master class in the novel's own seesaw (and Powers's career-long swivel) between document and concoction. And for this, there is not just a lesson plan "assigned" from the precincts of fictional design but a (meta)textbook. Primer, course bible, and brunt of many satiric asides, Russell's chosen required reading—the fictitious Frederick P. Harmon's fictitious *Make Your Writing Come Alive* (11)—is a thudding dud with the students, even though it is later consulted or recalled at times, by the narrator as well as his characters, when striving for a vitalization of event by mere prose.

The students' drive for self-expression proceeds in contrast, not just to the collapsed writerly ambition of the teacher assigned to guide it, but to the narrative energies that are piecing out his own story over his shoulder or behind his back. In all this, story is paradoxically striving to find a space within the unevenness of experience—including in particular written experience—that might fall under the radar of narrative, might escape the lot of plot, loosed to the bliss of contingency in the process. As such, and certainly without alluding to "secondary sources" beyond the required invented primer, Powers's own writing—as well this authorial polymath may realize—has entered tacitly into the heated recent debates in cognitive studies between the "episodic self" and the "narrative self": between contingent experience, taken intermittently and piecemeal, versus lifelines understood as inherently serial, looped, cumulative.[2] Such debates, as reflected in the novel before us, have to do in part with narrative time, with the merely punctuating moment under report versus the accrued and punctual increment in a masterplot. And it is on this issue—on creative writing's unique *way with time*, its way through and around it, in dilation or compression—that the novel is at its most compelling about the discourse of story. And about that sense of reflexive subjectivity long ago highlighted, as we saw in Chapter 2, by the very awkwardness of punctuation in *Three Farmers on the Way to a Dance* when the phrase "metaself-consciousness" came under the quasi-narrative lens.

Despite the intervention of a self-consciously obtrusive narrator in the doings of a failed novelist and nonfiction writing teacher, *Generosity* isn't just a tale about itself as written story, where all valorized agency is siphoned off by the telling alone, leaving the characters as playthings of fabrication. It's the tale of a story *being written*—frame-breaking, yes, in any number of ways, including its pedagogical puns, and braced by in-jokes on the pliable temporality of sequence, but not trapped in some airless circuit of world-building mastery. Especially when it borrows, as we'll see, some of the video or filmic techniques to which its protagonist's students are attached, the novel analogizes its own mechanism as an apparatus less for some fixed transcript in the mode of bookhood than for an access to time's rendered flow. Story, then, is in this case the image not just of itself being written—but, always and only in the moment, of life being lived. Not led; not dragged forward by plot. Not invented, but found. And given meaningful shape by the impulses of its finding in the track of a prose that skirts showiness on the one hand, tedium on the other, in the assertive showing of its own hand—and thus earns a conclusion that could well have been discounted as a bankrupt withdrawal from the true yields of realism. Instead, the narrative vanishing point, in its marked evanescence, has been carefully prepared for in just its final transvaluation of the metatext, where taking action is, and without taking up the pen, a figured triumph over writer's block—and this in story's longstanding contrast to the already-written of DNA codes.

Deciphering Genomic Script

As Russell's fascination with Miss Generosity increases, it soon turns fateful when he is indirectly responsible for her name making the papers after an attempted dorm rape by a fellow student in the class, whom in her generosity she forgives without bringing charges. With his teaching contract going un-renewed after this scandal, Russell gets progressively involved with Candace Weld, the college therapist Thassa has gone to for counseling. For their "charge," as student and patient respectively, an escalation in public scrutiny becomes intolerable once a visionary geneticist and frequent TV personality, one Thomas Kurton, has fixed Thassa in his sights as a unique biometric specimen. When a resulting mass media obsession, almost a national hysteria, turns this mysterious émigré into a poster child for genomic advantage, the intense affective triangle of teacher, student, and her staff psychologist becomes professionally toxic, compromising Candace's job—her whole career—and thus forcing her, against her own best instincts and those of Russell as well, to suspend any further contact with an increasingly dependent Thassa. All the while, the national furor increases—with warring audiences among her new media public either craving or decrying, in the terms of the novel's subtitle, the "enhancement" such genetic borrowing might provide.

In developing this increasingly stark contrast between biological determinism, on the one hand, and the alternate promise of creative nonfiction in neurological rescripting, on the other, we hear—read—that the genomic guru (and longevity entrepreneur) Kurton is famous for "a technique called rapid gene signature reading" (24). This is a hermeneutic procedure brought into line with his devotion to a cryonically aided human perpetuity, among other species improvements. In view of the polarized axis marked by interventionist genetic destiny versus existential free play—or in the book's antipodal mantra from here out, preferential "choice" versus the play of "chance"—we are led, almost inevitably, to contrast any such rabid messianism, a growing cult based on the molecular body as legible text, with the former utopian motives of Russell's own would-be fiction writing. In his grandiose youth, he was once a member of an informal creative cabal whose mission was to "change the way that writing worked, break the tyranny of convention, and reenchant the tired reading public with a runaway playfulness that not even the dead could resist" (33). Back from the grave of convention, in short, the idea had been a kind of visionary confrontation: bring your reader, not just your writing, to life.

In the novel's present, however, the real threat is the turning of lives into mere pre-scriptions. In a personal appeal to Russell at one point, Thassa seems to have become slightly unhinged. But Teacherman is dubious, as if aware—as audited in free indirect discourse—that some force beyond them may have staged the crisis for its own narrative sake (in allusion again to the textbook author Harmon): "Someone has invented the scene just to create rising action. Harmon: story starts when a character's core value no longer suffices to stabilize his world" (104). And our supervening storyteller steps in soon after, even more directly, this time no longer plausibly channeling Russell's own cross-reference to the writing primer. For it is the narrator, explicitly now, who wishes he could keep his characters "tucked away safely in exposition. But they've broken out now, despite me, into rising action" (109). Barely. A subsequent encounter still leaves Thassa "trying to figure out what kind of scene they're writing" (78). It's hard to know, because the character of her interlocutor hero is still incipient, diffuse, unfocused, and the narrator still on his elusive scent, resorting even to strategies pilfered from earlier metafiction: "I even loot those hall-of-mirrors avant-garde novels whose characters try to escape their authors, the kind he once loved, the kind he thought he'd write one day, before he gave up fiction" (40). Before he gave up that metafictional fantasy in particular. But not before the narrator may be having some lexical fun passing "loot" through the micronarrative looking glass, as if reverse-imaged to desperate narrative "tool" in the sentence's own chiastic chamber of mirrors. Next passing over in canted reflection toward the onetime "love" across its hyphenated shadow at "ha*ll-of*," this nostalgic recession of sheer phonetic fading serves to trace, yet again in Powers, the drift of signification toward the mimetically etched thing itself. But it is up to the narrator, from here out, to decide whether to let fiction as such give Russell up, let him be.

When such private encounters between Thassa and Russell are pitched against the grand plans of entrepreneurial genetics, let alone the self-reflecting enclaves of postmodern fiction-making in its extreme "hall-of-mirrors" mode, the novel's own differential scheme sharpens its outlines. The attempted translation of personal encounter to undecided scenario, in Thassa's own mind at least, is emblematic. Against the uncertain give and take between aleatory happenings and some tentative metanarrative that might organize them—might reward their being looked at again—is posed the macro sense of human evolution as a narrative through-line. It is as if the metafictonal urge were contagious in this book, since even the visionary geneticist also couches species genealogy in the language of story. The very fact of death has found humanity "stuck in a bad plot" (64). By the lights of visionary science, being mortal is nothing *but* a dead end. Becoming exceeds being as we know it. "We want to become something else. It's what we've wanted since the story started" (64). Besides evolution and its technical prostheses, there's another diachronic macroplot operating as well in this quadrant of the story, one that again circles round to the linguistic subplots of phrasing's own drama: the macro sphere of etymology rather than evolutionary biology. As the narrator wields and worries his own diction, he at one point explicitly alerts us to the molecular components of his novel's titular noun. But he does so before he's even spelled out the lexeme whose linguistic heritage he is rooting (pun no doubt implicit) around in. We are invited to catch on, catch up, as soon as we can, second guess his digression, get out ahead of language into meaning.

This segue-free transition is an unusual one. Arising from the white blank between sections, with no proximate antecedent: "I need a *genealogy* for the word" (85). *The* word? Which? The only plausible candidate we have for such a word is, right there before us, hovering suggestively: the noun "genealogy." Is this some kind of reflexive shortcut in syntax? All we can do is quickly read on. As if in a mark of textual rather than sexual selection, "it"—still no official antecedent, except as winked at there in the "gen" of "genealogy"—is a word that (the genealogical call heeded) "comes through the loins of that giant Latin *gens*" (85): a word to be pronounced, and thus confirming our ultimate suspicions about the lexeme in question, with the soft or short *e* of *generosity* rather than the first long vowel of *genealogy*. A personifying metaphor ("loins") as well as a recursive turn of phonetic byplay: two of Powers's trademark effects, mostly minimized by the unusual satiric cast of this deadpan "academic" narrative, are unleashed here in an unstinted barrage of lexical speculation. As well as in a typical flourish of "linguistic science" (among the author's other favored technical vocabularies)—while thrown into unique medial relief against the subtext of genomic code in the same investigation of shared genealogical prefixes. Picking up the passage again as it picks up steam, we hear how it is through the similar "loins" of a resulting rampant polygamy that this *gen* stem "so liberally shares its family name, family property, family ties, and"—wait for it, in its mortuary aura—"family plot" (85).

Both senses: words passed down and then on, in their own chronicle; words dying out, like people, like characters, in an entombed patrilineage. Words echoed against each other, words reflected back on one another—in the true if attenuated "hall-of-mirrors" mode this post-postmodern novel constitutes.

In this continuing materialist rumination on the linguistic trait as procreant "thing," an internal rhyme next emphasizes how "the original root of the thing has spread its genes into an absurd number of offspring"—including, in the continued withholding of the eponymous noun in question, the initial three progeny of a sixteen-item list (given at first in alphabetic order, but hinting at another erotic priority, both literary and pro-creative): "genial, genital, genre" (85). Genre, gener-. Diction is getting warm. We're still, however, expected to be filling in the blank in our reverse engineering of the word under such genealogic scrutiny, until finally it surfaces in adjectival form. This happens when it is said of this etymology, this whole genetic descent, that it is "generous to a fault" (85) in its family legacy of intermarriage. But the riddling spin of linguistic dissemination doesn't stop there, since the next summary objection is an immanent case in point (this time italics added): "Too many pro*geny* for any paternity test" (85). In sum, and proceeding in this same syllabically embedded vein, it is a "heterogeneous word" so "generative" that it naturally falls prey to "genomicists" as well as those who are merely "genuine" by nature in their desire to "make more kin," more intuitive "connections."

Point/counterpoint once more—and the emergent, the resistant, third term between. Against this heady philological genealogy, in its own parallel to traced *gen*omic mapping, one realizes that the branching lifeline of a lexical root—however multifarious—has a set of clearer trajectories than characters still struggling for a story line. In the largest disposition of the novel's irony, therefore, the wording—and weaving—of a narrowly populated human plot must thread its way as the combinatory middle track between a history of language and a history of biological code, between the powers of phrase for the shaping of "life stories" and the possibilities, otherwise coded, for a molecularly amplified human psyche. On the emphatic score of such plot options in *Generosity*, sometimes the undercurrent of making and make-belief flares to the surface in a bit of quickening book-market wit. If Russell had not become obsessed with Miss Generosity, he might have benefited from exactly her "generative" spirit, her energy, and have returned to his life, yes, "enhanced." But this is not enough for our publication-savvy character (in free indirect), let alone for his narrator, amounting to little more than a "vaguely midlist literary story" (93). Instead, even the dormant writer in Russell inclines, early on, to think "that such a plot has to go somewhere, that something has to happen" (94).

Micro / Macro: "The Story So Far"

New paragraph after the above recognition, with the narrator's aside licensing the exponential melodrama to come: "I know exactly how he feels" (94), how importunate the idea of event can seem as a narrative requirement. And so will Thassa, to whom that unknown mandatory "something" is first to happen. Once she is thrust into the national spotlight, we see in her agitated question, put to Candace and Russell at once, how the former's surname, Weld, may all along have been meant to bridge the instincts of therapy and fiction and thus solder the metaplot: "Do you think it's possible for people to change their own story?" (92). Faced with this query from Miss Generosity, this tacit plea for some offered lifeline in distress—a call for help probing to the very core of the psychiatrist's committed career, as well as the writing teacher's half-hearted and now furloughed one—the paired advisers are speechless: "Counselor and teacher both froze" (92). Recuperative therapy and forward plotting hang fire together, left bereft between history and potential. Partly, we're led to see, it's a matter of "genre"—as not *always* closely mated with "genial" after all.

 A struggle continues on the narrator's part to steer his triangulated characters clear of the mounting crisis he has himself been scripting, yet to do so without facile recourse to a hackneyed romance format. Once more, etymology dogs the heels of contemplated plotting. Lamentably, as a genre imperative, "Sexual selection, the surest and venerable form of eugenics"—our too-generous "gen" again—"has molded us into the fiction-needing readers we are today" (102). Urges sexual and textual are locked in an unholy embrace. "Part of me would love [the loaded word] to belong to a species free, now and then, to read about something other than its own imprisonment" (102)—its capture by the sex drive, by romance: something other than "love letters to the urge than has abducted us" (102). It is this kidnapping by sexual obsession whose syntax and lexicon the next chapter will take under its phrasal consideration in the dictional pornographics of Nicholson Baker. But in the dynamics of *Generosity*, including the usual countervailing swings of a Powers's novel, this critique of genre—and its hijacking grip on readerly desire—is matched (even in contrast) by the thinking of geneticist Kurton in his contempt altogether for the humanism of the novel form's individualist bias.

At a point of public crisis in his attempt to capitalize on Thassa's genomic code, Kurton drives for hours "listening to an audiobook of *The Plague*," deciding finally that the existentialist nonsense isn't Camus's fault, but rather that "the problem is with the craft of fiction" (249). In this sense "the whole grandiose idea that life's meaning plays out in individual negotiations makes the scientist wince" (229). Fiction is held hostage in this way to the myth of "self-making" in defiance of fate, blind to species-deep forces building toward the liberation from plot itself: in particular, from mortal closure. This is what is elsewhere and repeatedly celebrated by Kurtonists as the leap from an age of chance to the forever-after age of choice: an elective destiny genetically engineered as part of the monetized "tr*ade* in human tr*aits*" (250). Powers's programmatic metalinguistics again: his sentence intensification, even low-keyed, edging to the point of mimetic equivalence—where in this case phonetic interchange (*ade/ait*) replicates the barter denominated. Kurton's is a vision flagged in its spiritual reductiveness by that phrase's further lurking overtone, across the slant rhyme, of its own other sense: the trading-*in*—and upgrading—of personality, at whim and medical will. For Kurton, anything short of this biosynthetic fulfillment is an anodyne distraction, more broadly disabling even than fiction's romance fixation in the narrator's view. Yet for Kurton the problem lies with the novel form itself: "at best a scattershot mood-regulating concoction" (230), an "erratic cocktail"—"erotic" not far from earshot—whose pleasure principle is eventually to be replaced by "better, more precise molecular fine-tuning" (230). Instead, the novel that embeds this vision holds out for the luck of the contingent over against the genetic lockdown of such s/election, however "natural."

Counterswings, to say the least—or dialectical counter|points, with alternatives split down the middle of their own articulation. For it is demonstrably the case that the rhetoric of our sympathetic narrator himself, not just of his scientific foil in Kurton, also indulges in something of this same tropology: evolution as masterplot. This transpires, most obviously, in a freestanding set-piece in which, without attribution, the novel's allegorical prose seems almost ventriloquizing the synoptic voice of science in accounting for history after the advent of *homo scriptus*—as we might, so the inference goes, choose to denominate the human species all told as a missing link in a genetic eschatology: "Say that the six thousand years of writing are a six-hundred page novel," its "opening hook" being "secret marks that hurl meaning magically through time and space" (259).

Writing becomes the definitive new prosthesis of the tool-using animal. Long before any biomorphic destiny in forms of the transhuman, the storage function of script founds the very archive of the species—and this still in the historical present of the World Novel: "Freed from the present, papyrus starts to spawn new subplots." They split and lengthen and continually accelerate. In the evolutionary long view, a late avalanche of "quick reveals" gives way to "one of those massive finish-line sprints" in which "characters throw off the limits of the Story So Far and complete their revolt" (259). And so the "ultimate sentence" of the World Novel is a direct quote from its errant, defiant survivors: "Author, we're outta here" (259). Marked thereby, as a transcended "here," is the happy ending of the race's own making—in bold defiance of mortal limitation under the presumed sign of biogenetic escape. But this tacitly satirized macro critique of the human condition has, yet again, its micro alternative in resistance. In contrast to genetic reprogramming, the liberty ached for on behalf of the narrator's still-human characters is not a need to be "freed from time," but rather released to inhabit it outside the pressure of story, any story, including the one not just So Far but any prescribed one To Come.

So this apocalyptic teleology of biomorphic transcendence is fully quarantined by ironic contrast with other motives on which it nonetheless sheds a different scalar light. With no trace of this ventriloquized millenarian destiny in the compositional labors of his own fictional stance, Powers's narrator, instead, knows what he wishes he could do with his plot. But short of throwing it open to accident and chance, to life as lived, he senses his structure "starving to death between allegory and realism, fact and fable, *creative* and nonfiction" (129). Not creative writing versus nonfiction writing, note, but invention per se versus the given: making it up versus taking it on. At such moments Powers's metafiction doesn't outbid reality, but burrows into its own uncertainties, coming out the other side of the made into the still waiting. Speaking of his own characters: "I see now exactly who these people are and where they came from. But I can't quite make out what I'm to do with them" (129). Nor what they can do with and for themselves. That's the nonfictional burden. The narrator knows "what kind of story I'd make from this one, if I could: the kind that, from one word to the next, breaks free" (129). In other words, in two more parallel fragments broken away from the constraints of grammar itself: "The kind that invents itself out of meaningless detail and thin air. The kind in which there's no choice like chance" (129). Including, in this field of contingency, the "thin air" of silent enunciation. A breaking free, yes, but not into some autonomy of self-invention—as also resisted by Kurton from his antithetical faith in posthuman apotheosis. The active setting-free dreamed of is instead a sense of liberation effected in the grain of onwardness "from one word to the next"—as sensed in miniature with so many chance collisions in Powers's own style.

Inscription, that is, may generate its "next" worded motive from the inside out, coterminous with what it builds on—as is the case with the alliteratively slanted idiom "no choice like chance" in redefining accident as the ground of the most natural, so to speak, selection: contingency as the true field of decisive action. Modeled by prose as much as by plot. Not long after this preferential vision of fictional release from assigned script into inscriptive liberty—from the pat and pre-formulated to the fortuitous in the place and play of words—we come upon what may be the metatext's quintessential wordplay, skewering the book's self-stultified hero even under sympathetic treatment by his alter ego, the unfailed and in-progress novelist. This is a passage in which Russell Stone is seen, fully in character, to evince yet again, oxymoronically phrased, "the *steadfast failure of nerve* that has penned his whole life" (122; emphasis added). And beyond paradox, the pun: "penned," scribed and caged at once. It is from that simultaneous perspective, verbally and narratively superimposed, that the hero seems living a life that has written itself into a corner—and needs the revision, as such, that only a final trope of inscription, reversed and redeemed, can, however unexpectedly, provide. By which the writer's life, through a force figured as script, is finally unpent.

But not until the throes of inscription, of depiction, necessary to get there have been further highlighted en route—and transferred from the discourse of narration to its own embodied plot turns. Indeed, the onetime writing hero, after a long celibate dry spell, first warms to his new relation with Candace in the mode of prolonged verbal foreplay. The affair finds its early bloom, that is, in nightly telephone calls whose intimacy is not likely to be demoted by our narrating fictionist, who speaks for the hero in free indirect prose about "the tangled inventions of their nightly sentences" (155), or, in other words, the erotic reciprocity of their "free trade of signs" (155)—more Russell's natural "real medium" for communing than the so-called "community of touch" (155). And once semiosis has given way to frequent overnight beddings, the couple thinks of their affair as a kind of coauthored if still hesitant adventure (the effort, in short, recalling the conclusion to *The Gold Bug Variations*, to "draft an imaginary book together" [222]), each of them content, so far, with an open-ended development.

For his part, and against the drift (and "draft") of his own invention, the narrator, when trouble erupts between them over Thassa, recoils from what he has set in motion: "All I want is for my friends to survive the story intact. All the story wants is to wreck anything solid in them" (246). And in a double helix of this same ironic "story," the media-hounded Miss Generosity turns to nonfiction pedagogy as an escapist bedtime text when she "makes herself drowsy" at night by "reading Frederick P. Harmon," falling asleep "thinking of all the ways that a creative narrative might rescue her from nonfiction" (237): save her, in short, from the real. And the slippage between story and its telling can become weirdly vexed at times, so that one loses the sense of priority between the made up and the taken down. In this regard, a curious phrasing has pulled back, at one earlier point, farther yet than we had anticipated from the auto-commentary of the plot-in-progress. And in tense structure itself. Russell the would-have-been metafictionist is made uncomfortable by a casual invitation, at the incipient stage of the romance plot overtaking him—at which point the narrator goes about unsetting, we might say, his own scene, opening a supposed gulf between biography and fiction: "I watch him twist, the way he did so often in real life" (103). The twist is rhetorical before bodily. Tapping again the surveillance aesthetic installed on the opening train ride, the trope "I watch him" is verbal, fictional, not lived, but preternaturally cognate with reality even in its translation to the page—where watching supposedly becomes our decipherment of a rehearsed and embodied scenario in its truest past contours. Where to read right is to "look again." As we just did, reflexively, puzzled by the near paradox of that phrasal extratext whereby the invented reverts to its conditioning reality.

Imprint, Time-Stamp, Plot: Narrative Unpenned

In just such passages on the way to the novel's climax, the no-longer-plenary spheres of the real and the written uniquely interpenetrate, addressing each other from their previous tangency—or unstable overlap. As details are revealed only to congeal, narration finds some of its own sought freedom in an overt play with time. Beyond the narrator begging our tolerance for that "massive jump cut" (85) mentioned earlier, there are various episodes of slowed or accelerated motion that, out in the open, strategize fiction's "defeat of time" (168)—as in those ratios of acceleration, for instance, that offer remission and sometimes redirection for the characters. This defiance and ultimate "defeat" is the "single most useful trick of fiction for our repair and refreshment" (168). No correlations are mandatory between event and its rendering: "A century of family saga and a ride up an escalator [here he might well be alluding to Baker's *The Mezzanine*] can take the same number of pages. In this way, in the clocking of real versus reading time: "Fiction sets any conversion rate, then changes it in a syllable" (168). Yet story's "defeat of time" is itself only intermittent and provisional. Any total submission to such a supervening narrative force, a ceding of all agency to the pace of writing and its editorial license, cannot be settled for. The too-facile elision or ellipsis is resisted. Closure is not the "happily ever after" of a couple presumed on the road to marriage, Russell and Candace in this case, but the mere suspension of their story, letting them go their own "probable" way. But before that, the story has to be wrested from the devastations of chance by a decisive choice of action, an impulse split-second but redemptive. The long "penned" (pent-up) character of the hero—cramping his own options, in ways he himself well recognizes—is offered reprieve from within its very own term(s). It is at this point suddenly, as we've more than once anticipated, that, turning in this case on a single (monosyllabic) about-face, he must take control of his own life in saving another's, rewriting her endgame.

His every self-doubt prepares him for failure in the clichéd escape plot he is now living—without being able to write a part in it for himself. His modus operandi has always been an escape *from* plot. The timeworn "getaway car" story into which he's now plunged suspends him in an insecure and unfolding dramatic present, tensed in every sense in and by the still uncertain. "Just beyond South Bend," in his attempted return of Thassa to Montreal, and mapped in narrative time present, "Stone has an epiphany. He knows," once and for all, "why he could never in his life or anytime thereafter write fiction: he's crushed under the unbearable burden of a plot"—a plot that will not bear up. "He could never survive the responsibility of making something happen" (297)—even, so he would think, the responsibility of a survival itself. "Plot is preposterous" (297), he complains. That adjective lands as an ultimate metaword in this context: an etymological oxymoron formed of an impossibly coupled before-behind dyad, pre|post, a paradox enacted rather than signified—and thus a metonymy for all else illogical and ridiculous in the arbitrary structurings of fiction. What, for the hero, is most rudely preposterous about plot is the normative sense of serial order: "event following event in a chain of clean causes, rising action building to inevitable climax and resolving into meaning. Who could be suckered by that?" (297). Story isn't an arc but a stall, postponing doom by distraction. Handbook bromides are called out again, immediately to be put down: "The classic tension graph is a vicious lie, the negation of a mature grasp of reality" (297). Nonfiction should be stricter than this, and the novel truer in this respect to its antithesis in journalism: "Story is antilife, the brain protecting itself from its only possible finale" (297)—fending off death by intervals of ersatz meaning and false plateaus of achievement. Russell Stone, as a once self-styled writer, would have been a different transcriber of existence. For life seems to him, in its own right, a "failed avant-garde experiment"—a joyless revel in the aleatory, which any true writing would acknowledge. Result: "Sales: zip. Critical reception: total bewilderment... not even a decent allegory. Even the cutout bin doesn't want it" (298). No remaindered half-life for the true-to-life, for any such shapeless authenticity.

Thus might have concluded the novel's own seminar in creative writing, schooling attention in a principled resistance to plot, inculcating a sense that to scaffold a story with indecision is its surest engineering and its truest measure of human pertinence—that, in short, chanciness is the choicest of formal options. But, within story, on the part of—rather than just on behalf of—its characters, that option (all options open!) still needs to be taken up, engaged, enacted. At which point reading in *Generosity* finds its most emphatic reflex action, in ways less abstract than this inevitably sounds, in the trope, the sheer metaphor, of writing as event. How this is accomplished requires nothing less than a metatextual introversion of desire. Or puzzle it out this way: If "story is antilife," and plot absurd in its staving off death, what is the best fictional name, or analog, for what saves a life? Is a story, so to speak, possible by accident? And in that case, if not shaping up as a novel, avant-garde or otherwise, how might it be imagined—as for instance by the "penned" energies of a failed writer and "unrenewed" writing teacher—as a scribal vaunt nonetheless?

The recuperative move thus negatively anticipated is as disruptive and unexpected as the "scene" that Thassa has chosen to write for herself, for both of them, at this late turn. When, along their escape route to Canada, Russell discovers her attempted suicide by an overdose of assorted pills from his dopp kit, the man who never did anything "anyone could construe as resolute" (290) in his life, including any literary commitment, collapses in front of her unconscious body. He is rescued from inertia only by the narrator—and in an author's terms. Giving up on Generosity, Russell "sits down on the floor, shaking, clouded, and adrift. And in that instant of annihilation"—the canceling moment both of her death and of his active commitment to her—"art at last over-takes him" (314). How so? How in the world? How in any world other than the one spun by narration? A swollen moment of obliteration, distended and locked down by those delayed modifiers of spasmodic inertia ("shaking, clouded, and adrift"). And then—as if to review the earlier tabulated premises of fictional temporality—it all (via "conversion rate") turns on a dime ("changes... in a syllable") in a breakout passage "from word to word." For here, recovering the dialectical shunts of figuration that build toward this moment of achieved agency, comes the metaphor of all metaphors: when, in the fifth and final part of the novel, and in a climactic sentence's final *two-syllable* clause, "art at last overtakes him, and *he writes*" (314; emphasis added). It would be hard to exaggerate the deliberate *lack* of histrionic exaggeration here, with that minor breath-catching of the comma offering the most dramatic gesture of the two clauses, and the preceding hyphen its only lexical twist. With what torsion exerted? In a total collapse after long torpor, art finally catches up with him, "over-takes" in that sense? In the collapse of his defenses, art takes him over? In either case, "writing" has become simply a figure of speech, not for inscribed speech, but for intentionality per se: aroused will—to vary the Harmon textbook, a "rising" *to* as well as *of* "action."

    Faced with her breathless body, he knows all too well, this time, "what kind of scene" they were in, what kind of creative nonfiction they "were writing"—and sets about, true to his day job as pulp magazine hack, but with a purpose far exceeding those stylistic fixes to which he is consigned in his schlock-rag editorial work on *Becoming You*, to bring his writing student back to life by swinging into gear and dialing for help. This surge of commitment, this call to action from the voice of instinct, imagined as a textual rescue from the inexorability of an unwanted plot, has been anticipated in reverse early in this automative escape route, Russell at the wheel, Thassa telling him, with a depth of feeling beyond sex, that "I just love you" (300). The embarrassed blush is figured as a topographic journey in itself, then a wished for excision in this lived journal of their flight: "Blood runs uphill into his face, and he wants to red-pen his whole existence" (276). Instead, it is panic that italicizes his leap into action soon after. The onetime aspiring fictionist—emptied out by a loss of drive on the page and in social space alike, everywhere hemmed in by inefficacy—rises for once to the occasion, engages with the "rising action" (and narcotized body) of the tragic turn confronting him—and, in the now intransitive form of a monosyllabic verb with no object, authoring a peripety without content as yet, quite instinctively for once, and without block, "he writes." And caught by this surprising predication—at a new pitch of reflexive investigation—*we read*. The odd flatfooted downbeat of those two monosyllables executes a back-flip in the novel-long figuration of the so-called "life-story." After this instantaneous flashpoint for such synonymies of being and textual doing, the trope is prolonged during Thassa's hospitalization, where Russell "can do nothing for her but revise. And he has time to rework entire world anthologies" (315)—the sense of "revision" here answering to the free indirect discourse in the paragraph immediately following "and he writes": namely "He can rescind this" (314). She survives, and as this last phase of the novel closes upon her release from plot, and her last valedictory manifestation by (and before) the narrative voice rather than Russell's, she is "still alive, just as I conceived her, still uncrushed" (321). Adding, from that Harmon textbook mantra again, now an existential rather than a textual paradigm: "All writing is rewriting" (321). In that sense, the true plot is exactly that which can be fixed.

To earn the climactic reprise of this proposal, more has happened at the turning point than a mere figure of speech—more than a last-ditch gesture in the mode of a metaphysical conceit: for experience as revision. The self-signaled discursive build-up of the novel has, in all this, pressed a passing trope over into an emblem and almost a parable. Daunted by the demands of plot, of plan, of purpose, nonetheless the aimless hero has snapped out of it to help get the lethal pills out of the heroine's system. Riddance is revision. Taking his dictation from disastrous chance, and then script-doctoring it sideways toward the emergency lane of choice, his initiative has helped see her through. He has hauled the comatose body of this national idol back toward life before the helicopter ambulance—*machina ex dea*—arrives. Unproductive as an author until now, he at least forestalls a premature closure, for her and the novel alike, and thus keeps the story open, going. "All writing is rewriting"? If so, beyond that tolerable pedagogic paradox, a revisionary *chiasm* has also set in. Its corollary notion is one that goes far toward motivating the entire subtext of "creative nonfiction"—anchor of the novel's resolute fictional metatext—as a mode of thought more deeply embedded than a ramified joke about authorial omniscience and its breakdowns. Under the aegis of this self-composed narrative, if writing is always a revision of the given, then, symmetrically, all corrective action, any rectifying scenario, any resuscitated energy, *is a kind of writing*: the sketching out of another way forward, an alternate path of commitment palpably subscribed to, with agency drafted into service along a freshly marked-out line of inscribed thought. Each new event is a rewriting of its imagined prototype, a bypass, some self-authorized rite of passage. Not for writers only, or in particular, are we to imagine this trail broken forward from discursive constraint: not just some privileged way with words. Instead, *revision* shows forth as a name for going forward, bearing down, leaning in, changing action's own course: revision as righting. Red-lining included, as well as interpolations, reversals of sequence and consequence. Dead-ended by events otherwise, "rewriting" delineates a newly articulated right of way, with every "journey"—the tacky classroom gambit come home to roost—activated as well as tracked by its own tacit journaling. From the inside out.

Fade to White

So has our reading proceeded "between allegory and realism"—but, instead of "starving to death" in that way, it has managed to feed on its own reflex action in reader investment. Here, then, has been the story of a failed postmodern storyteller (and fallback writing instructor), onetime aspirant to the metafictional avant-garde, so little able to shape a plot for his own feckless life that he retreats into the mindless editing of self-help testimonials in the periodical rebirths of *Becoming You*. Unexpectedly recruited to proselytize the very writing he has lost faith in, accident throws our hero in the way of a part-time teaching post and across the path of two women who bring him at least halfway back from a self-inflicted grave of disengagement. But one of them, after the commercialized reading of her genomic script, finds her life aggressively rewritten into a larger cultural narrative of neurobiology and evolutionary advance, swept up in a national passion for cannibalizing her genetic profile and its closely read (and guarded) DNA code. Coming to a head in this collapsed dichotomy between the terms of organic vitality and its inscription, the novel has sustained in many comparable ways a recurrent flip-flop between life and text. Though fostering a certain stylistic restraint within the orbit of narrative dubiety and inhibition alike, the story's ironies keep in repeated touch, understood this way, with the hero's ill-chosen classroom text, *How to Make Your Writing Come Alive*.

Any plot summary of this novel is therefore at one with a rhetoric of fiction in any phenomenology of reading such a novel. Invented lives come to consciousness not unlike our own in the throes of self-narration. The oscillation between dead letters and the breath of life persists until the melodramatic peripety passes the baton of composition itself—as sheer metaphor—back from narrator to character. A writing textbook's bland figurative advice—regarding the animation machine of prose—has by now been literalized around a "trigger point" (that flagged term for the reflexive nodes of historical transformation in Powers's first novel) wrought by personal catastrophe and emergency resuscitation: precisely as a life story's scribal imperative. Plot is thereby reformatted as a kind of metalinguistic syllogism. If words on a page can in any sense come alive, then—in a reciprocal figuration—bringing a character back from the dead is a kind of primal writing: a resistant redraft of the otherwise intractable. Unforeseen by the protagonist who has abandoned creativity in his frustration with plot, the only way out is for this man "penned" by inertia to take corrective action as an engaged "writer" anyway—such is the "hall-of-mirrors" shape of his own consciousness—and thus free himself from any imposed story but his own in progress, including the stories of those whose fate he can affect. In extremity, desperation is redeemed, after all, by creative nonfiction: by the act of one's writing some articulated way out of suspended animation.

With such a metaplot-summary behind us, we are ready to follow out the novel's remaining (and barely narrative) language in tapering off within a nest of audiovisual analogies: story's last steps being taken, beyond plot, in an open coda of withdrawn depiction. Building toward it, in the restless conceptual turns of the narrator's tropes for event and its plotting, and as a kind of structural obverse to fiction's "defeat of time" by ellipsis, the exhausted Russell, collapsing into sleep, "wakes several pages later" (288)—as if a disappeared text-time were only a measure of "real time." In just this final phase of the novel, the cinematic tropes increase as well, so that driving on from Chicago, over such an endless stretch of similar terrain, seems to trap the renegades in "an enormous loop" (297). And later yet in this escape plot, after Thassa's nervous slow-motion methodical fussing in a motel, the narrator's mechanical sense of temporality—channeling his hero's—suggests that the "film speed gradually returns to normal" (310). All this seems preparing us for the interlace of video record and textual erasure on the novel's enigmatic last pages.

The vise-like deadlock of the pre-posteriorized has been rescued from implosion, broken out to the unknown after all, and thus submerged, we are to find, in the aural blur of language without text, immemorial—before the disappearance of the world itself as text. All this transpires, expires, when the TV anchorwoman, Tonia, first responsible for the national scale of Thassa's unwanted publicity, has tracked her down in the Maghreb, at some unspecified point after the heroine's return from Montreal. On hand, of course, and up to his old tricks, the narrator intervenes, by quasi-cinematic machination, in the visitor's rush through the congested streets: "I slow her down" (317) and shortly afterwards, seeking direction, she "switches to French. The whole point of giving her a Brussels childhood" (317). With all real plot subsided, this throwaway metajoke at narrative's eleventh hour can only cast its shadow back on the whole double-tracked progress of story and its shaping discourse. Authorial first cause arrives as an unmistakable reflex of secondary effect: the aftertext of recognition in a nutshell—and its happy cracked joke.

Other resolutions attend as well this suspension of plot in the very disclosure of plotting, in even its least descriptive backstory. With unseen voices singing, in competition, an advertising jingle in the street beyond the café where the two women so inconsequentially meet, it is as if any vocal conflict is abstracted to harmony—and a phonetically realized one at that—when, in a sibilant ripple, "the co*nt*est of t*en*ors cr*esc*endos and a*scen*ds" (320). Set off in a kind of parable, and inflected by perhaps the most characteristic stretch of Powers's audialized prose in the whole novel, the clear emblematic gesture guiding this passage is to escape the already-written, commercial or otherwise: to get back to a language unshackled by the accrued formulas of historical time. Incurred in this is the audial reverb—or say the acoustic chamber of mirrors—in which the primordial sounds of human word forms are found cresting unshackled in the now, rather than tugged back or yanked forward in the pre-posteriority of referential constriction. With the rarefaction of words into pure melody, here too is where the paracinematic and the metatextual collide with and elide each other, ceding their force back to the blankness of thrown light and unmarked page. For this last nominal interview between Thassa and Tonia now tails off in a video fade of the entire intimate scene, but with its optical dissolve concentrated first on the space of wording in an everyday text (of restaurant choices) when reverting to tabula rasa: "As the two look on, the menu's French fades. The Arabic follows it into white" (321). The prototype has come just before, as Thassa suggests that the gift brought to her should be given to Russell instead, a copy of Harmon's *Make Your Writing Come Alive*. No sooner is it handed back than "the text disappears" (321): whether the bound volume itself or its imprinted prescriptions, like menu options, it no longer matters.

The fade-out implicitly continues, as if telescoped back beyond evolution's whole Story So Far, when audial blur is figured, in a wider illegibility yet, as following the imprinted letters "into white": "So, too, do the sounds in the air around the café, until the only language running through the nearby streets is the one that existed in these parts long before the arrival of writing" (321)—a communal murmur free of text. The living effort, that is, remains still phonic, still latently linguistic, but has passed back beyond any clear messaging, pre-narrative, to the oral propulsion, and somatic pulse, of its sheer sounding out. All this in an apogee of scriptive dematerialization—until finally, in suspending this last confrontation between the amateur camcorder journal-maker and her broadcast nemesis, the parting of the ways is made unmistakable, graphic, pictorial. Here "the filmmaker herself," her footage in the can, her use in the novel exhausted, "vanishes back into documentary, banished to nonfiction" (321). As the echoic sound play enforces (the slant rhyme of "van"/ "ban"—indulging again in the deliberate consignment of life to text), narrative exit is always a kind of exile. The banishment is followed in this case by a segue from metafilmic to metanarrative denouement in the next paragraph, with our narrative chronicler taking the vacated place of the documentarian in a last evocation of Thassa: "And I'm here again, across from the daughter of happiness as I never will be again, in anything but story" (321). To repeat, to linger, to accomplish the reflex action of a lone preposition: "in anything but." Limned by its own exit lines, "story" has just such an *inside*, not merely a direction, and thus its relief from the driven linearity of plot.

Story, too, is its own kind of storage and perpetuation: "She's still alive, my invented friend, just as I conceived her," and remains "still uncrushed by the collective need"—that macro trope of the species in its evolutionary through-line once more—"for happier endings" (321). Above even the syllabic chime, the acoustic mirror is here a hinged reflection verging on anagrammed replication: "in*vented friend*." Instead of acceding to the evolutionary demand for the ever "happier ending," the title figure's continued nicknamed presence allows a closure that defiantly keeps things open, generously, generatively. The impetus achieved by stylistic echo in capturing this open rhythm is, aptly enough, at its most delicate and moving in the chiastic mirror organizing two final sentences in characterization of Thassa's surviving spirit. Instancing Powers's style in epitome—approximating what it names in the reduced mood it must here settle for—such phrasing marks a reflex interplay between syllables that operates only through our own activated reflection. "The ecstasy is gone now, the untouchable buoyancy muted." Muted too, by reversal, the *sy* and the *cy* of that levitation, come down to earth in "What's left to take its place can at best be called ease" (317). So is the very sound *eez* extracted and distilled from the trailing syllables (*see, cee*) it replaces. By such enacted relaxation in the metanarrative hall of mirrors, closure can be forestalled: "What we have been is as nothing; what we will be is ever beyond us. But what kind of story would ever end with *us?*" (321). Or with that? Only a story, one might answer, that has relinquished authorization, has released its characters from both fiction and nonfiction alike: let them loose, rather seen them through, and only in the sense of letting them "outta here"—released to chance rather than ontogenetic choice. Which returns us yet again to the tacit etymology of the *meta*, the "ever beyond us," scripted as extratext from the realm of sheer potential. And returns us once more, as well, to a crucial iteration two paragraphs before—in the unabashed admission of a work-still-in-progress for a set of characterizations holding on for dear life in the refusal of closure: "All writing is rewriting" (321). Even as the text goes off to press, there is still time, both real and emblematic.

Given our interwoven cast of characters in the narrative push, the whole evolutionary drive, toward the "outta here," it is not just an exit, of course, but an exeunt (plural) that is necessary. We've seen the narrator—not in propria persona as the author Powers, but only as a narrational construct operating within the interspace of script—maneuvering to effect his last confrontation with his heroine, via pure evocation, in the conceptual zone of reverie and residual invention. At the same time, he has moved his hero Russell off stage without a word, left him to his own resources, verbal and otherwise. In this final tacit dilation of narrative time into raw unwritten possibility, narrative agency—once having released its surrogate, its "adjunct," from all further "assignment"—serves in this way to locate the metaplot's fullest relaxation of narrative tension, narrative design, narrative signage. Stone is on his own—and by now, even more than before, he'd no doubt "be pleased to know that... he's still mostly white space." Not least because he's learned to write, and then definitively revise, his own way into the unknown blank of that space's constitutive "beyond"—where choice is as indeterminate as that bleached-out sheet of bilingual menu options in the elapsing scene. Or, more encompassing yet, in the novel's last vanishing words—where Thassa and her narrator, watching day dim away as if the world were yet another open book, "sit and watch" the punning "Atlas go dark" (322): place and page over together, mountain range and its mapping, sunset and typeset.

So it is that these last two chapters on Powers offer a kind of diptych under the (subsequently published) paradigm of an overstory: a diptych within its own kind of trilogy. If *Plowing the Dark*, by analogy with immersive digital, reflects on the augmented reality of reading, including actual script and its cruel proscription in captivity, *Generosity* reflects on writing—but only as the two functions, writing and its reading, coincide, in this later metatext, upon the role of speculative duration, avoided foreclosure, and the lure of the unsaid.

A writer's career may come into perspective around a single formulation. What we found Powers identifying in his very first novel as literary "constructivism" has, in the *writing event* of a later reflexive text called *Generosity*, penetrated to the shaping of human agency per se as some empowering combination, at once, of model and mode and trope.

But what, then, more specifically, about these last two chapters in light of our previous exploration of Powers's more recent novel and its overt structural logic, its overstance? If the frame of our reading is pulled back far enough to include again *The Overstory*, a medial perspective takes sharper focus. In any contemporary faceting of the reflexive extratext, the recurrent demands made by Powers's fiction upon the phenomenology of reading are exemplary. If the center is to hold, it is often up to us to construct it. Reading is an organizing configuration, a supplement to structure, an inbuilt destination. We have examined this synthesizing function at work—more necessary than ever in Powers's challenging narrative formats, and as recently as 2018—with the eight interlaced plotlines of *The Overstory*, before backing up to 2000 and 2009. We have in fact found this will to synthesis intimately signaled across all three novels: by the density of lexical *play* in *The Overstory* (patterns of verbal echo and their imploded punning nodes), by narrative *counterplay* in *Plowing the Dark* (polarized locales, virtual and eviscerating by turns), and by inscriptive *freeplay* in *Generosity* (in the always as-yet-unwritten shape of lived narrative), including its transient enhancements—genomic coding notwithstanding, and with stylistic flourish in that novel kept in check by a sardonic attitude toward the very pressure of fictional format upon human motive.

As evidenced in this way, textual orientations grow distinct within a closed authorial system. But rethought in chronological order, instead, we might best register the sequence from *Plowing the Dark* to *Generosity* to *The Overstory* as predominantly a move from the metanarrative to the metatextual to the metalingual—and in widening circles of inclusion. *Plowing* is radically (de)centered along the continuous rift of its plotting, with our call to reading cast into slant reflection by the hero's agonized need for some reading of his own. *Generosity*, in contrast to the genetic masterplots it invokes for human evolution, turns on a stylistically low-keyed and often tentative script for narrative advance, with reader activation completing in turn the destiny of "life writing" in its figurative animation as unfinished business. *The Overstory* is aimed finally at sign systems extending well beyond human language but bound up with the text's own concerted linguistic mission—in the need, that is, via whatever twists of legibility, to comprehend (if never quite translate) the signaletic network of arboreal messaging. The novelistic sequence thus moves, in these overlapping terms, from the crux—both goal and gauntlet—of *reading* (in encounter with antiphonal plotting) through that of *writing* (life as nonfiction prose) to the understory of *medium* at work (semiotic ec[h]osystems). But only with the extra sense in each case—regarding precisely the synthesizing reflex of the extratext—of *medium writing into possibility its own reading*. And doing so through the filters of Powers's shifting panoply of specialist technological, cybernetic, genomic, arboreal, televisual, and ecological vocabularies. To name only some of the restive, witty cerebrations to whose challenges we're invited to rise—in all their various modulations of prose rhythm and lexical stress, whether in full phrasal bravura or dialed down by narrative mood, as in *Generosity*, to a more impassive neutrality of tone.

And another way to sum this up. Each of the three Powers novels we've considered at length ends by a freeing of readers from the mirror of our constructive investment. Satellite scans finally take up our burden in *The Overstory*, deciphering the tree-trunk adverb/adjective "still" in which nature tells its own story. Before this, the triangular knot of narrator, character, and reader has been variously undone in closure. Whereas distant characters meet briefly and unrecognized, at the hallucinatory climax of *Plowing the Dark*, in a disembodied reciprocal epiphany—some kind of synaptic electrode meld beyond technology—in *Generosity* it is narrator and character who finally enter into a detaching interchange on exit. The "white space" of the unwritten to which they are equally released after that last trope of global fade-out recalls the blank beyond explicit picturing at the end of *Plowing*. Taimur, released from captors to caretakers, is beginning to catch up with the "news," with time itself, in the *International Herald Tribune*. "You see yourself staring out from page 3: the forced prison picture, the one that bears no living resemblance to you" (412). And soon, in effect, a freeze-frame. Three pages later, when you exit a plane in Istanbul, you see your daughter and her mother "as in the world newspaper photo they instantly become" (415). Within a moment, as previously detailed, you're given a hug that for the girl makes the story of stories real at last, brings to life "the fable she's grown up on"—while, in the brief last paragraph, she shoves into "your shaking hands" a drawing made "for you" (415). In what immediately follows, there is only a noun fragment, amounting to a freeze-frame again, and with no more second-person grammar, no more tacit solicitation of the reader, no more digital sophistication of the graphic image: "A crayon man, returning to a crayon home" (415). After all this electronic picturing in *Plowing*, then, only now the white blank of possibility, in which—as print breaks off, along with the ekphrastic trace of child's scribble—imagined life might reassert itself outside the solipsistic closed circuit of that previously beleaguered "you."

What might come next in recuperation is now beyond counterplotting in *Plowing the Dark*, just as what might succeed to the novel's "story" in *Generosity* is that lived rather than written "enhancement" (in the form of textual effacement) to whose latency the narrator releases both the reader and all control. Yet one tiny detail deserves revisiting, via what may now seem like something of a false lead—or cover story—in the mind-game of narrative "enhancement" transacted in the interplay between writing getting done and reading catching up and on. To repeat the narrator's thieving recourse in maneuvering to rescue his characters from the plot that seems all too inevitably unfolding, he speaks of his belated raid on the literary-historical mode of metafiction that he pretends only his failed-writer protagonist was once attached to: "I even loot those hall-of-mirrors avant-garde novels whose characters try to escape their authors" (40). As we read on in the novel, we soon sense this looting as indeed a fitful retooling of the mode, one in which the "mirrors" are angled to ensnare reader rather than character or fictive world in their inverted image: snare us in speculation over our own textual discernment and its sometimes involuntary recognitions. No detail is more quietly telling in this respect than the logical (at least analogical) obverse of fiction as the "defeat of time" that occurs well along in the novel in mentioning our exhausted hero—still insomniac through his fatigue—waking restless, as noted above, "several pages later" (288). Tutored often enough by now in the notion that time is as the mercy of textuality's s/pace, we well recognize how ellipsis and dilation are the defining features of story as opposed to life. But here, suddenly, the metaphor for unconscious respite, for narrative intermission, is reversed to an accelerated turning of material pages themselves. Mirrored in this surprise, once and for all, if only by analogy: our own present reading act as the ground of all fictional duration.

We soon turn, in the coming final chapter, away from Powers's demanding *scientific fiction*, as it were, back to a variant of the Hollywood sci-fi we began with—parsing there, so we once did, the pixel deconstruction of film narrative as the telos of an inherently technological media reflex in screen viewing. I refer in particular, given what's ahead, to the magic freeze-frame empowerments of Baker's *The Fermata*, with their mad-scientist overtones. Even within the precincts of prose fiction exclusively now, we are thus moving far afield from either the metalinguual schematics of an encoded global botany and its climate science, or the different technological reach of its predecessors—within Powers's signature themes—in computerized virtual environments, weaponized digital tracing, electronic DNA decoding, and so forth. In a swerve that involves a curious bridge as well, we also exit here the premises (both senses) of Powers's typical narrative formats—in their contrapuntal scalar displacements—to enter upon the monolithic implementation, through a premise closer to sci-fi fantasy, of a sequestered textual erotics. But what unfolds, in part by obsessive female undraping, is a narratival sexology whose heatedly metafictive mix of fact and techno-fantasy maintains, nonetheless, a familiar contemporary focus on the phenomenological force (and sometimes counterforce) of the readerly reflex—though under a weird duress in such writing's kinks and randy linkages of phrase. Prose maintains this focus even while delivering, to ear as well as eye, the highly questionable pleasures of its tacit lexical extratext as at once absurd, perverse, furtive, dubious, and pruriently metalingual. But first....

Bewilderment: An Enhancement

Powers's lauded thirteenth fiction arrived on my desk in September of 2021 at almost the same time as the copyedited manuscript into which these attached paragraphs were soon inserted. Given the timing of the novel's long-awaited publication, it would have been understandable to table discussion of this new book for now, I had been thinking in advance, sight unseen. But no. That its plot returns to the combined ethical and media crisis of *Generosity: An Enhancement* in a new leaner style of consummate narrative economy and unusually engrossing characterization, sustained and punctuated by arresting turns of dialogue—even that wouldn't have necessitated a lingering mention here. Nor even the way it works to enhance and interlace the psychology of *Generosity* with the planetary critique of *The Overstory*. Such a thematic weave could have been noted pretty much in passing. What instead claims direct attention, if all too brief at that, is the way *Bewilderment* prosecutes—by verbal instance and emblematic apparatus alike, even in its newly lucid and streamlined first-person prose—that deep principle of literary phenomenology we are to find surfaced and perverted in the next chapter. This is the reflex internalization in reading by which the thoughts of others become ours. In the combined narration and demonstration of this, Powers's novel is so immediately cogent and moving that it can make other books by him seem too clever by half. It certainly risks sentimentality—but in a speculative gamble repaid by its sci-fi vision of sentiment itself in sedimentation and palimpsest, with spirits of the dead nested as the very principle of endurance.

Bewilderment is the story of a widowed father, Theo, and a troubled nine-year-old son, Robin, named for his dead mother's favorite bird, and called Robbie by his worried father. Troubled kid—yes, troubled by the kind of planetary anxieties about animal rights and endangered species to which his lawyer mother devoted her life before being killed in swerving to avoid an animal on the road. Troubled, angry, intractably brilliant—in ways that get the boy targeted for the usual raft of pre-teen distraction and spectrum drugs. The most relevant diagnostic buzzword is never directly used, but after celebrating his son's ready focus on the things he loves, and his lack of concentration only when bored, the narrating father, resisting the boy's medicalization, asks rhetorically: "Tell me what deficit matched up with all that? What disorder explained him?"[3] From here out, we're often meeting this low-keyed style halfway, precisely by reading in.

To avoid the routine drugging, Theo is convinced by an entrepreneurial scientist to let Robbie take part in a cognitive experiment to ameliorate the mother's loss. Something like attention surfeit might facilitate a preternatural intimacy with the missing maternal energy. Technically, this involves the AI-assisted apparatus of Decoded Neurofeedback (DecNef), in which the "brain print" of the mother's best and most characteristic moods, including "ecstasy"—having been recorded for an earlier experiment—are retrieved from the fMRI record ("functional magnetic resonance imaging": the graphing of brain *function* per se from the wavelengths of blood pulse). Robbie is weaned from video images of his mother, which he has been watching obsessively, by the promise that this new fMRI regimen will remind him of the videogame interactivity he's so drawn to as well. In this new version of interface, what results from plugging-in to the biorhythms of maternal exultation comes to resemble a return to the tubular MRI womb of his own gestation, the child made present again to his mother's stored magnetic aura in a new kind of blood relation.

Symbolism aside, the actual procedure works. Robbie quickly sheds his anger—and transforms his anxiety to passionate artistic activity and eventual public activism on behalf of our depleted biosphere. At this point, in respect to the therapy, if not the activism, the novel becomes a clear and self-conscious variant on the ethical crisis of *Generosity*. The latest book's young hero of happiness enhancement finds peace and purpose in an instrumental feedback loop with his beloved dead mother rather than through a genetic anomaly of a mutant DNA inheritance. But like Thassa in *Generosity*, his highly fragile private story goes dangerously viral. Just as her "happiness gene" turned her into an emotional phenomenon and prodigy in TV interviews, Robbie ends up appearing in broadcast video under supposed digitized facial anonymity—but is soon discovered, by a slip of his own tongue, to be an easily traceable astrobiologist's brainy son and emotional wunderkind. The genomic wild card in the earlier novel has been replaced by cognitive transference, cloneable DNA by repurposed fMRI—yet each potentially marketable, and each tending to victimize the unwilling poster child caught up in the public frenzy. Further, the metafictional loop so prominent in *Generosity* has been profoundly rethought. We are no longer concerned with anything like that book's narrating novel-maker coaxing his failed fiction-writer hero into acting on behalf of the heroine and her genetic miracle in order to *rescript* her fate. In *Bewilderment*, we follow instead the travails of an astrobiologist father shifting from his day job—as the probabilistic computer modeler of unobserved planetary biosystems—to deploy similar invention in the sci-fi bedtime stories about weird distant planets that serve to soothe his son to sleep, eleven of these "visits" paced across the text. By a striking and wholly effective structural reorientation, the usual bald counterpoint of Powers's fiction is refocused on the play between traumatic frame story and inset visionary narratives: a smooth enfolding of framed tales rather than the sharp structural disjunctions of his typical formats. And with this taming of disparities by a closely focalized first-person narrator comes a more personally compelling story than ever—and a style distilled to a smiting new purity.

Beyond regular sessions of mood-elevation in the fMRI lab, the inquisitive child increasingly takes on—by a kind of ethical osmosis, as if by a delayed "environmental" rather than genetic effect—the mother's particular environmental causes. He ends up making colorful hand drawings of the world's endangered birds and animals. In this way, too, as in his bouts of electromagnetic brain imaging in the recapture of maternal energy, the trace preserved in the pending absence of creature extinction offers a greater longevity than the thing itself, even at species level. After Robbie dies in an icy river in the overwrought service of his ecological mission, wrapped at the last, for futile warmth, in his father's desperate arms, he ends up enfolded by the mourning survivor in another way—his joy, his curiosity, his passion all internalized by the father in his own surreptitious recourse to DecNef's cognitive transfer, letting the boy's spirit live again in him. And, by this intimate mediation of the son (a now internal "medium" all but spiritualist or clairvoyant as well as electromagnetic), the lost wife and mother lives again as well. This tiered but immersive restoration of feeling begins with an assonant phrasal chord change in the manner of magnetic *prose* resonance and its enacted gravitational pulls (emphasis added): "I lie in the *tube* and *tune* myself to a print of Robbie" so that "my brain learns to resemble what it loves" (277). It is a kind of wired memory-work. "And then one day, my son is in there, inside my head as sure as life." What's more, by an embedding braced by the assonant echo of "life": "My wife, too, still inside him" (278). As with the gentle jolt of that clipped spin on the colloquial "as sure as your life"—in this case, the son's life, rather than "yours" in vernacular address—such sinuous idiomatic wordplay, always one of the Powers trademarks, is so exquisitely simplified in this novel that you sometimes can't even be sure it's there. This is perhaps even more the case with the slightly awkward "my son is in there" if heard to operate as a redemptive subliminal rehearing of a grieving and bereft "my son isn't there." However resonant, readers may well think they are merely hearing things. But there they are, those things, those auditory cues, in you: operating by way of exactly the stylistic reflex action this book has been tracing. In this reversible shadow play of phonetic self-negation, what is(n't) there of Robbie in death, and in turn of the mother channeled through him, but here in the father instead, has a further transformative momentum in the train of phrase. "What they felt, then, I now feel" (277), with the adverb both retrospective and consequential at once: a recovered "then" under the force of a mediating technological "therefore." They think, therefore I am—am the repository of their continuance: their feelings not *for* (in the everyday sense of affection) but *in* me.

A related idiomatic ambiguity, this time a shadowing of paradox by colloquialism, soon occurs in the brilliant capstone line, falling into place after all the far-flung planetary voyage stories in a sci-fi mode. In Theo's final channeling of Robbie the non-robot: "The thought occurs to him—and I have it" (277). Direct thought transference, yes, in what the book has earlier called "emotional telepathy" (93). But here with the overtone of a eureka moment as well: "[Ah] I have it." I get it! The secret found—and a new foundation for living on. To complete that thought in its neural relay to the reader, citing Robbie in the italics of a now nonmortal tongue: "... and I have it. *Can you believe where we just were?*" (277). One more planetary excursion complete. You and I, Dad, joined in the remembered experience called terrestrial existence. After all the made worlds of nocturnal expedition, those narrated planets strictly made up or biologically modeled, this, too, says Robbie from beyond the grave—in a slide from present to past tense ("believe" to "were" in a journey over too soon)—has been our shared astrobiological probe: this always-too-brief visit, for any of us, to planet Earth, confronted there, here, by both its natural splendor and its threatened biodiversity. It has been a sojourn as imponderable as that on any imagined galactic body we wouldn't presume to call our own: a prolonged alien visitation, in effect, amid our own failing stewardship. Bringing the previous eleven bedtime fictions to a round, a very round, dozen, the whole novel circles back on itself as, globally, inclusively, the last but not least of these episodes. Except in its overall existence as a narrative fable, no unique suspension of disbelief is required for this encompassing terrestrial "story"—so that phrasing has flipped at once from epistemology to the childlike idiom of sheer innocent wonderment in the strictly rhetorical "can you believe...?"

Make that innocent bewilderment: at the baffling profusion of life forms wild rather than human. Such is, by title, the story Powers rather than Theo has just moved *us* with, reinscribed by an eleventh-hour recognition. Signaled in closure by the stunningly understated "constructivism" of Powers's residual narrative disposition, the author's surviving postmodernist habits are summarily reframed for a creative nonfiction of the Anthropocene. And of course there is, in all this, the extra metanarrative turn in the wake of those sci-fi bedtime stories as models for prose fiction as well as biological probability. The novel, after all, has been transmitted to us by literary narrative's everyday version of neurofeedback, with a sorcery all its own. Just as with this story of postmortem "brain prints," so with the phenomenology of reading according to its most famous formulation by theorist Georges Poulet—to which the next chapter will turn for its warped operation in Nicholson Baker's *The Fermata*. In reading's ordinary mental ventriloquism (Poulet's claim), the worded thoughts of another are "had" (Theo's word) as mine in their very decoding and articulation. As much as with DecNef decipherment, then, the absent other can live on in me.

To be sure, writing is a hedge against time—including the recoverable measures of its own verbal pacing and the narrative rhythms it clocks. Verbal pacing—and cognitive. In this sense *Bewilderment* is the fulfillment of a longstanding aspiration on the author's part. Two decades ago now, acknowledging in the *Paris Review* interview cited in Chapter 3 that the "structure" of his books, though of course "important," takes second seat in compositional priority, he insists that "it's really the individual sentence that I work at again and again until it becomes the thing it's trying to describe." That effort of hypermimesis, concentrated in the newest novel on the thematic power of resonant empathy, operates almost by direct transference to the reader in the sympathetic vibration of wording's reflex recognition. For whenever the novelist-as-writer, as Powers goes on to phrase it in that interview, succeeds in his hope to "build sentences that are equal to mental states"—and never more markedly than at the end of *Bewilderment*—the conduit is directly opened to any reflective reading mind. Opened, that is, across the tempo of word-formation itself.

In a typical oscillation of Powers's phrasing, even in its unusually crystalline flow this time out, there is again, as noted, the engrained reflex action of thickened phonetic response. It is a tendency we might want to hear derived in this case not just from voice-recognition software (the author's touted compositional habit) but, via synecdoche, from the feedback loops of the "cosmic symphony" that is always "both playing and listening to itself" (67). So with the performative act of reading, producing what it attends to—and in the process noting at times a certain restless nesting of sounds not unlike the snug g/hosting of affect from wife through offspring to narrator in the AI circuit of this one metaplot. As with crossword puzzling, literal and otherwise, in *The Overstory*—especially that pervasive but unspelled pun on *bark code*—even the technical term for the neurofeedback scan in the later elegiac context of *Bewilderment*, the laboratory lingo of "fMRI," may be heard to carry rebus overtones of the transient and fleeting, overtones themselves evanescent and self-vanishing. The particular effect in question transpires, in subvocal breath itself, at the level not just of mortal characters, in other words, but in the othering of words from themselves in fugitive alphabetic play. For it is a special prose version of "magnetic resonance" that might seem tenuously compressed in the very acronym of fMRI. The novel's cautionary environmentalist emphasis is the same, with or without such extra phonetic vibration—but it can only seem more eerily infused and distributed when audited at this level of signification. Like the terrestrial biosphere on any one inhabitable planet, the private circuit of human psychic ecology—without a will to preserve while persevering—becomes (with the electronics, but not the phonetics, of *f*MRI quite aside) a matter of the fiercely *ephemeral*, in human as well as geological time. Ready to hand among the lexical array of his technical expertise, the applied science of phonology has always been one of the cards most deftly played in the strategic punning of Powers's "mind-game" prose.

Notes

1 Richard Powers, *Generosity: An Enhancement* (New York: Picador, 1969), 168.
2 In his role as the chief spokesman for an episodic ontology of the human "self," a position strenuously debated by psychologists as well as cognitive narratologists, see philosopher Galen Strawson, "Against Narrativity," *Ratio* 17.4 (2004): 428–52, as followed up, a few years after *Generosity*, by Strawson's "We live beyond any tale that we happen to enact," *Harvard Review of Philosophy* 18.1 (2012): 73–90. The countervailing notion, that one can only live as the reflexive performance of one's own autobiography, is of course a model this book's Preview found slotted ironically by Powers into his first written narrative, *Three Farmers on the Way to a Dance*.
3 Richard Powers, *Bewilderment* (New York: W. W. Norton, 2021), 5.

6

Reading: In Decent Exposure

Decently enough exposed as a rule in reflexive writing, even if not exhaustively anatomized, is a reader's contributory work in the energizing of prose. This deciphering labor at the receiving end, the very activation of the text as "work," is reflected on the slant—by episode and inference alike—in the kind of metanarrative tendencies we've been examining. But what if the writing is itself "indecent," in that term's own etymological descent from "unfitting" to "dishonorable"? What then is the fit of any vestigial metatext with the force of reader investment, however dubious or enthused? The question takes us to a limit test in this study that, for all the extremity of obscene detail in such an inflamed fictional experiment as Nicholson Baker's *The Fermata* (and related novels by the same author), falls demonstrably, if not quite comfortably, within the spectrum of the self-tuned responses we've been examining. That's the main shock of such a text: that its grossly guilty pleasures, however much warmed to, only serve to measure again—and all but explicitly—the way literary readers are always the implicated co-authors of the narrative fantasies they help activate. Fantasies however fleeting. How else, as just suspected with *Bewilderment*, could an overtone of the ephemeral make its mark on a bewildering fMRI effect, a transient matter of verbal rather than neural imaging?

We've come far enough to stand back—before lunging ahead to this very different kind (if not force) of prose. In methodological terms, it has been one premise of this study that pointedly metatextual dispositions don't just manage somehow to outlast their temporary apogee or canonization (Modernism, say, followed by its "post" repositioning)—and survive the respective fading glories that follow—but may, in the process, take more lucid shape when backlit by a dimming limelight. One question it should therefore be a good time to ask, rather than in any way too late: After *Pale Fire*, after *Gravity's Rainbow*, after Borges and Calvino, after everyone from John Fowles through E.L. Doctorow to Don DeLillo and Mark Z. Danielewski, what explains the continuing reflexive kick, or demystifying charm, of the metatexual turn? Or which devices in particular best work its trick? Such questions share a sense that tendencies may be clearest when they are neither trending nor even crystalized in a richly accomplished instance. That assumption is what brackets this study. Nothing, on the face of it, about Marvel Universe franchise cinema or highbrow literary porn (Chapters 1 and now 6) advertises any unique value in the estimation of medial self-reference in their respective narrative formats. But worn thin by the rhetorical or genre demands of each mode respectively, including the narrowly and barely dodged exhaustion of its scenarios and tropes alike, a certain textual overexertion on the part of director or writer may reveal an abiding *stress*—in the form of a new *strain*—regarding the identified medial resources, optical and verbal, recruited under such genre duress.

That's one way to think of it. A related way: unenriched by complexities other than those designed for snaring attention, and thus for leashing an audience to the plane of display—whether the screen of digital spectacle or the page of scandalous prose—such bare-bones storylines are likely to reveal not just the skeletal structure of their narrative effects but their points of definitive *medial* articulation, whether in screen technology or literary technique. The lures, and limits, of both viewing and reading may come through more or less unimpeded at such disclosed nodes of structure and affect—such divulged generators of textual pleasure in reductions specular or phrasal. But they come through, as diagnosed here, not in ways made clear by traditional narrative explication, but rather in their local pockets of intensity and linguistic indemnification. Neither with works as dizzyingly complex as Powers's novels, nor with the roving sexaholic picaresques of Nicholson Baker's up next, which boast their own exacting kinky detailism, is an effort made by this commentary at any sustained interpretation—in some traditional synoptic sense—for a given work. Discussion is closely embroiled, yes, with the unfolding details of plot and its sponsored imagery, event and its syntax, and so forth: not, though, in an effort to offer a comprehensive narrative analysis, but rather so that this study's main claim would be felt to emerge—where alone it could carry conviction—from just such a textured mesh of literary expression and plot development. For this is a claim—quite apart from the traditional sense of "*a* reading"—about the way in which even antithetical texts like these by Powers and Baker can bring unexpected reflexive pressure to bear on the fact of their *being read*.

Read—or with their counterparts on screen, being viewed. Where the very idea of the specular becomes a theme. So the latest *Spider-Man*—in the trivial digital implosion, and quintessential Hollywood mise en abyme, of its ironically brandished and ballistically targeted special effects—casts its spun web widely enough to net, not just a virtual reality novel like *Plowing the Dark* in a shared field of augmented reality, but a pair of pornofictions by Baker from the same American literary establishment as Powers, an A-lister gone X. These last flourishes of comic raunch are overwrought texts that manage to do to, and with, a sexualized lexicography, via abrasive disintegrations, something of what—and, more importantly, the *kind* of thing—that the self-conscious Hollywood blockbuster does with the CGI fraying of its own narrative plane. Each reductiveness is an instructive condensation. On screen and page alike, across any of the works we've been considering, the impact of genre, medium, audience investment—all give way under analysis, and before that under general audience attention, to the reflexive textuality that otherwise furnishes their medium's normal transmission of narrative event. In this sense everything one can think to care about—or care to think about—in reflexive narrative manifestations has to do with the weight of reception at the medial level, whether (in the case of prose) with a texture of writing luminously witty, immanently sensuous, pointedly self-elucidating, showy, reticent, crassly erogenous, slyly lexigraphic, boldly obscene, or naughtily slap-happy. You name it—and do so there at the flashpoint of its affect. You have to be paying a certain degree of invested close attention to see what pays off in reflexive estimation. Which includes, in a "trick" film or novel, how the medium has been complicit in taxing or short-changing your comprehension. And so standing back, to emphasize as much, can only send us forward again into the thick of textual—even when barely narrative—action.

After the categorical metanarrative template laid out with the opening two chapters on film, this study's literary gambit has been based on sampling effects, in a more exploratory fashion, from two striking poles of contemporary practice. On the one hand, so far, the prolific maximalism of Richard Powers: a kind of "blockbuster" fiction in its own interlaced montage scope, its disciplinary range and ricochet of specialist vocabularies—amounting in their own lexical sense to a kind of hyperliterate technical infrastructure. At the other pole now: the minimalist precisions, turned at times mock-obsessional, of Nicholson Baker, including a lexicon not fetched far and wide from different scientific masteries, as in Powers, but confected for lascivious frantic exactitude in the hothouse of a narrowing erotic preoccupation. Cast into a far sharper contrast than just that between scientific fiction and the sci-fi fantasy on which our main exhibit from Baker is based, these polar extremes in contemporary American writing don't divide against each other, or parse a tacit spectrum, so much as bring forward the common denominators of reflexivity across remote alternatives.

Here, too, one question above all—or beyond all—is begotten again under *meta* duress. This we've seen repeatedly. Aired in action by a given text of this stamp, when exposed to sufficient notice, is the primal inquiry into just *what* about its mechanics, its operation, its intake, its uptake is being developed for inspection—or unleashed by inference. In statistical probability, given the frequency of the strictly fictive reflex, one ready answer might easily miss the mark. Like movies about "the movies," books *about books*, or about themselves as such, don't necessarily bear down on the process of their verbal deciphering. They more often implicate their own fictiveness. You are, as at times you're either abruptly or subtly reminded, *only reading*: only imagining in words these people and their tribulations, or elsewhere their furious sexual convulsions. If narrated things are getting out of control, they're still wholly in hand—all safely within the covers of a book. It's a rarer reflex that—beyond any such reminder, however disruptive as well as obvious, that you're only now turning pages—that adds the calibrated sensory specifics of that reading function as word processing, figural decipherment, rhetorical competency, what have you.

Those are, of course, the textual investments—and ingrown investigative gestures—at stake in this discussion. And surprisingly enough, perhaps, Baker's 1990s hermetic sex fantasies, *Vox* and *The Fermata*, do, in just this regard, make common cause with Richard Powers's densely technocultural novels, often happily prudish by comparison, around the two authors' shared emphasis on exactly that operational (and in its own way seductive) facet of the *meta*: the verbal *manner* rather than topical *matter* of reading, a recognition site-specific more than categorical, yet as much temporal as spatial or physical. It's not that you've been merely lost in a book, an open codex, a paged space; it's that you've been whirled away by sequenced words. Beyond, then, the frequent and generalized literary turnabout (and sometimes turn-off)—'Don't forget this is only a book you're moving through, a made-up story'—is the *meta* of specified mediation. Lifted to attention at this level instead: just *how* you are making your way across its depictions—or, in other words, and always in words of its own, the means by which such reading is made to happen over linguistic time. The reflex action of fiction in this regard is at its most immediate and probing, on the issue of mediation itself, when it engages the cognitive activity of reading rather than the fixed form of the text, when it zeros in on the generative rather than the generic, the formative before the formal. Call it the lexical—rather than generalized textual—reflex.

That's where certain novels come into surprise alignment across entirely different narrative demands, tone, and rhetorical terrain. Even when the energies of reading, figured in this way, reflect on the status of the codex object (as in Baker's *The Fermata*, so we'll find, as much as with Taimur's craving in *Plowing the Dark*), they do so—in those exemplary cases of the *meta*, when pressing beyond their own separate evidence from within its rhythms—by sending us, ultimately, back to the palpability of words. These are words that, once found on the page, find activation in the echo chamber of the inner ear. Their "beyond" of mere designation is registered in this way, so we've repeatedly noted, as an extratext— over and above (while still about) their straightforward cumulative function, but less as a mere surplus resonance than as a raison d'tre in the delayed playback of recognition. How *so* is again the issue. Certainly all this is easier done up in summary than seen demonstrated in the said—or inferred by the heard. So we need yet again, in the name of reading, some sustained effort at it. An effort attempted here in the unstable rhetorical context of a book, *The Fermata*, that figures the reading act in exorbitant metaphors—extended and literally metaphysical (or at least sci-fi) conceits—even while isolating it for more intimate apprehension as a work of words. And all this in a novel where the mere reminder of codex form is meant to be so little a downer, amid the novel's unabashed pornographic rigors, that the page Fold becomes, including by borrowed name, a model aphrodisiac. In examining the ongoing pull of the *meta*—through and beyond the narrative it reframes by beveled refaceting—we've looked so far, in the wide-ranging disciplinary and technological masteries of Powers's fiction, at such disparate structuring thematics as ecological understory, militarist counterplot, and even an academic satire on writing pedagogy itself. The sample could scarcely have been narrower, more arbitrary, or, I hope, more revealing. The noncongruence of topic—and topicality—optimizes the common denominator. Regardless of divergent thematic emphases, the persisting vitality of what we might call *self-reversion* in the conduct of story, the leverage of reflex, has to do in these works, and those coming next, less with bookhood or fictionality straight off than with the recognized grain of phrasing, of sentence-making. Wording comes forward as object in itself, the stuff of material production rather than its mere conduit— with that production emerging in turn as the very nub, or even hub, the true nerve center, of transmission. As we're now to see, this is no less the case when the words thus flagged as such might be eminently bleepable if circulated in any medium but uncensored text.

But first, a reiterated caveat regarding this book's narrative sampling. As made clear from the start, I trust, these chapters haven't set out to study the latter-day fulfillment of a modernist mode, nor even its post-millennial highpoints, but rather the fact of its endurance: the stamina of the *meta* in exactly those various longevities—including the highlighting of form as content's direct medium, the force of structure in textured execution—that it tends to bring with it, and thereby to reveal by iteration from work to work. Long after anything that could be termed the heyday of ontological metafiction, what does explain the staying power of the *meta*? If some dimension of an answer to this involves a writerly stretch at times toward the "pleasure of the text," with Barthes's emphasis on a sensory force that quite literally "comes" across in reading, then raw erotica—for better or worse, at least when putatively subsumed to literary experimentation—ought to be one touchstone of such pleasure under reflexive audit.[1] And if serious literary ambition and unhampered verbal talent lead a certain celebrated writer into the realm of pornographic low comedy—in ways that feel, not at first, but ultimately, more or less hardwired into the self-consciousness of his broader writer's project, there and elsewhere—then the results don't have to be deemed triumphant in their literary showiness, any more than in their erotic pretensions, to offer a laboratory sample of salacious reflexivity as one terminus ad quem for narrative's self-mirroring bias, its indulgent slant. One can think of this grouping of final test cases from Baker's pen, then, as a matter of autoerotic wording.

Apart from the obvious imbalance between film and literary evidence in the assigned chapters of this study, there is no last-minute effort at a false literary symmetry: say, three novels by Powers, albeit for a chapter each, followed and scrupulously matched with three by Baker, if mostly one in particular, and all in one chapter. The count and scope are irrelevant. The book's broad effort in comparing the reflexive triggers of attention in a reading across media has been to offer less a method than a mnemonic, a reminder of what we always do when, if caught by a visual or verbal effect, we get caught up in its inferences. This point is important in looking back. Only if you've moved through this book remembering similar jolts of medial recognition in your own viewing and reading are you likely to have responded fully, in however loose a connection with those recollected reflexes, to the effects paused over in these chapters. In this respect as well as others, Baker's pornographic writing, even in its deliberately blunt contrast to the prose of Powers, might seem unnecessary to the argument, running the risk of making the same point twiceover with a second chosen writer. But what a revealing double jeopardy this constitutes—and how unexpected from the writer whose breakout book was the fiendishly low-keyed *The Mezzanine*. If this final chapter is more than just an appendix or bonus, some extraneous icing on the layer-cake of exemplification, that's ultimately because the pornographic genre it wrestles with and transcends, but only from the inside out, depends on the most reader-directed yet *meta*-squelching of all prose, overstepping any mere rhetoric of persuasion into a solicited prurience so obvious in Baker's hands that reading is thrown back, and prose with it, on its own resourceful eros.

And again it behooves us to consider that broader literary-historical transformation we've previously entertained, begun with modernist epistemology and long since compounded by ontological irony, in gauging Baker's place in *The Metanarrative Hall of Mirrors*. This chapter arrives not as an addendum or a mere countercase, as I say. Nor is the attenuated metafiction of Power's evolving work felt to be somehow, in an imagined contemporary spectrum, definitively complemented, rather than just contrasted, by such overblown and thus undermined pornography as Baker's—thereby rendering the comparison integral, if not inevitable. Instead, the reflexivity of linguistic mimesis in Powers's sentence-building practice—attempting its heady fence-sits between phenomenological conviction and fictive construct, between realism and metatext, characters and characterization—is directly inverted (and hence tacitly reconceived) by Baker's licentious send-ups. Standard-issue pornography is the most phenomenological of prose genres. The depicted world must be made as close to present as possible in erotic charge; you need to feel like you're there, there to feel the sensations traced in language. And the most narratological: climax mandatory. Neither Modernism nor postmodernism are the mode's best friends. In Baker's work, the phenomenal presencing of desiring bodies and their affect ends up defaulting to a linguistic ontology of its presentational effect as medium, as language. Instead of the aesthetic telos of the word-becoming-thing in Powers, or of language lifting its own veil on the charged amatory body in the standard contortions of such genre writing, an overcalculated eroticism like Baker's would dissolve the fetishized thing itself back into fondled language, hardcore gone over to a strictly vocabular friction and relief. Baker's words are so dirty that their clouded syllabic opacity is its own reward, their tongued one-offs becoming by default, in their kinky linguistics, the performative deed done. And always in the self-pleasuring urgency of its continuous renewal.

Seeing print a quarter of a century earlier in his prurient ventures than the orgastic phantasmagoria of his no-holes-barred *House of Holes* (2011), Baker's *Vox* (1992) and *The Fermata* (1994) are textual experiments more inquisitively situated within the scope of literary innovation than is the later unchecked and ultimately bland carnival of manic gargoyle penetrations. With the earlier works, however, *The Fermata* in particular, it is important to note that even the justified slings of professional literary critique may miss at least one definitive mark: the verbal reflex rather than merely the descriptive exertion. In a painstaking takedown of Baker's "para-pornography" in the *London Review of Books*, acknowledging its cleverness along with its suspect ethics, novelist-critic Adam Mars-Jones sees *The Fermata* as a book—being ultimately and only about masturbation—that is likely, in his clinching line, "to give self-abuse a bad name."[2] A review needn't be wrong, in its main complaint, to have narrowed the view that a more dispassionate (if that's the word) analysis might wish to take regarding such a work. And precisely in its verbal inferences. In the case of Mars-Jones's dismissal, there remains the unexplored fact that, along with Baker's previous "phone sex" novel *Vox*, this aggravated "sequel" is preoccupied with more than private gratification. Not least, in a quite resolute if intermittent fashion, it concerns the relation of book reading to any such closeted eroticism, including the associated textures of page and flesh to which a certain reading may give rise. To apprehend this doesn't in itself bridle any sweeping aesthetic objections to the book's mode and ambition, whether regarding imaginative laxity or sexist effrontery. But it does reframe the adduced shortcomings of a fetid onanistic focus by entertaining the writing's potential reach, less heated, more searching, after something intrinsic to textual excitation per se.

In this respect, a searing review like that of Mars-Jones that scores against *The Fermata* with a chiasm cutting to the quick of the novel's style—its sporadic brilliance only working to "make sex wordy, when the plan was actually to make words sexy"—has actually targeted a larger question. The barb has struck, without pursuing, exactly the *meta* note about literary lexicons and their contortions that points well past sheer syllabic massage, in Baker's trashiest mash-up coinages and collocations, to broader questions of wording in circulation along the capillary channels of readerly desire. Questions this novel itself takes up. But make no mistake. *The Fermata* doesn't just risk, it courts and wallows in, the potential single-minded tedium of selfishly cultivated male desire, of coveted solo relief and its demeaning fantasies of female subjection (make that effacement). For all its comic panache, it's certainly not an easy novel to like—nor, for all its dexterity, to steadily admire. But what it repeatedly folds over itself in *likening* its eroticism *to*: these effects concern what we do like in reading, what we do desire from the open book, what we do admire when mired in the rhetorical intricacies—even syllabic twists—of literature's depicted turmoil. The relentlessly lewd or lurid quite aside from the general textual investments that these obscene features of reading here serve nonetheless to emblemize, Baker's fixated pornography is, like Powers's encyclopedic sweep, deeply "bookish" and lexigraphic at once—and in a correlation that is itself exploratory, where the physicality of the bound volume knows no divorce from the tangible surface of its every aurally (as well as manually) stroked page. But how, more specifically, as a strategy rather than an accident, does Baker "make sex wordy"—rather than the other way around? In what way does this justify my early reference to his vocabular provocations as lechemes rather than lexemes? Or say lech-semes rather than lex-semes in such invented semantics. Answers begin in following out the dilations (in every sense) of its plot, not just far-fetched but downright fantastic.

Tempus Interruptus

There are, now and then, novels that can seem to retell one story, and in some detail, while telling another instead—or, more accurately, along with it. The effect can be a kind of allegory—but with tenor and vehicle, overt and coded plot, less than steadily separate, hard at times to peel apart. To show what I mean about such tandem narration—by not quite meaning what I show the first time through—let me abstract only one through-line of a 1994 American novel about storytelling in a memoirist vein. No title mentioned (again) as yet. I do so by deliberately pulling the punches of its plot on this "first read"—instructively, I trust. Breaking stride with this study's layout so far, here are two novelized plots by the same author that could never lay claim to separate chapters; unlike the interchanged episodes of *Plowing the Dark*, for instance, these plots in Baker are coextensive, each the blurred double of the other in reading's prescription monocle.

The main narrative taking shape, if only at one level, goes this way. A thirty-five-year old "secretarial" office worker, whose temp status baffles his serial employers and shifting cohort in various typing pools, tries explaining away his lack of permanence by pretending he's mainly "a writer" in other than the obvious clerical sense.[3] But the fib has by now been internalized. That plausible cover story, filled in for us as we read, has held up well enough for years. But now this part-timer has gone so far as to activate the excuse and—shortly after our novel opens, or perhaps coincident with its launch—has set about actually drafting the first stabs at an autobiography. He strikes—strokes—these off on a portable electric typewriter, a Cassio C-W 16, thus deliberately eschewing, for privacy's sake, his current office's computer network. In the confessional mode he has embarked upon, bursting its seams with extraordinary disclosures, privacy is at quite a premium.

A belated and more candid David Copperfield is Arnold Strine, who begins his life in the middle of his life, recording that he was born eventually to record it. Forget any bogus superstitions about David's amniotic caul being a talisman against drowning: entirely my allusion, not Strine's, who was instead "born with a knot in my umbilical cord" (20)—which may help explain his powers of elective removal from the world's natural biorhythms. This part-timer can part time itself. For our narrator's is a life story of a genuinely magical gift, unsourced, inexplicable. With the snap of his fingers lately—as well as by other more prosthetic affordances in the past, like garage door openers—he can flip on his uncanny powers and stop time for everyone around him but himself: a "fermata," or musical "hold" on duration itself. This goes beyond anything conjured by David's lyrical plateaus of present-tense retrospect in Dickens. Strine doesn't retrieve time but intervenes in its halted continuum—for his own strategic relief.

His is the power to leverage a respite from dailiness, to spread any moment open to his inhabited mastery. To speak in metaphors like that of a pried-wide gap in the everyday, a hinged ingress to temporal release, a driven wedge of exemption—figures of speech that Strine doesn't in fact use, among many other tropes like them that he does—is only (for now) to suggest how the immobilized world becomes his shucked oyster. Strine's own model or mastertrope—marking "the crucial importance of hinges to my pleasure in life" (9)—involves the spread stems of his eyeglasses when lifting them (unfolding them) into place. And this for none other than his own aggressive mode of enhanced vision: his prolonged contemplation of an unwitting world (albeit exclusively female in his case) suspended in a limbo from which it can't look back. Suspicion effortlessly dawns (in addition to what has already been made confessionally obvious): such, mutatis mutandis, are the writer's own powers, prowess, dispensation—all in some uncanny crystallization behind ground-glass lenses.

Cautious enough, Strine indulges this preternatural gift sparingly in his professional life and its official office chores, only occasionally deploying its forced interregnum to transcribe a tape at the Dictaphone console—so that, when bureaucratic duration is resumed, he has accomplished this in seemingly half the time needed by other expert typists. He wants to impress, in this second sense, but only infrequently enough not to arouse suspicion. The impressions he really cares about are those hand-tapped marks on the page of a life story. For now, beginning just now, he is taking time out, as it were, to type up the anomaly of his own way with time—eight single-spaced sheets proudly completed at the point where we are a corresponding number of pages (18) into the printed text. Thus has his magic "Fold" or "Cleft" (11) allowed him to furlough himself intermittently from his day job for private satisfaction: any half-time writer's fantasy come true.

A kunstlerroman in a downbeat supernatural key? More than that, a writerly parable might well be thought to coalesce here under the banner—and extravagance—of magic realism: writing, as if by definition, serving to effect the arrest of lived time for transcription, whether of business files or "life writing." Calling this magic option, as its perpetrator does, a "Drop" (11, as in *out*) as well as a Fold—the latter as in a provided swivel from one time frame to another, a crease or furrow or hinge: these are only further metaphors added to the *Fermata* trope of the novel's title. For named there is the "hold" in music that prolongs a single note—beyond its initial direct sounding—for its rounding out in the retardation of sequence, completing its remission from assigned tempo. Fermata as "rest" with sound: a lingering, a suspended retention, indicated in graphic code on the musical staff and reproduced by the text (at the head of each chapter) as a dot overarched by a horizontal parenthesis. The recurrence of such a "time signature" in this novel's own eponymous context—given the defenselessness of other bodies when stopped cold under the force of the narrator's freeze-frames—reads as well like the piercing eye of empowered voyeurism under the arched eyebrow of sardonic authorial description. 🍂

In a certain sense it's always true: one must stop the world, "hold" back its own flow—if only in one's head—so as to write about it. But Fold is the dominant metaphor within the text, rather than the echoic hold or fermata: Fold in the sense of a temporal collapse, inward upon itself, via the secret pause button, if only finger snap, of an "open sesame" that goes without the narrator's saying a word. When Strine reflects on how much his life depends on "hinges" (9), beginning with those glasses of enhanced vision, first tool of typist and writer alike—he extends his rhapsody of indebtedness, by optical metonymy, to the throwing open of french windows, even the swung shutters giving out upon motel parking lots, all by tacit analogy with the remote leverage effected by a garage door opener in its normal implementation. For it is that mobile device, before snapped fingers alone have been doing the trick, that was one of his more trusted implementations in the past, deployed as a kind of stun gun in the technotrickery of his calculated time warps: inducing what we might call the fugue states of the world, not of himself as subject. At such willed moments, time itself doubles inward upon itself, folds over, swings shut—or open—depending on which side of the fermata you find yourself on. Even to invoke the uncanny procedure in these terms suggests that it hardly remains, in the precincts of clerical drudgery, just a "writer's fantasy" of time carved out from (and for other) work—unless part of what is being written up involves some unholy power over other lived bodies in their separate walks of life.

But I'm jumping the gun, blowing my cover in this heuristically curtailed effort to channel at first only half the plot, its "upper" layer, its mocking tale of writing's higher calling and its wondrous facilitations. As such an allegory of representation might be imagined—at least in redacted form—to continue unpacking itself, it is as if the time taken from the drudgery of keyboard transcription (taken out, borrowed), in order to chronicle a lifelong magic dispensation from exactly time's uninterrupted grind, entails *at the same time* a redoubling of manual dexterity (more hours of alternate typing commitments than the laws of physics allow) that does no little physical damage to the keyboarding anatomy. Such, certainly, is the strain of Strine's double life. He ends up undergoing diagnostic tests in a neurological lab, submitted to MRI scans by a female radiologist in her research into carpal-tunnel syndrome—Strine still masking his magic by claiming only his day job as culprit, plus a frequent snapping his figures to the music of his choice. The innocent exercise would seem incidental, even if understood by us (rather than the doctors) in its abracadabra valence, to the forearm pain that besets him. Writing takes its more obvious tolls, autobiography not least—where the time set aside for retrospect, explanation, confession, does not escape the real salaried duration of exertion and its palpable symptoms. It is by this logic that the novel's "time-travel" sci-fi plot—about implausible jaunts within the orbit of a dilated present tense—might well secure a thematic of scriptive versus lived temporality, art versus life, figured in the magic apparatus of stop-action as the sine qua non of the world's very transcription. An allegory rounded out, rounded up, with the last chapter's modest coda in which the self-deprecating narrator goes on to imagine self-publishing a simulated Random House version of his autobiographic chronicle (303)—with color-Xerox cover and miniature logo—if the said Press won't actually take it.

Which of course, instead, it has by the time we hear of this worry—in the same bestselling edition we're reading. All told, the duration taken up by Strine at his keyboard has thus been partially answered by us in our preferred reading space. Space—and whatever time, in variable intervals, has been "set aside" for it in our own readerly rhythm, bracketed off, carved out, all this without, on our relaxed part, that occupational hazard of his right arm's muscular and neural discomfort. All told, that is, and obviously enough, our reading syncs up with a typescript already underway in its destined print incarnation: an autobiography already engraved. But so far, "all" has *not* been "told" here—but only in the actual published book as we have it. Which I've only half read back to you in rough summary, even if from beginning to end. I haven't been euphemizing so much as just reducing, narrowing, normalizing: giving only one facet of the beveled auto-allegory. If this novel is in part about the passional drive of writing, and the very "defeat of time" (Powers) it necessitates in at least one sense, it has, however, been all the more obviously a record of sexual obsession in the narrator's magically activated erotomania.

These are the two layers I began by saying it is hard to peel apart. That's because, unremittingly, each has laid the other bare in their own entwined sequencing, already stripped the other naked in their reciprocity. Case (study) in point: that radiogram scrutiny by the female neurologist attending to the stinging distress of Strine's right arm near the book's close. By this point, when almost all has been scabrously done and said, the scan's finds would pointedly diagnose, on their display monitor, what amounts to the full-screen view I've forestalled at one level of summary. For it is high time to admit that these MRI experiments are on the track of a less flattering diagnosis than keyboard over-exertion. Strine hasn't revealed to the doctors that his finger-snapping lateral rather than vertical "drops" into spooky omnipotence should be understood as his true pre-existent condition, but he's said enough about his solitary eroticism that the medical experts have set about distinguishing, if possible, between alternate causes for the same effect of neural aggravation. The scans are taken to see if science can determine whether the damage to Strine's strained right forearm is the result predominantly of his portable typing, a kind of writer's cramp, or traceable instead to the exertions that his particular writing reports upon—and which, he confesses, alternate quite rapidly with composition in real time at his desk (260). By his own admission, then, as onanist more than autobiographer, such is the inveterate wear and tear incurred in jerking himself off—and out of time's flow—until his nerve ends are frayed, along with his sexual fantasies, to the point of chronic tingling irritation. It is only this sexual relief, then, *un*enhanced by any magic but his own presumed erotic projections, that he admits to the doctors—for which all supernatural empowerment is merely, as we've long recognized in any actual reading of the novel, not just a secret aphrodisiac but a trope.

Beating the Clock

Yes, time to come clean on my part, in narrative summary, about the unstinted "filth," what he repeatedly calls the "rot," of his raunchiness. It doesn't just *turn out*, but has been blatant from the start in any (nonbifurcated) reading—despite my studied abstraction of the parable—that it is sex as well as exposition that "drops" the narrator out of clerical duration into time-tumescent fixation. When sexual (rather than diurnal) abstention deserts him, as it so punctually does, he willfully enters the temporal hold, the Fold, the gap—as if it were the vaginal crevice itself, or the "vadge" as he repeatedly calls it—by arresting women in their tracks so as to undress and fondle them. His temporal respite is not a diurnal intermission for writing but for something engrossing enough to write about. A typical minor molestation of his female neurologist in that MRI lab late in the book—on whose nipple he leaves a Post-it of warm thanks after a few surreptitious time-out licks and sucks (272–3)—is only the latest and last of his time-warped perversions in the appropriation of wanted bodies (his "fer*mata*," etymology aside, being complete with unwitting mates). These women, like time, simply stand still for him on quasi-telepathic demand. Within the swollen moments of such temporal leveraging, his is the power to pleasure himself in the face (often literally) of female stasis, a victimized oblivion. And it is in the *now* of the text we are reading that he has been transcribing all this—including inset examples of his earlier experiments in non-autobiographical prose pornography—as the shamelessly straightforward episodic drama, the erotic picaresque, of his improbable life story.

This is the true fascination of the work's two-ply parabolic arc—that what it says about time out for text production and time out for sex speak very much the same, as it were, language. These phases of the story turn out not just to alternate with, but to converge upon and refigure, each other through the word play of the latter. But the result isn't an eros of the seminal pen, some ecstasy of expression. On offer, rather, is mostly a keen-eyed observant precision and low-octane wit, harder to identify with in genre terms, whether lyric or pornographic, but almost as difficult to look away from. So more than that too: an authorial power play—and ultimately reader complicity: each of us, reader and fixated narrator, held hostage wittingly, electively, to episodes of obsessive one-way intimacy over which its female subjects have no control. We've never been kept in the dark by Strine, only you by me in the previous selective précis. Right from the first, with the opening fantasia on (*about*, and played out *upon*) a co-worker's secretly exposed body, Strine celebrates, with no more than a lightly poeticized euphonious assonance, her "exuberant pubic hair" (50). My own summary notwithstanding, the "hold" is admitted up front as a license to grope as well as to stroke and ejaculate. Its pried-apart gap in time, its hinged entry, its driven wedge, the capitalized term "Fold" itself—all are evocations of erotic topography. The titular preference for the musical root of his expansive term "fermatization" may have caught on, for all we know, despite the other kinky nomenclature, by association with *spermatization*. But what we do certainly know, first hand, is our tendency to get hooked on these nonsensical obscenities, playing along with our own verbal equivalents of his described "aftergasms" (132). The prurience unfurls, throughout, as the magically accommodated (and thus madly exacerbated) symptomatology of a normal life's fleeting fantasies: escap(ad)es in every sense—*distended* into full-scale scenarios of one-sided consummation. Fold, hold, hiatus: giving himself a libidinal break by breaking a hole in time, he's more completely "in the zone" of erotic fantasy than mere metaphor could suggest.

So another thing we know at close range: how the relentlessly pursued options of masturbatory release and finger-tip self-narration on the keyed-up page—the spasmodically expressed over against the verbally expressive; sex drive per se versus the libidinous impulse behind the spew of typescript—cannot leave our own *attention spans* unimplicated. This is the case well before we've read our autobiographer's own first effort at detached textual (rather than lived) pornography—as a practicing apprentice "porniste." From early on, we're in on the very game—already textual—that, as we play along, is *playing us*. Nothing really sneaks up on us in this regard, so blatant are the signals. Long before we are reminded that the whole fictional autobiography (as authorial luck would have it, at least in the case of such a lubricious potential bestseller) bears indeed the prestige imprimatur of a major New York "house"—in the form of exactly the Random House imprint we've been holding—we can't have failed to sense our so-called audience participation, precisely as book readers, proceeding under implied dubious scrutiny. For we, too, have suspended other chores—put any plausible reality utterly on hold—to share in Strine's flatly descriptive bouts of impossible erotic predation. Such is the reflexive trick of our proxy's stop-action lechery—in its punning "hold" on us—even with its strangely low-keyed delectation. These Folds of his—these embodied variants of porno centerfolds, these snapped-fingered or remote controlled upgrades of finger-triggered videotape searches (previous staple of the porn industry, at least for allusion by a book seeing print only in the first year of the web)—are always couched (though usually without furniture, bedroom or otherwise) more as respite than desperation. Strine breaks open these holes in his day not so much to give some intense sexual frustration a break—the "hinge"-worthy, cringe-worthy version of the voyeur's vulval release valve (as he might have put it)—but rather as a titillating libidinal mode of killing time.

But how are we to take this, to come to grips with the sober methodical perseverance of this masturbatory persona? Can the narrator's detailed seriousness be serious? Is the pornography itself burlesqued? Are its prolonged efforts at getting-off just a take-off? Cartoon, lampoon—or loony tribute to the ingenuities of need? The prose is so clinical in its observed detail, evincing such meticulous and patient lechery, that the potential for comic hyperbole is almost undercut by its monomania. It isn't that the sex is joyless for Strine, but rather so impeccably annotated as to lose all sense of abandon in the very act of representation. It exceeds the text of fetishism by becoming the fetishism of text—or almost. If it went all the way, into Nabokovian realms of caressed euphony, that would be its higher comedy, its pathos, or its perversion. Instead, it leaves us guessing about the tone at every turn, whether appropriation or parody, and thus vexing the "pleasure of the text" in unstable and unprecedented—which is partly to say *meta*—ways of its own.

The inescapably comic absurdity of his uncoupled (never bedded) consummations, in their sheer selfish use of the female body, goes way beyond anything we might call sex farce. Taking time out from clerical transcription to scribe his own preternatural erotic career, and within that impossible first-person retrospect to interpolate his further experiments in the penning of freestanding omniscient smut, equally incredible, Arno Strine (in the company of ghost writer

Nicholson Baker) may seem to have invented a whole new genre: porno farce. And a new stylistic register. There is even a deep etymology to this concocted genre, its textuality cross-fertilized between Baker's longstanding fascination with linguistic detail, alphabetic and phonic by turns, before and beyond his erotica, and the comparable obsessiveness of his obscene conjurations. To read the relevant dictionary entry bottom to top in this regard is to track the philological unfolding of a pertinent term—*facetiae*: (2) archaic, humorous or witty sayings; (1) dated, pornography. Up to date with a vengeance, however, is the facetiousness, in its very flatness, of Baker's "higher" porn, which is rarefied only in the preciosities of its excess—and only as its fantastic premise, the narrator's omnipotent mastery over time and its arrests, is meant to emblemize, by hyperbole, life's everyday fantasy interludes of routine arousal and "drop out." In his intermittent bouts of "*jamming* time" (59)—often (in the other sense) viscous enough in the upshot—our own verbal instincts in particular, other sensual affect aside, are piqued, pleasured, and now and then thrown for a loop. For in this respect, if this is porn farce, the tone of travesty is scarcely either consistent or confessed.

As the book goes unequivocally *meta* in its bound-volume mode, its readers are consistently angled in, Folded back, "held" captive, to the deliberately equivocal tweaks and twitches of textuality in the erotics of reading. We may think of this as happening at two strata of sensory gratification: both material and linguistic (as the very difference is ultimately rendered moot), or, in other words, both palpable and phonetic (ditto). Apprehend the former first, the physicality of our own bodily contact with Strine's confessional delivery system: a book in the making (in the days before Kindle), a concrete object sewn and bound, but already open to us in the pseudo-temporality of its draft form as we read along with its hormone-juiced composition. Even Powers's work, from the "make a baby" trope of narrative gestation in *The Gold Bug Variations* down through *Generosity*, couldn't haul out its metanarrative mirrors more openly, couldn't be more up front about fiction's need to get on with it. Materiality is in this sense figured and confirmed by being ratcheted down to the manually operated paper substrate of a weighted volume, the codex format itself, rather than being deferred exclusively to the subvocal text production its surfaces furnish the somatic need for. But that vocal enunciation is "on hand" as well—and in its own form of tangible pulsation, pressure, and release.

Such necessitated enunciation certainly has its own literary libido in, not just material, but active *bodily* engagement—a latent oral activation on which is bestowed much fervid rhetoric in Baker's subsequent *The Anthologist* (2009), whose persona cements a literary-historical manifesto for the "whispering aloud" of poetry in its role as "prose in slow motion."[4] It is no accident that this phrase might well define the erotic dilations of Strine's day job in the transcription of cassette-taped business dictation, well before he moves on, within his porno vacations, to the eroticizing of the bound codex. His clerical audition is for him especially delicious when it is a woman's voice he can mechanically interrupt, back-pedal, and caress in the labor of transcription. Still less an accident that the explicitly literary characterization of the phrase "prose in slow motion" would apply as well to the clutch and jam-up, the abutted morphemes and hyphenated cross-poundings, of Strine's anti-euphemistic newspeak coinages. At any speed, and however otherwise breathless in *The Fermata*, the aural charms—and sexual surcharge—of speech in action (this as in V*ox* before it) are complemented in turn by overt wordplay. Witness Strine's kinky metaphors and metonymies for the salving "hinge" in time (rather than saving stitch) that provides him both respite and release in what he at one point characterizes as sex's shattering orgastic "clasm" (134). Such seismic fissures in a quotidian vernacular tend to arrive in just such granular verbal turns: in the fore- and after-play of throated language and its surprise emissions, the very shivers of extratext. Strine's own self-stroked word play, along with ours vicariously in performing (or running further with) it, offers the truly original if limited titillation, such as it is, of this text—including the kind of syllabic hold-over, or alphabetic fold, as we find in the portmanteau categorization of the narrator's preternatural mastery: his "chrononanistic experience" (13), or later his coveted "chronanisms" (20). Under such interpenetrating compression, lexical activity seems aspiring less to the stuffed bag of the valise (or portmanteau) than to the proverbial beast with two backs. Everywhere, in fact, onanism subsumes chronos to its own purposes.

And if we are inclined to play along at the lexical level, we may find our own cognate coinages riding out the whole prurient recursion of desire in the reading mind: the prolonged, or say elongated, interval of time's appeasing *masturbatement*. Such is literature's way, pushed to a limit by Baker, of getting us to talk dirty as we forge ahead. Here is the contagious vocal eros of *phonanism* itself, what Barthes so unabashedly figures, otherwise, as a penetration of the ear. Recall the famous conclusion of *The Pleasure of the Text*, offering, with "the grain of the voice," its title's fullest definition—as if it might have lent inspiration, albeit gone over-literal, to the frictional static of phone sex in Baker's previous novel *Vox*. Barthes stresses the intimacy of a "writing aloud" (predecessor to

Baker's poetics of "whispering aloud" in *The Anthologist*) that entails "language lined with flesh, a text where we can hear the grain of the throat"—as by his own analogy with voice in cinema, where Barthes can feel "the anonymous body" of a verbal "actor" projected into "my ear"—and where this vocal pressure roughens to ecstasy: "it granulates, it crackles, it caresses, it grates, it cuts, it comes: that is bliss."[5] It is just this mode of phonic script, heard as such along the fault lines of its every lexical "clasm" and re-latch, that Baker's concupiscent wordplay (and ours if so inclined, and quite parenthetically, in its wake) may evoke—even while seeming further to trivialize it: removing its whacky cadences far afield from anything like the avant-garde privilege of writerly innovation in Barthes.

But not so far from that brand of "caressing" invited by the material book. To this aspect of the readerly reflex, however, we can best return by precedent in Baker's previous and more popular, if hardly more notorious, novel from two years before, *Vox*. There, too, the slide between phrasal and anatomical manipulation carries over into an erotics of the bound volume itself and its opened pages, as both metaphor for the spread potential of sexual gratification and as the available surface for vicarious stroking. It's hard to say any of this with a straight face, of course. And what *Vox* has already broached so bluntly in these matters of codex sexiness—material and otherwise, figurative and actually fingered—we'll return to *The Fermata* to find exacerbated to the point of loony delirium. And, no less dubiously, further transfigured to textual parable.

Sex in Lexical Reflex: The *Gold Bug* Variant

But first, a clear contrast to Baker's text: instead of an anatomical explicitness so extreme that it must invent the diction of its candor, as if no normal obscene designations will do, there is certainly an erotic charge to be had from the innovative new conjunctions—and figurative interpenetrations—of normal descriptive rhetoric. To appreciate the distance of Baker's pornography from passages of literary erotica—and from a more suffused verbal erotics—a ready comparison suggests itself within an already sampled text. In Powers's *The Gold Bug Variations*, whose metatextual co-authorship we saw in the Preview figured as baby-making insemination and biograft, the main sexual partners of that research plot enjoy their first fully erotic entanglement, as detailed by the then-narrating heroine, at a deserted neighborhood playground, where—though in their science-nerd fetishism they would be thought the opposite of (unsaid) urban "swingers," still "swinging seemed the thing."⁶ And one thing, so we'll hear, soon leads to another. "I would rock on mine, hardly kicking, dragging my feet in the gravel beneath. Franklin, male, shot for escape trajectory" (303), his instinct to "pump to apogee and bail out" (303). A funny and passing bit of gender sociology? So we might think, until many pages later, in one of the novel's encyclopedic litanies of colorfully phrased factoids about terrestrial life's vertiginous shifts of scale, we get explicitly confirmed what we had every reason to suspect has happened next, that long-past night, on the commandeered private swing. Every reason to suspect, that is, across the crests and dips of the prose at work, whose reflex action on the reader's part, as so often when faced with Powers's open-weave wording, is to wonder whether we are reading in—or actually out, eliciting the rhythms of inscription's own inbuilt lilt.

So here's the rub, with its alert to prose's own frictional excitation. In that subsequent section's speculative excursus on the terrestrial biosphere, the heroine-narrator, Jan, meditating on the "prodigal gene" in her ode to DNA, and awed by the unsaid cliché Book of Nature, puts it this way: "If the volumes are beyond listing, I try at least to locate life's bookends" (319)—one of this one book's typical metatextual tropes. But then right away—by deliberated mixed metaphor for another paper containment?—"How large is the envelope?" Extremes meet in a biocentric wonderment: "Living cells have been snagged miles high in the stratosphere." And from that passive verb of abstract research ("have been snagged"), we move to a noun, in back-formation from a verb, plunging ahead as a new syntactical subject: "*Dives* into the deepest sea trench, under several atmospheres, turn up diaphanous fictions that explode before they can be brought to the surface" (319)—as fragile, at least, as not just paper-thin narrative "fictions" but as the phonetic slant rhyme *dive/diaph*. But then, out of the blue of our narrative (rather than the heroine's encyclopedic) backlog— as a capping example of scale's paradoxical disjunctions—it occurs to her, not accidentally, if with new precision: "One male ejaculate—on the swings in a dark abandoned playground—releases 300 million half lives" (320). Ah, right all along, says the reader. I thought so: all of that sinuous rhetoric adding up to his orgasm. Where Baker would have clocked the stages of a final "pecker pulse," or the like, Powers has educed a reciprocal transfusion between the couple—to which many readers would now return (critical readers not alone, I imagine) for a second run through. And what we find is what we might have expected from Powers. Though the aftertext of explicit mention ("ejaculate") has been deferred by nearly twenty pages, the extratext of recognition was carried in place by syntactic motion itself rather than clinical nomenclature, figure and idiom rather than terminology.

The scene in question—under phrasal self-interrogation as it goes—couldn't be farther from the one-note annotations of the Baker persona in the throes of orgastic choreography—except perhaps in its shared (though hardly stressed) implausibility. In a bit of apparatus ingenuity almost as far-fetched as Baker's mail-order battery-operated mechanisms, Franklin convinces Jan to straddle him in his perch on the swing seat, for what he says is called "Swinging Double Dutch" (303)—well before we find that he has trouble learning Dutch when outposted for research to the, yes, Nether-lands. Here, on the expanding arcs of the propelled swing, it is up to prose rhythm rather than mimesis to, as it were, complete the act. As Jan adjusts herself, it is "just enough to shatter his equanimity" (303)—with just enough extra fricative phonetics, as well, to secure the next point before the rhyme with the couple's punctually timed and synchronized "kicks." Thus: "He rolled his eyes at my little *flick* of *friction*." And they're off: "At the top of each arc we would press, pretending innocence, ignorance of contact." After that staggered lexical seriality of "press" into "pretending," the generic "innocence" is etymologically specified by expansion into a disingenuous "ignorance"—until the heavily patterned syntax aids in the botanical troping of sexual pulse and release, with orgasm approached by chiasm: "I kicked in rhythm, climbing a sapling on each upswing, and on each swing back, the sapling me" (303). In the Newtonian reciprocity of this swinging cling, equal and opposite forces trigger the reader's own reflex return for rereading.

We may let the rhythm wash over us the first time through, before even registering the sexualized vegetal pun on "sapling"—let alone the fourfold rhyme of *pling/swing*—until taking a second or third loop through this pivotal wording in the privileged rescanning of textual concentration. Not a case of an explicit "backswing" matching "upswing," as we might also note on third read, but "back" delayed for an extra notch of chiastic symmetry ("and on each swing back"), after which, in this phallicism of the man's sap-filled wood, the ellipsis ("the sapling [riding] me") has its own way, without penetration, of fusing the playground partners in an undertone of the colloquially ungrammatical and far more shatteringly romantic "the sapling [being] me." This operates in something of the same way that the phonetic charge of "each" has more nearly breached the sibilant onset of "swing" ("ea<u>ch s</u>wing" over against the former "each upswing") in the freefall of return. The reversible arcs of the described scene are no sooner over, that is, in the traced gesture and return of their unique literary kinesis, than the eager reader has swung back, as often as necessary, to assess them.

In the never more than implied ejaculatory release of Franklin's desire, a subsequent metonymic rigidity operates as an upward displacement (in the psychoanalytic sense) of the unsaid: "A slight *stiffening* ran up his arms where I held them" (303). Up from we well know where. And for her part, vibration and flow and temperature are all subsumed to figuration on the cusp of the too-literal: "Warm oscillation rippled across the gap to me—unforced, unconscious" (304). And the appositive grammar continues to unfurl without subordination in an extended and assonant noun fragment, rising from soft to hard *u*: "A r*u*sh of cond*u*ctance, animal-perfect r*u*bato" (304)—even while putting the visible frictional *rub* back in the otherwise pronounced Italian terminology. And then a simple declarative clause headed by the metaphor of flux and undertow—and spilling out into further specification: "Backwash erased all difference between us. No burst. Just sweet, spreading infusion, for one instant complete" (304)—with that cadencing of the bivalent grammar sealing the trans-fusion: itself merely instantaneous? or realized in its "completeness" only for a moment? The questioned difference answers itself in vanishing. In the meantime, though, readers see that their grammatical second guess was right: "the sapling [climbing] me." New paragraph with paraphallic relaxation: "We went slack" (304).

But even before the indirection of this figuratively erected male relief, together with its complete female reciprocation, a yet more remarkable sentence has been channeled through the libido of the female narrator, in a wording that can only be said to keep coming at us, never over till it's over: "I felt myself at my coat cuffs, against underwear, inside my silk collar come within seconds of anything" (304). That's it: hard to read, hard to parse, hard to see through to conclusion. Certainly hard to imagine a dozen and a half words being busier, more variably vectored—or more in need of reflex estimation. Here is the phrasing again, with its internal enjambments marked: "I felt myself / at my coat cuffs, against underwear, inside my silk collar / come / within seconds / of / anything." Right off, the grammar seems expansive, self-consuming, not so much self-corrective as centrifugal, spinning out / phrase by phrase / of control. Any paraphrase must be terraced, itself spaced out. Nothing in the wavering grammar stays put, even for as long as it seems. The fluctuant utterance—at least not for more than a split syntactic second—says neither 'I felt myself [at last],' in the vernacular sense, nor something like 'felt myself on edge,' but rather declares how she feels her bodily self materially, along the edges and surfaces of her clothed skin: 'I had the sensation of myself in friction with them.' Yet also, as the grammar pulses on, "felt myself come," but not in just those so many words of sexual idiom, but spreading out immediately (mimetically?) into another vernacular rhythm. For the female narrator "felt myself... come within"—as, say, within the circle of his desire, or rather, a second later, "within seconds of"—what? of *his* coming? Maybe, but not specifically: just within seconds of that or of "anything," anything at all. Indexed there is an infinitesimal limit, a kind of inward asymptote of the possible, defying representation itself in a throbbing loss of focus: pure intensified potential tracked across its sensory basis as a revivified metaphor of arrival. The author who rewrites his prose until signification "becomes the thing itself" has here—when that thing is "anything" at all, including the diffused nothingness, the self-loss, of orgasm—has not just matched his meaning in words but consummated it. Prose friction, by any name.

Compare this to the lighter wit of a coupling in, for instance, another contemporary novelist, Zadie Smith in *NW* (2012), where the partners "came swiftly to reliably separate, reliably pleasurable, conclusions"[7]—an achievement in prose with its own bipartite rhythm. In contrast, Powers's twist of idiom has a reciprocal topography all its own, rather than just a euphemistic vernacular flair. "Cut loose," as the next sentence opens, the heroine's "coming" is reiterated as approach, advent—since, so modified, "I was closer than ever to learning who this boy was" (303): a carnal knowledge well underway before he takes his lead on the upswing. Such a teasing reticence between them here—and between prose and its reader—is abandoned later in the novel in the throes of their rocky erotic commitment. So that, a year before *Vox*, in fact, phone sex in *The Gold Bug Variations* has replaced in full candor the phonetic and figural gratifications of the earlier passage. Admitting (by transferred epithet) to calls at "obscene hours of the night," Jan's narration, figuring her life as a bound text, seeks to know "how depraved I might, under the prose binding, really be," and asks: "Do you mind if I touch myself while you talk? Say something that might get me bothered" (510), with the truncated 'hot and bothered' hardly missed in the idiom. In Baker's opposite treatment of any such expressed desire—and let this encapsulate the whole point of the comparison between Powers's sculpted erotica and Baker's half-lampooned rubbishy smut—an effort or two toward meeting her request would be graphically forthcoming.

Vox and Its Vocables

In pursuit of the metatextual extremis staged by Baker's pornographisms in *The Fermata*, it is certainly clarifying to work backward to his breakout excursion in this mode, where the prurience was so purely verbal as to be, in one sense, nearly disembodied. But what so strikingly prepares the ground, in his 1992 bestseller *Vox*, for the escalated raunch apocalypse of *The Fermata* two years later isn't what one would be led to expect in a novel not just about, but comprised entirely by, anonymous "phone sex" between its unnamed couple. It isn't the sexual so much as the lexical thrills that help seed the "sci-fi" frictionalities to come in the anti-time-travel novel of suspended mobility. Call it phonic sex. In *Vox*, the couple's credit cards are overcharged, along with their libidos, as they meet "in the fiber-optical 'back room'"[8] of the Vox call site—where the fibers that bind constitute the mere audio feeds of a non-optical hook-up. And their intimacy is twice displaced, not just by wired virtual contact but by the nature of their reciprocal turn-ons, induced not by immediate behavior and its self-description but by the freestanding stories they make up for each other—and the words they find as substitutes for an already surrogate erotic conjuncture. Improvisatory and vividly specific, but patient and exacting, He and She (my caps on the subject positions of their otherwise-unattributed dialogue) are collaborative pornographers first of all, not long-distance debauchees, devoted at least as much to the verbally inventive as to the manually dexterous. Those who can, do; those who can't, talk—but not just talk: lavishly narrate, spin scrupulously paced tales, coin phrases, take authorial pleasure in holding the attention, and feeding the desire, of a never quite captive (but entirely captivated) audience, back and forth across the cables that bind them.

Improbably articulate and in every sense composed, this long-distance couple squanders several metered hours in the pursuit of narrative distraction, postponing their own final climaxes for those—Aristotelian and otherwise—of their several stories. And amid the seemingly effortless tale-telling, they generate not just crisply detailed salacious fiction, but extrude, *Fermata*-like, its verbal synecdoche—or at times reductio ad absurdum: the single dirty word, with another repeatedly close on its heels. As if with no diminution in the smut factor, they frankly exchange inapt and colorless synonyms for intimate body parts that turn received common names into new coded terms less metaphoric than the existing thesaurus of obscenity more widely available to the everyday adept. For our nameless male lecher, female breasts are ripe for lackluster coinages, his arcane version of *pet* names. As he explains in one somewhat hesitant disclosure (the ellipses his, though with the pauses leaving nothing unsaid): "Frans is the main one. Sometimes... frannies. Frans, nans, and Kleins... Sometimes I think of a woman's ass as a tock" (59). Leaving us to think this through along the unsaid pulsing conjuncture of dick/tock, not to mention the even louder gender symmetry of another male-membered *ock* rhyme. When our nameless She admits to the phrasing "dithering myself off," it is left to Him to contemplate instead, with philological finesse, "Fiddlin yourself off? The dropped g is kind of racy. No, no, *Strum*" (32). Such is the sometimes cacophonous, sometimes euphonious, music of their quirky handmade coinages. This shared jabberwocky of private wankery is insisted on, in these ways, as also a prose poetry, open to the tucks and wrinkles of a daft linguistic ingenuity—and emblemizing it in the process. She, too, indulges in her little hesitations, marked by the dot dot dot of building expectations. In sharing one of her private verbal usages in the context of her "dithering" preferences, a specified gendered form of genitalia, she admits to a fondness for streams of water aimed "directly on my... femalia" (141)—as if the suspected slight shyness, absurd in the midst of this fetishized candor, might mark, with that ellipsis, a "wait for it" moment of self-celebration over the word itself.

For all their ingenuity of nomenclature, telephonic crossed wires can result from such strumming off-beats. A single example can illustrate the potential confusion that results from such private dictionaries of the indecent—with the reader again yanked gladly along as co-conspirator. Mentioning after the fact that she likes thinking of the male member as a common noun derived from the proper name of a high school boy she was long ago "infatuated with" (60), she uses this secret language of her aroused secretions to explain, in the present conversation, her momentary sense of freakish coincidence when mishearing, in their breathy teleforeplay, his ludicrous term "sperm-dowel" as instead her favored "Delgado" (60). In this way, as with *dick*'s latent response to *tock*, she leaves the reader to hear in turn, within this phonetic bracket of the immortalized "Delgado," the hinted alphabetic core of the *dIdo* that would, if need be, substitute for it. As in all of Baker's pornograms, the lewd is as much ludic as crude. And as much a fleeting self-consuming treat, at least if you're in the mood, as any other instigated self-gratification. In this case, the phone(tics) of obscenic rather than aesthetic distance can lift anonymity from the Joycean "phonem*anon*"[9] so as to give desire a local habitation and a name, with the ennobled synecdochic "Delgado" derived in Spanish from the Latin *delecatus* by way of, in this case, her willed and coveted indelicacy.

Certainly the lexical is sexualized at every available turn, with anything we might call wordiness valorized as an overexcited tantalization all its own. Along with the tongue flicks of words like "clit-trickery" (122), the clunky portmanteau of "nastybation" (88) is answered later by the faux etymology implied by the woman's imagined inviting vagina as "that nice nasturtium" (162). Speech is mated to desire in all this, the voicings transcribed even as a deeper script is sometimes left implicit or deferred. Three sibilant triplets, for instance, bring heavy breathing into line with the very audio technology she warms to: "I *like* the *s*ound of the pau*s*es in long-di*s*tance conver*s*ation*s*—the ca*ss*ette hi*ss s*ound" (25). And the pinpricked mesh of the phone receiver induces another fantasy that may well seem to reframe their entire conversation in an idiomatic pun (not her own). With the reader again on call, so to speak, the phone receiver is imagined by her "like a sieve"—rather like the filters "over the bathtub drain." But in this case what goes through is hardly strained clean. "Sometimes I think with the telephone"—a clause that might seem momentarily complete unto itself, until she pushes on—"think that if I concentrate enough I could pour myself into it and I'd be turned into a mist and I would rematerialize in the room of the person I'm talking to." The result would be "some kind of conscious vapor" (95). He knows what she means, but only we are asked to say it to ourselves: call it *steaminess* (dis)embodied.

All this self-pleasuring banter is familiar enough from the subsequent *Fermata*—and placed here too, by Baker, under the pressure of metafictional invention as well as erotic inventory. But there are two even more pointed anticipations of Strine's fermational exertions in the earlier *Vox*, each caught up in explicit metanarrative nodes of the sort we've considered in that later novel: first about reading as thought transference, then about the book as erotic corpus. Beyond caressed scabrous lingo, one of the lecherous reminiscences in *Vox* takes our nameless Him, like Strine later, to a bookstore, in this case stocked with used and well-rubbed volumes. Smitten by the mere materiality of "historical romances" with titles like *Love's Hurry*, or a shameless potboiler like *Love's Tender Fender Bender*, our intrepid sensualist is moved by their being much thumbed—for him fondled—by women readers. "They looked *handled. All* of their pages were turned. And turned by whom? Turned by women. My heart started going. I had entered this enchanted glade" (65) graced by the erectile thrill of "owning this pre-enjoyed book" (66). It is only one notch further into erotic fantasy, as prosecuted in *The Fermata*, to imagine his own spreading of the text as an access not just to female reading habits and their stroked pages but to the vaginal cleft itself.

Well short of this later apogee of the sexed codex, in *Vox* it's not just the touch of palpated pages, of course, but—by present exemplum—the words on them that are meant, however briefly, to transport the reader. And that do so by inset example as well. For this novel's long phonic intercourse does not just deposit well-crafted obscenities by way of narrative anecdotes but more directly meditates on the inflammatory power of the written word. Following his bookstore confession, the next scene finds his phone mate declaring her preference for Victorian pornography over "X-vids." This surprises him, but it makes sense when pondered. Whereas he still "needs the images" (75), it is possible to recognize, as we'll see Strine appreciating in *The Fermata*, that pure words have the value of direct thought transference—so that the lubricity of a given pornogrammar "surrounds all images with thoughts," becoming (as again would the novelist Baker like to think) "the hottest medium of all. Telepathy on a budget" (75). We are thus back—which is to say glancing forward, one novel ahead—at the barely rarefied erotic zone of Strine's dictagraphic tapes. From this later point of vantage, hindsight finds in *Vox*'s deference to the thought-transference of words—reflexive enough even within the novel that poses it—a direct foreglimpse of Strine's erotic relation to the verbal transcriptions of his day job in *The Fermata*, so often upping the temperature of his temp work to a kind of phoneto-porn. About which more needs soon to be said.

But in the oral wear and tear to which the eponymous *vox* is submitted in the preceding fiction—where telepathy is textured further by telephony, and where, given the long hours of chafing chat, it is the voice that has done more mutual work than His and Her exercised private parts—the question at the end is not just a joke: "Is your voice sore?" (163). She has admitted—in a shared fantasy about the moans of her bathroom raptures being transmitted by prosthetic technology to passing male motorists—to feeling "as if my voice was this *thing*, this disembodied body, out there" (163): a perfect match for his fantasy of an "Mmmmm-Detector" (152) leaving no female orgasm, however remote, unnoted. But words, more than the inarticulate groans of release they help to instigate, are at a premium in Baker's saturnalia. And if the fictive as well as frictional emphasis of all this weren't clear enough from the incorporated stories and corporeal monikers made up along the way, proper names at the end, long withheld and now confected, take on a kind of strictly lexical rather than sexual sense of alphabetic play. "Thank you. Bye Jim," our She signs off, with the inescapable whiff of by-jiminy, as answered, beyond a modest alliteration and deflected assonance, with a strictly legible tangle of puckered morphemes: "Bye Abby. Bye."

Reading Between the Sheets

Language is one thing, bodily delivered; its physical platform another, yet comparably sexualized in Baker's depiction of Strine's fantasy life—as before him in the bookshop haptics of *Vox*. Such is the material erotics of the codex as a hinged prosthetic. And not just in respect to its caressed front, back, or spine, nor even the twice-palpated pages that the avid reminiscence in *Vox* might be thought to have prepared us for. As the author of an award-winning nonfiction lament for the devastation of newsprint archives in American libraries, called *Double Fold* (2000), Baker is so aware of the imprint mechanics of the material (before temporal) "fold" that he has his earlier fictional protagonist in *The Fermata* thinking at one point to distract himself from the temptations of fermaterial caress by a more conventional interlude with a book. But even there the momentary satiety Strine seeks is in its own right reductively eroticized, since what he contemplates is the organic fix that the gullies of certain freshly bound volumes can, in their glued aroma, induce. The mounting compound grammar of his reference to this seems all by itself to up the erotic stakes; instead of indulging in the Fold: "I could go to a bookstore *and* select a new beautiful paperback *and* buy it *and* put my nose in it to smell the pukey smell that books often have" (117). And that, just midway through the novel, is still only a material, if indeed a visceral, anticipation of the yet more explicitly erogenous association, figurative this time, of the fermata's hold—its central Fold—in regard to reading matter in its more than olfactory fascinations.

Yes, that heady scent of pagination is more than a tucked-way, funky clue. Such a generic book-within-the book, untitled, speaks volumes. If we're really reading, that is. As posed in my latest subheading, the idiom "between the sheets" is deliberately misleading. Given the errant orgasms launched upon in *The Fermata* in various office settings, sheets have more to do with codex production—or with business typescript—than with sex. Almost no one is traditionally bedded in this novel, whether in its autobiographical plot (where women are passive and usually upright tools of Strine's satisfaction) or in its inset experimental tales, where imagined women take madcap equipmental charge of their own thrills. Aided most of the time by some mail-order form of "sex utensil" (7), too serious for mere "toys" in non-bedroom settings, cascading female orgasms are accomplished on truckbeds, bathtub rims, front-mount "ridem" lawnmowers, washing machines in their last vibratory spin-cycle, or, in a final projection of the narrator's (ultimately balked) anticipation, when his enamorata is squatted on the floor at the ajar chained door of a fantasized motel room. Satirized there is an "interface" of *mutuality* (or perhaps *simultaneity* is more like it) that, far more often, goes untapped by the female "partner" entirely on "hold" in the alternate workplace fermata of halted cognition—and entirely elided coition. In most of the episodes from Strine's memoirist litany, not of conquests but of surreptitious arrests, the woman's oblivion is not first of all orgasmic but ontic, the male narrator having repeatedly stopped his chosen female body dead in its tracks—as if in a parody of some mesmeric charm—in order to work his intrusive one-sided will.

My own paraphrases and derivative wordplay aside, and the phrasal contraptions of Baker's that have instigated them, one remarks again on a certain bland straightforwardness in even the most voluptuary passages of these novels. The tone, its equilibration, its pace: that's what's so extraordinary in the rough-and-ready erogenous zones of Baker's never manic style, free of opulence, frenzy, or elation. Even in detailing its most burning throes of desire, the prose feels sedulously anatomical, perfunctory, matter-of-fact. For the most part there is only a meticulous scopophiliac release—and then whatever haptic advances seem mandated. The whole overblown comic premise is more than tawdry, but its operations are often timed in a quite clear-headed way to the moderated rhythms of desire. Shall I or shan't I? To beat or not to beat: mostly an open, if always the only, question. There is no rape, no bodily penetration, just a continual displacement of somatic coupling by solo and often utensiled gratification—even in his own first effort at pornographic fiction, his initial text-within-the-sex. That apprentice venture is a novice fantasy, as ludicrous as it is explicit, about separate simultaneous orgasms shared between a vibrator-availed lawn-mowing woman, subsequently taken for a joy ride with her battery-powered dildo in the bump and grind of a UPS truck, and the seduced driver who enjoys hearing the writhings of her passion as he brings himself, still at the wheel, to the on-time delivery of his own "united parcel of peckerpaste" (142). It is as if his last "upward fist-stroke" (142) were implicit, along with the woman's insertions, in his delivery company's own acronymic plural. Two UPs better than one. Like *Vox* before it, this is a text—there is no other way to put it—for playing (along) with. Yet readers—perhaps tickled with themselves in this way at first, for going the jokes one better, doubling down on the dumb fun—may eventually tire of such nudged associations. Given the number of latent teases found seeding the text at its most vulgar, we may in the long run feel less spurred to our own scuzzy wit than co-opted as dupes of the deliberately insinuated residue from Baker's own occasional reticence.

Everything in Strine's personally recounted stunts of untoward gratification depends, as I've suggested, on confession's odd monotone. Framing that last inset fictional text of outré vehicular ecstasy, and another pending "porniste" excursion like it, is a quite methodical account of his magical, rather than merely exaggerated, encounters, where the autobiographically unbelievable is never overheated so much as overworked, even in its fetishistic detail. There is no obsessive, aching rapture in any of this, just the lurid precisions of an expeditious dispatch: call it the anti-*Lolita*, both in its rhetoric and in its wordplay. Detailed here are a series of everyday intermittent fantasies made serviceable by a superadded fantastic premise, often wryly phrased. And where, for us, as suggested, the extra fetish thrill comes instead—gratification writ small—from Strine's (Baker's) syllabic couplings and interpenetrations, the salacious slam-bangs of their neologisms at a far pole from Nabokov's swooning cadences. But a prose poetry nonetheless: leiric, sexphrastic, and satyric all at once, even *onanomatopoetic* in its pulsional build-ups. All is part of the flagrant cutting edge—if not quite Barthes's grating abrasive bliss—of permissive deviance. But don't take my word (my sense of silent wording) for this, any of it. Baker spells it out by a complex parable of cross-mapped auditory stimulations, part and parcel of a broader sense of the *fermata* as metaphor: figuring above all an emblematic space for textual as well as sexual interpolations—and thus for their comparable indulgences.

The analogies gain momentum as follows. When Strine at his desk job jacks in, as it were, to the coveted spells of his fermatted interims, he turns the world off and himself on, getting down to business before returning to it. The textual reflex in this has been impossible to miss. The world must be suspended as much for erotic description, in the separate time of writing, as it is for the private delights that feed on any fantastically accessed flesh. Strine suggests early on that he plans to do most of his autobiographical composition while his life is *on hold*, "sunk in the Fold" (74), but instead the Fold remains merely a trope for composition. "Writing is solitary enough" (74), he decides (and erotic enough, too, he might have added) without wasting his powers of arrest on it—just as he has earlier proposed solitude per se as the "solvent medium" (59) of reading. Though Strine has insisted that he has no idea where his powers of the Fold come from, he does guess that they may have been boosted further by one palpably entrancing aspect of his day job. He enthuses especially, as we know, about his real-time assignments in Dictaphone transcription, using his machine's foot-pedals to stop and start the tapes at clarifying intervals. Beyond the merely functional, "there is, without a doubt, a strong chrononanistic element to my doing of tapes" (38). And not merely because he revels in the timbre and pitch of the oral record, especially when that of "women dictators" (37): each a kind of lexical dominatrix whose "forward-luring rough-smooth voice on the tapes" (37) is what has most "hypnotized" him all these years. It is not just sensuous attention alone, though, but the power of (reasserted) control, that enthralls him in its linguistic particulars: "The daily regimen of microcassettes has kept me unusually sensitive, perhaps, to the editability of the temporal continuum" (38–9)—that span of phonic combination known as wording.

The implicit "rest" that is for Baker the hidden metric secret of English poetry, as polemically illustrated in *The Anthologist*—namely, the recursively caught breath of rhythm itself—is here controlled by his foot-pedals in the manipulated voice of the other. Strine's delight in the massaging of phonic sequence goes to implicate further, of course, our own "sensitivity" to speech pattern in Baker's transcribed text. Across the narrowest holds and gives, pauses and ligatures, we stall over the syllabic tension and release, the jams and ejaculations, of his spasmatic neologisms. In the combinatory glee of his wordsplay, it is as if word borders were being abraded by sexual friction itself, its pacing a matter of "chrononanistic" upbeats and elisions. Indeed Chronos meets Onan at the Fold of just such a prefix in its premature succumbing to the stem: the whole crude, rude vehemence of the Drop scaled down to an alphabetic syncope rather than a temporal blackout. So goes the triplex structure of reflex identification in this book about lubricious dilation-as-temporal-deletion: in regard at once to solitary writing, the shared solitude of its reading, and the fetishized orality of its phonetic couplings and syllabic jump cuts—those last the inherent layerings and viscous lap dissolves of literature's "solvent" verbal medium. Even to recall for a moment how far this falls from the passive arboreal semiosis, played out in words, that we tracked in the echosystem of *The Overstory* is to recognize once again the true extremes of this study in a polarized stylistics.

But such a verbal contrast of Baker to Powers is only part of the larger-scale accommodation of writing to reading achieved by the former in the invaded privacies, the erotic intimacies, of textual identification. If Strine's rhapsody on the contours of the vocal trace on tape recalls Roland Barthes on the grain of the voice, the temp cleric's delight in the serial decipherment of vocal record offers an equally close replay of literary phenomenology in the work of theorist Georges Poulet, who stresses the ventriloquized ideas of a text in the enunciating head of the reader. In reading, "I am the subject of thoughts other than my own"[10]—meaning that I am silently saying them, from the subjective focal point of their own grammar, in order to make them out in the first place: the text's "I" borrowed as mine. Recorded dictation does nothing to spoil, for Baker's protagonist, that silent co-optation at the reading end, where, as so often in the strained borders of Strine's world, the very idea of "presence" is entirely compromised in the context of subsequent tape playback: "It is a great privilege *to be present* when a person slowly puts his thoughts into words, phrase by phrase, doing the best he can" (36). Such is a mode of "presence" that begs its own designation—and with an extra twist. Despite the erotic privilege accorded to the ear-opening pleasures of the female mouth in such voicing, the gender bias ("his") that seems to have set in here—merely for the purposes of a vernacular sexist generality in the slide from "person" to "he"—has, nonetheless, an extra way of entailing the male narrator himself as the implicit target of our own invested attention, at one definitive remove, in the wording of his own thoughts. And not in least the contagious tonguing of his own lascivious diction. With or without Poulet's theorization in mind, here is an emphasis on the *meta*, emerged from the midst of erotic investment, that has departed from an epistemological Modernism and an ontological postmodernism alike in taking a more immanent and reader-oriented phenomenological turn, however coarse-grained its particular filters in this pornographic transference. And here, with his Dictaphone ear-plugs inserted, is Strine in the unexpected role of Powers's own imagined reader, pronouncing the words of his voice-dictated novels at the receiving end.

But wait. Put a fermata over this moment. For there is a second Fold in our slowing over the language of this early (and tutor) passage. What immediately follows from the last citation about the dictating subject doing the "best he can" in the rush of transcribed dictation—about the unique vantage point of such list(en)ing in ("Because you are traveling right along with him" [36])—begins as if were an explanatory fragment, until subordinated to the condition of the main clause. "Because you are traveling right along with him as he forms his sentences, making each word he says appear as a little clump of letters on a screen"—because of just this, as the no longer fragmentary grammar now lands on its feet in completion—"you begin to feel as if you are doing the thinking yourself; you occupy some dark space in the interior of his mind as he goes about his job" (36). Plowing the dark again. Yes, in a sense we are back with Taimur in the prophet's cave of transference. The words you read are as if projected directly from the lair of enunciation, traced out of thin air in an obscure space of inception indistinguishable from the cortex and core of your own ideas—and not just some dramatized "you" pedaling your way across the unreeling of microcassette record. The "you" here is apostrophic as well as generic: you my reader, as Strine would have it—and as Baker does. Or hear Baker, Powers, and Poulet on the same keynote: literature as "Telepathy on a budget." However high-tech such neural matching has become in *Bewilderment*.

Strine's great erotic payoff, until now, as any reader of Baker's can't have been surprised to find, is having watched a female reader bringing herself to climax after perusing his first novice porn tale, that UPS story, once he has anonymously and invisibly slipped it to her on the beach. The fermata, it turns out, serves to facilitate porn's distribution as well as production. In the novel's last extended episode, Strine hopes for the same result from an unidentified motorist into whose car, for tape deck enjoyment, he has stopped traffic to slip an oral recording of his latest repugnant tale: an extemporized fiction about a coprophilic orgy. In his imagined rendezvous with the woman who in fact r/ejects his CD indecency, he nicknames his pending semen bursts by a metatextual coinage based—it is again for the reader to note—on the term for brief satiric scripts ("squibs"). These are, we may preen ourselves on recognizing, *strokes* of pen, rather than of cupped hand, that have brought him as verbal confabulator—in a spurt of lexical nonsense for something like "cum squirts"—to the brink of those "scumsquibs that were imminent in my bloated factotum" (230). It is as if—and Baker the novelist, rather than Strine the autobiographer, has us again on the cusp of just such speculation—as if this whole phrase is no more than a spasm of satiric prose in a mock-up of sexual dyslexia, with the "factotum" yet again an unsaid (reader-invited) play on "jack of all trades." In any case, a routine assonance in that "bloated factotum" has gone so far as to operate its usual recurrence under the special sign of glandular pressure—as if with one hard *o* for each testicular release.

And beyond the in-jokes of rhetoric and textual production, there is the grammatical infrastructure of this whole erectile stretch of Strine's fantasy. The entire episode has been cast by his invention into the subjunctive: about what "would" happen in both the conditional and the optative mood of his frenetic predicates, all in service to his insatiably girded "gender-beam" (249), twin brother to the "sperm-dowel" of *Vox*. But grammar isn't by any means, as we've just noted, made to bear the entire metalinguistic burden of this encounter. Under the gaze of our porno protagonist, or in other words our author/lecher, the prose-seduced imaginary partner reveals, to the further perturbation of Strine's overloaded odd-job-man (or factotum), her own cloven sex: the equally assonant "seam of her open peach" (252). In shifting the "seam" metaphor within its own sliding association, the next moment is almost shocking—if only in its sudden simplicity. In conjuring a view of her cleft succulence in this imagined future episode, our autobiographer realizes, in one more convulsion of subjunctive textual reflex, that it "would look oddly like an open book" (252). One man's oddity is another and more seasoned author's tickled wink—as the "vadge" (his recurrent term) turns paginal more explicitly, but no more suggestively, than in the many spread pages we've moved through, if not nosed out, in the recursive build-up to any such febrile epiphany. This plus the unsaid idiom in its lurking pun: peach without a pit—*pulp* erotica indeed. Seam, fold, cleft: such are the passing mechanics of the so-call page-turner, the body of the pornographic codex in hand. But the body of the reader is involved in the massage of language as well, phrase by phrase. Taking our own book's dictation at the level of phonic impulse, in the seductions of a silent listen, we traverse these brief Fold-overs of enunciation—in all their deaf holds and resumed collusions—by tracing out their tantalizing if sometimes daft undertones, however unseemly, not in the seams of the folio format but in the tucks and creases of script's own undulant silent tonguing. Strine's surprise at his own simile ("oddly like an open book") shouldn't really surprise us in turn, given his bookstore interest in the wedged visceral scent of paperback interiors.[11]

Whether or not featuring it as sexual act, in fact or in fantasy, both these works by Baker, *Vox* and *The Fermata*—by being equally, in medial terms, about "oral sex"—are about themselves as aural prose. This is the *meta* in which they eventuate: the beyond of reframed perspective and its adjusted scale of focus, the extratext of their lexical exertions. Whether transcribing only salacious chit-chat in *Vox*, with the couple's sustained and inflammatory commitment to each other's spoken wording, or isolating the male libido of *The Fermata* within an unstable transit zone between self-expression and self-manipulation, in each case the book—about the unwritten or the being-written—is a novel whose exposed plot armatures may be erotic, in one degree of satiric send-up or another, but whose true textual fulcrum is defiantly verbal. And reflexive as such. These are works that put the reader through paces ungraced by any aesthetic but that of the impertinently filthy—and thus hyper-material—word. The force of the *meta* could in this sense scarcely be clearer than in such recognition. Not *above* enacted desire in its exposition, but nudging just beyond it by inference, prose of this stamp expends its energies in being not just about sex, or even in itself sexy, but in bearing by association—and baring unabashed—a lust for new moves of wording.

Beside the solo exertions of such exhibitionist metasex, there is literary history at work here as well, long term and shorter. From the many mansions of Henry James's "House of Fiction" through Mark Z. Danielewski's *House of Leaves* to Baker's 2014 *House of Holes*, it's not just that we've come an almost unrecognizable way past the dramatic ascents of Modernism and postmodernism. Within the tradition of obscenity itself, charged uninvited or courted by design, Baker has his far and near precedents. "What is pornography to one man," wrote D.H. Lawrence in "Pornography and Obscenity" (1929), "is the laughter of genius to another."[12] That could have been an epigraph to any one of Baker's three exercises in the erectile *risibility* of sex, however deadpan its exposition at times in the earlier works. And nearer in literary history, he has a more explicit model for his own genital candor. Exploring his admiration for John Updike in the eponymous *U and I* (1991), Baker singles out his American predecessor, in a famous accolade, and just the year before publishing *Vox*, for being the first author "to take the penile sensorium under the wing of elaborate metaphysical prose."[13] Gone, in Baker, the metaphysics, and with any anxiety of influence placated, it would seem, by unflinching satiric hyperbole. If there could be the least doubt about the prominently lexical burden borne in *Vox* and *The Fermata* by the quest for fresh pleasures in sexual experiment, the absurdist copulations of *The House of Holes* would lay this, along with its characters, to exhaustive rest.

From the Greek for a graphic rendering of the prostituted female body (*porne*), emphasis in the application of the word "pornography" has of course evolved to apply, generalized, to any such raw exploitation, whether trafficking in "graphic" words or actual images. In Baker, language seeks on its own terms the final titillation. Obvious enough early on, this language ache has become programmatic with the splatter-shot depravities of *The House of Holes*. Everything this chapter has meant to suggest about the rejuvenating (if often sophomoric) metasexiness of wordplay in Baker's early 1990s porno sprees is made incontestable with the turned-on spigots of carnal nonsense in *The House of Holes*. With realism already thoroughly overthrown by the time-machinic Fold, the hold and clutch, of *The Fermata*, it is an equally magic scatology that conjures up the later eponymous hothouse as a kind of pornographic theme park in which, as it were, its pre-paid amusements ride you. Yet the pleasures are more those of a seething private thesaurus than the augmented realities of a virtual brothel. From the Latin again, rather than the Greek, we arrive here at the historical reversion from extravagant filth to mere *facetiae*. There is, for instance, entirely typical, this documented climax among one of the couples synchronizing their satisfactions in a penultimate ménage: "Suddenly, Glenn's orgasm slammed into gear, and he threw the first hot clot of a busted nutload of jizzling twizzlering sperm up inside her." The character's own throbbing heave aside, language has spent itself four times over in the gasps of *ot/lot, ust/nut, izz/wizz*, and finally, fractionally more relaxed and spaced out, *zler/sper/her*. A sentence later, and the clot has gone more thickly phonic in the curdle of hyperbolic redundancy—a result felt when (italics added, though hardly needed) "Shandee let out a ragged *joyous scream cry* of pure consummated cockfuckedfulness" (256). The whole phrasing is so strained out of shape that its last cresting lexeme might as well be summoning some lost participial archaism like "cockfuck'd." Under the investigated pressure of a literary appreciation no more ridiculous (or redundant) than this phrasing's own unchecked intricacy, the mind reels—reels out, that is, its teased rush of free association. In the outsize *fulsome* abstraction of this "pure" all-consuming mating, that last unhyphenated and overstuffed noun can seem to be merely completing a verbal auto-mimesis in the preceding phrase. For there, in the anomalous use of a substantive as intensifying adjective in the tautological "joyou*s s*cream cry," a paroxysm of vocal ejaculation—answering in overheated phonemes to her partner's "hot clot"—releases its own viscous "cream" by the thickened elisional hiss of juncture itself. Parody has, yes, its way of inviting parody.

To say the least, there is no over-reading of such overworked prose. Nor any shaking the suspicion that Baker is tempting us with just this sort of seduced hermeneutic amusements. Such are the true reflex actions of this textual experience. The deliberately rhythmic piston-thrusts of such phrasing push every button—and limit—imaginable while pulling no punches in their slavering assonance and compactions: a drooling aural sex displaced from carnal to phrasal obsession, from soma to sema, in the disseminations of the fondled word. Whether the "turning" is ultimately on or off, the troping of such pornophilology bends attention backwards into wording at every turn of such reflexive lexical ferment. And reminds us—in line with our treatment of technical estrangements on screen, from celluloid freeze-frames to CGI glitches—that the grip of audience reflex is always, at the textual stratum we've been investigating, a medium-deep recognition.

So that if an inevitable suggestion of this last chapter is that when wording gets its erotic license, in Powers, from recognizing rhythm as one verbally translatable medium of sex (the orgastic upswing of the playground episode in *The Gold Bug Variations*), and, in Baker, from exaggerating compression and effusion as another such medium (as caught in the frequent burst of his phonoclasms), then the reading of such prose has, going in, not only its clearly framed prompts but its own inbuilt reflex inspection—however compromising or embarrassing—in the serial cues of uptake. And there is of course a deeper connection between these two writers, beyond the occasional or the habitual sex scene, respectively. Powers dictating his prose by voice-recognition on his paperless "tablet" and Baker's Strine at the bodily levers of his Dictaphone, in the variable bliss of transcription, dawdling over vocables, dithering in sympathetic vibration with the push and pull of sound, meet halfway along Barthes's grain of enunciation. In Baker's later prose, to be sure, the house of fiction has gone so far as to include the ceiling as well as hall mirrors of a narrative brothel, reducing the contextual dimension of a literary model like prose\plot/topic to the plotless and hermetic confines of lexicon\text/sex. But through it all reading is kept very much on view in the medium, and phenomenological valence, of its investigated discount telepathy, where literary language still, even in reductive travesty, can be watched putting ideas in our heads through words.

Hence the true fermatas under celebration in prose like Baker's and its instigated responses: the lingering holds and delectations available to the remote voice control of text's essential hardware as a platform for enunciated wording. This last chapter's early effort was to pry as wide apart as possible the overlapped "holding" patterns in the temporal manipulations of *The Fermata*—between the sci-fi premise of time out for sexual exploitation and the would-be autobiographer's space for narrative writing and its reading. If this succeeded in exposing a narratological allegory of verbal duration narratographically engaged, then it worked to condense, as it was meant to, a bonding emphasis across all the preceding chapters, probing as they do the literary medium of lexical accretion in comparison to that of celluloid sequence and pixel mapping.

Refocused by the broadest metanarrative concerns of this study, one can now rewrite the contrastive practice of its two main authors more succinctly. For the imploded crux around *wordy sex/y words* in Baker's phrasal pornoramas—in its fanatic narrowing of the *thing/nifier* dialectic in Powers, whose phrasing works toward *achieving* its referent in material form—closes the circle of comparison upon the stimulus-response reflex of a medium-steeped readerly alert.

Notes

1 Roland Barthes, *The Pleasure of the Text* (New York: Hill and Wang, 1975), trans. Richard Miller, a text that itself closes in rapturous captivation by the kind of writing of which Barthes can only say that "it granulates, it crackles, it caresses, it grates, it cuts, it comes: that is bliss" (67).
2 Adam Mars-Jones, "Larceny," *The London Review of Books* 16, no. 6, March 24, 1994, in a review named for the theft of time in the plot's underworked sci-fi premise, https://www.lrb.co.uk/the-paper/v16/n06/adam-mars-jones/larceny (accessed October 4, 2021).
3 Nicholson Baker, *The Fermata* (New York: Vintage, 1994), 12.
4 Nicholson Baker, *The Anthologist* (New York: Simon & Schuster, 2009), 1.
5 Roland Barthes, *The Pleasure of the Text* (see n. 1 above), where the prose comparison to this audible voicing is "*writing aloud*" (italicized, 66), rephrased as "vocal writing" (67). The last multiple run-on sentence (previously quoted in n. 1) about the grating orgastic release of textual bliss, in the original French, captures the irritation and release more evocatively yet via the sibilant liaison (and fermata?) of a caressing "*ça care_sse ça_ rape*."
6 Richard Powers, *The Gold Bug Variations* (New York: William Morrow, 1991), 303.
7 Zadie Smith, *NW* (New York: Penguin, 2012), 156.
8 Nicholson Baker, *Vox* (New York: Vintage, 1992), 10.
9 James Joyce, *Finnegans Wake* (Harmondsworth, UK: Penguin, 1992), 258.
10 Georges Poulet, "The Phenomenology of Reading," *New Literary History* I (1969), 58.
11 Then, too, Picasso's many reading women often leave open on their laps a cloven folio in a muted version of this same erotics of interiority. Strine might have found his own fantasy—book as sexual organ—less gratifyingly "odd" if he had spent more time at galleries than at his dictaphonic labors. See Garrett Stewart, *The Look of Reading: Book, Painting, Text* (Chicago: University of Chicago Press, 2006), ch. 6, "Sujet d'Art: Picasso and the Crisis of Interiority" (275–328).

12 D.H. Lawrence, "Pornography and Obscenity," *Complete Essays of D.H. Lawrence* (Pickering, UK: Blackthorn, 2009), 515.

13 Nicholson Baker, *U and I: A True Story* (New York: Vintage, 1991), 18. Bearing in mind the stylistics of Updike's psycho-physiological candor in his own erotic writing, as contextualized of course by social norms and their testing in postwar American culture, one notes how the approach to tallying "bad words" in this chapter differs from the broad cultural canvas, for instance, in an earlier American moment, explored by Michael Millner's *Fever Reading: Affect and Reading Badly in the Early-American Public Sphere* (Durham, NH: University of New Hampshire Press, 2012). In the orientations of the present chapter, instead, any public sphere—and public's fear—meets the text head-on only at the kind of reflex angle of wording canted toward the one-on-one encounter with the cues and goads, however ludicrous, of lexical provocation and its vocalized response.

Afterthoughts \ The Angle of Incidents

In the tipping-point year of 1970, the inveterate *writer* William H. Gass—experimental novelist inhabiting his alter ego as philosopher and textual theorist, even while working to spill into each other those three separately sanctioned roles—coined, as we know, the buzzword of a literary epoch with "metafiction." Two definitive decades later, it was time in 1991 for a prominent brainchild of the fictional succession, Richard Powers, to ask "what's a meta for?" At more than one level, his question began to answer itself: not in so many words, but in many others of his own narrative production. Including a self-exemplifying twist of idiom earlier in the same sentence, shifting the proverbial "man's reach... exceed his grasp" to the transverbal "man's speech... exceed his lapse": call it a metaphrase. Not since a dear friend of mine, literary scholar Elliot L. Gilbert, walking on the beach with me in California just before his untimely death in that same year, 1991, quipped that "They also surf who only stand and wade"—not since then, at least in my hearing, has a line (Browning's in Powers's case, rather than Milton's in Elliot's) been more nimbly permuted across its crisply phrased contraries.

Solecisms, speech lapses, comprehended under the rubric of metalinguistics: what else is new? But what really—even if elapsing from word to word—is the "meta for"? Just there, in the full ambit of Powers's droll transfusing wordplay, might lurk a broader and more compelling answer yet to his own question. Compared to the engineered girders of high-rise metafiction dominant at the time, what may be hinted at in that double punning are other ways, say more foundational, more bedrock, to exceed—to survive—the inevitable lapse of postmodernist self-enclosure. Shaping the texts brought into evidence, and submitted to verbal attention, in *The Metanarrative Hall of Mirrors*, this is where the *labor* of reading, always reflexive under certain textual pressures, finds itself already inscribed in the *work* as an inside job. What's a meta for? It's formative. And it is in this sense that specifying anything like a readerly double-take as an *after* thought, let alone an integral aftertext, is productively paradoxical—since the deciphering reaction is indeed already *written in* as a latency awaiting response, both interpretive hurdle and a reassurance at once. Already written—and often in the lapse of explicit sense, the secretly styled life of signification: the lapsus, the parapraxis. Such word-wrung metatextuality can seem decipherable as a kind of prolonged Freudian slip, speaking forth—to the surmising eye and ear—its true inferences accidentally on purpose. As the first epigraph of our Preview, Powers's jokey provocation looked forward to confirming turns we've heard him venturing ever since, including the double play on Sheherazadian narrative reach and a daughter's paternal "grasp" at the close of *Plowing the Dark*. And most recently the lapsed monosyllabic language ghosting "is in there"—in locating the son's renewable energy—as reflex trace of his own transcended absence ('isn't there') at the close of *Bewilderment*.

In light of the technique\text/context paradigm established in the opening consideration of reflexive film, when transferred to the interplay between verbal style and thematic pattern in fiction, these chapters—bolstered by that cinematic contrast, and building on Powers's jesting question—have essentially asked four questions of their own from novel to novel. Clearer perhaps now in retrospect, these are inquiries regarding literary (broadly textual) self-consciousness in the continued vitality of its narrative inflections. First, how is it (Chapter 3) that an ecological novel can overstep standard representation in an effort actually to translate the signals of nature when understood as already their own message systems, their own texts? Through what (Chapter 4) micromanaged effort of textual attention does a book become *a* novel when it reads for most of its length like two in alternation? How (Chapter 5) does a narrative struggling against the hesitations of its own writer's block get finally written from within the story itself when masked as a mutant form of creative nonfiction? And wherefore (Chapter 6) do unmitigated pornographic fantasies become "literary"—lexical as much as sexual—apart from any flavor of rhetorical elevation or narrative power?

Though the answers vary widely, of course, their accounts are part of the same unfolding study because they locate, each in its way, the gravitational pull of style, of wording, at the sentence level—or below. In the circuit of inquiry rounded out by these reflexes of reading (seen against their cinematic counterparts in Chapters 1 and 2), a defining narrative charge in each novel answers to (Chapter 3) the extrahuman root system mapped by echoic phrasing and its punning tentacles under the sign of an arboreal masterplot, (Chapter 4) language's plot-bridging and theme-binding tropes across insistently severed story lines, (Chapter 5) the specialized vocabulary of narrative composition per se, and its place in the creativity of nonfiction, as mobilized from within the coils—and toils—of depicted events, and, more narrowly, (Chapter 6) the linguistic twitch of dirty words in their strictly self-remunerative coinage. One way to broach a post-postmodern stylistics of this sort is to read your own verbal reactions—as if the text were doing it for you. Forwarding a storyline is the work of narrative. Certain afterthoughts are the work of the metatext in the near simultaneity of verbal—of medial—reflection. The latter, in its narratographic traction, defines the onset of uptake in the engaged sorting of response.

This mode of phrasal double-take is a reading continued on "beyond" ("meta") the normal course of wording in further registration of the same elapsed phrase, sentence, or paragraph. Its induced response is thereby angled back on itself in interpretive recursion. It is, as Powers assigns it to his hero in *Generosity* in the pedagogical form of "life philosophy," a mode of looking twice, looking harder. Where that looking, when at narrative words, is inseparable from lending the ear of your own silent voicing. Ultimately, it is a degree of attention aligned and framed for us, cued and guided, by the self-signaling rigors of texts themselves, their surprises and unpacked compressions, their mimic glints. In the geometry of optics that helps orient such extra "looking," the angle of incidence—in etymological link to the "coincidence" (as intersection) of a light ray with a planar surface—applies, as functional measure, to reflection and refraction alike. It is Emily Dickinson's "certain slant of light" made quantifiable. It is what this book, from its Preview on, has meant to evoke around the edges of narrative mimesis: namely, the slant faceting necessitated when narrative is arranged, at however oblique or canted an angle, to mirror its own field of operation in the reading mind. To mirror acoustically, that is, as well as visually. For our most recent examples of this, of course, we have a certain slant of sound in *Bewilderment* to thank, where what both "isn't there" and "is in there" is the very stuff of *fMRI*'s 'ephemera' when set in echo along a framing phonetic bevel. At whose unexpected angle, in context, we are *inclined* to hear the said in the unwritten.

By cinematic comparison, the last four chapters have been directed at a multifaceted textual rather than retinal spectrum, separating out overlapped layers of effect in the recurrent deflections and filterings of metanarrative afterthought. Plot delivers incidents; *meta* reading takes them up, if also sometimes to pieces, along the worded face of their manifestation. It does so at whatever angle of incidence—including a vocalization often aurally awry—such wording admits or delimits. Since the technical terminology of "incidence" does apply to acoustics as well as optics, to sound waves as well as light rays in their encounter with—and bounce-back from—the surface of page-like planes of whatever sort, this figurative vocabulary retains its flexible interpretive value. Such angular geometry invokes an apt scope for the phonetic as well as mimetic events of prose narrative in the immediate reverb of its extratext. Immediate: the coincident processing of plot and its medial process—the latter precipitated from story in the blinked eye, or cocked ear, of its reflex action. All told, for both screen and verbal narrative, the close-gauged medial awareness invited and channeled by such metatextual works—in an immersive encounter very different from either "surface" or "symptomatic" reading (in the buzzwords of current debate)—engages narrative consumption via a reflexive action of medium itself, optical or phrasal.

Limit cases can help measure and deliberate a spectrum—and in prose fiction as much as in cinema. Now, it would be strained and overly schematic to claim a definitive sea change from the late twentieth to the very dawn of this century, especially when signaled at mid-career by two novelists still active at this writing. But the difference between the late metafictional *Underworld*, from DeLillo in 1997, with its networked *omniplot* of subterranean connectivity, and the global *counterplot* of 2000's *Plowing the Dark* does offer a template for distinguishing the fictive monolith of self-referential *construction* (in the mode of a canonical metafiction) from the dialectical reflex of reader *comprehension* negotiated at both phrasal as well as narrative levels. One speaks there, in that third italicized case, etymologically. It is a matter of shape *apprehended* by internal signals in the build-up to understanding. If Powers would be inclined to number his own novels among ongoing variants of that self-referential "constructivist" sort dubbed as such in his first book, the term would seem best applied, in the case of his typical later works, to the way, at one remove, a *constructive reading* gets foregrounded in its trained prehensile reach across the divided vectors of plotted event.

Thrown back reflexively on its own resources, and precisely as the conduit of a verbal medium, reading in Powers is enlisted, phrase by phrase, to *construe* the encompassing tacit construct. And to monitor the nuances of attention's own reactive shaping. We began with a late writing in this vein, and have worked back up to it, for the way—beyond illustrating certain refined quirks in his echoic lexical ironies—the fertile "understory" of *The Overstory* serves to thematize "language" per se: language, as it were, regardless of medium, forest signals in this case, as before with this same author's ode to genomic code in *The Gold Bug Variations*. But perhaps we can best think of these works, in retrospect, as part of an evolving trilogy. One novel (*Plowing the Dark*) gives its half-time hero something to read in translation, a space other than his own imprisoned one to plow through, before bringing to light (in experimental pixel lumens) his indirect electronic co-share in the "translation algorithms" of the militarist overplot we have finally learned how to read. One novel (*Generosity: An Enhancement*) gives its hero something to write in getting its own climax written. One novel (*The Overstory*) branches across multiple storylines in giving their separate characters a chance at interpreting nature, in its botanical subscript and otherwise—until deforestation contrives its own translated message, in global English, out of the trees' severed limbs and trunks. These related texts steer us to separate narrative closures across a density and breadth of earned scientific language—tracing virtual imaging via algorithmic ciphers, genomic signature in translation, botanical messaging in bioorganic code. All the while keeping literary reading, as reflex action, in homologous train. And if they gather to a kind of trilogy, then *Bewilderment* arrives as its supplement and summa: a stylistically tracked allegory of reading as neural transference.

And then, by pointed contrast, Baker—who has taken to circumscribing the self-recognitions of literary reading within the narrow lexical sphere of carefully curated and long-postponed verbal ejaculations, in all their neologist bursts, tonal effrontery, and requisite double takes. Baker, in whom the metatextual has been reduced to the verbally autoerotic. In *Vox* and *The Fermata* alike, as first marked by the estrangement of foreign nouns recruited for English titles, it is the inventive lexical densities of voiced filth that keep language at high heat in the recognitions of reading rather than the projections of the flesh. The figurative term *fermata* could hardly be farther from the musical overtones of theme and variations, of bark ode, in Powers. More parodic than odic, with a body talk more fluorescent and tacky than erotically incandescent, Baker's anomalous fermata names the unsaid but equally euphemistic *fixation* that turns pornographic compulsion into an obsessive testament to graphomania—and to the seizing up of its restless lexical pulse in certain obscene throbs of, uh, neolojism in his perverse spunk aesthetic.

Oddly enough, then, the present book's commentary happens to find itself bookended by the logic of the freeze-frame—first as technological disclosure in film, then as metaphor for stopped time in the scatological narrative dilations of *The Fermata*. It is also the case that the near-instantaneous reverb of metafictional "pleasure" (or at least internal pressure) these chapters have been positing—as it complicates the very phenomenology of mimetic attention—can be understood as modeled on such an arrest of intrinsic sequence for the held-breath recoils of textual duration itself in afterthought. Turns of phrase that turn back on themselves are the registers, in this sense, of textual episodes whose impact plays out only in the reflex off-angle of recognition. The freeze-frame, that is, doesn't just instance reflexivity; it can figure it. Put it that certain narrative incidents come fully clear only as verbal events in analytic arrest. But the angle of incidence thus skews even when it renews attention. The whole process is brought to a rude salience—and travesty—in Baker's prurient musicology of stave time, with its fermatas magically furnished for depraved invasions of privacy: the freeze-frame as the displaced erectile stiffening of the world in frozen abjection.

In such prose's underlying channels of affect, certainly the literary-historical distinction between the metanarrative touchstones of modernist epistemology, on the one hand, and postmodern ontology, on the other, have passed over, in *The Fermata*'s supernatural technology of erotic empowerment and invasive surveillance, into a contaminating phenomenophilia—whose lines of transmission and transference could scarcely be more openly scrutinized. And worried—at least worked over. An emphasis on the vested fascination in us that Baker's obscenity elicits is foregrounded in part by the reflex action of that novel's own narrator, "phrase by phrase," in the flaunted textual erotics of audition and tape transcription as its own "chrononanistic" fondling of writing's time-based medium. This tingly sense of things doesn't just subtend the plot's low erotic hijinks but often upends them altogether, turning untoward lusts toward textual addiction itself—with even a codex fetish thrown in for good queasy measure.

An exacerbated case, to say the least. Certainly this study falls far short of its main hope if it hasn't come across as a book about something more than—"beyond" in its own *meta* sense—the scope of quite limited evidence. Analysis is meant to prime any number of extrapolations in a slant reading of other contemporary as well as classic narratives, literary and cinematic alike: a beveling of perspective far more widely on view in the reflex action of each medium separately. But the tendency, it must be said, strikes a richer vein lately in fiction than in film. Examined in these chapters is not a vestigial literary subgenre in the wake of its po-mo apogee. Seen more clearly in its dispersed, and deeper, service—as well textual pleasure—rhetoric's prompt to reflex action marks an intermittent and subliminal stimulus in an ongoing recharge of narrative's verbal field. So the triptych mirrors of technique\text/context, meant to cover the two media at once, can also be purposefully specified—with "context" isolated at its nearest edge and interpretive interface—as prose\narrative/audience. Reading, like viewing, yes, is often written-in to the fictions that solicit it. But it is more than simply enlisted. What analysis has wanted most to bring out—primarily by noting it framed by glancing moments across the linguistic face of many a narrative's cannily faceted expanses—is the narrowest measure of our captivation: the fact, in the intensities of certain prose incidents, as well as in the keenest *decipherings* of film technique, that reading reads us. Reads, that is, the level of attention it implants, seeds, machinates, triggers. Such is the sparking action that this book's argument takes to mark, by dint of medial interest and by way of definition, exactly the reflex by which we recognize our own function in narrative's variable mirror.

With montage prototypes in mind from numerous revealing anomalies of the narrative screen, we've turned to comparable arrests and extremities in prose storytelling: test cases that actively test our reading. Or think of them as trials of our own novelistic attention in the face of a broad, if selective, spectrum of reflexive gauntlets: a quartet of texts (three main narratives by Powers, one by Baker, with side glances, of course, at *Vox* and *Bewilderment*) investigating in chapter rather than chronological sequence, first, the transhuman limits of the legible, next a transnational rift in narrative coherence, then the enervation of scriptive will in the prosecution of plot, and finally a festering of the lexical libido itself in various stalemates of narrative development. Under assumption beneath all this, the axiom in recap: we read *language* first of all, not novels, as some novels—in their semantic antics—want us expressly to know and acknowledge. These are signal texts that italicize the work of their own signal system, the code of its messaging as the very condition of their texting, sorted out in the *meta* of afterthought, of extratext.

In the uncommon writing under consideration in these chapters, then, the highest common factor: *prose that wakes us to our own reading.* Structurally, the hardwired armatures of narratology are found grounded in narratography. Mimetically, the narrated world comes across as an assemblage as much as a semblance, strung on the rungs of stylistic enunciation. Affectively, we respond twice over to a certain intensity of written story, first to the writing, then to the story—as we do to the filming of screen plots in either their fullest medial persuasion or their trivial digital showiness. Technically as well as psychologically, writing, too, operates as an apparatus for double identification, both with wording and with the world it works into shape. Immersively, that latter phenomenological engagement may at certain points reach to the place where stories and their store of words must unlearn each other's limits in an earned access to the weft—and resonance—of sheer text, of textuality per se: where the *meta* is inseparable from narrative process in all its after rings of phrasing, its afterings in response. Reflexively, then, we read *in* as well as *on*: moved in moving *through the words*—and regularly amused to glimpse our own labor as if anticipated, paid forward, mirrored in advance.

Index

acoustic mirroring 165, 221
aftertext 15, 17, 51, 121, 132. *See also* extratext
Allen, William 103 n.2
apparatus reading 19, 29–30, 46, 61, 71

Baker, Nicholson 2, 18, 154, 181–2, 223; *The Anthologist* 196–7, 209; compared to D.H. Lawrence on obscenity 213; *Double Fold* 206; material books eroticized 204–05, 206, 212; minimalist versus Powers as maximalist 3, 71–2, 84, 215; on the "penile sensorium" in John Updike 213. *See also The Fermata, House of Holes, The Mezzanine, Vox*
Barthes, Roland; erotics of voice 24 n.13, 196–7, 210
Baudrillard, Jean 103 n.2
Benjamin, Walter; on photography 65, 68
Bergman, Ingmar ?, 20
Bewilderment (Powers) 223; "decoded neural feedback" and the phenomenology of reading 173–4; mind-game prose 176, 179, 220, 221; oscillating idioms 174–5
Bordwell; compared to Powers on the film's audience as narrative catalyst 32; narration (versus narrative) defined 30–1
Brando, Marlon 35
Brooks, Peter 77

Camus, Albert 155
Cavell, Stanley; "assertions in technique" 29
Christensen, Jerome 47 n.7
Citizen Kane 10; abyssal hall of mirrors 25–7; as metacinema 26–8, 34–5
computer-generated imagery (CGI) 28, 30, 39

Connor, J.D. 47 n.5
Conrad, Joseph, *Heart of Darkness* 34
constructivist novels 83. *See also Three Farmers on the Way to a Dance*
Coppola, Francis Ford, *Apocalypse Now* 34–5
corporate Hollywood logos (as reflexive screen metatexts) 38–9
Corrigan, Timothy 23 n.9
Currie, Mark, 22 n.4

Danielewski, Mark Z. 179, 213
Deleuze, Gilles 103 n.2
DeLillo, Don 3, 88; *Cosmopolis* 70; *Underworld* 10, 70, 222; as "writer of sentences" 10–11, 17, 20
Dickens, *Our Mutual Friend* 85
Dickinson, Emily 221

Echo Maker, The (Powers) 8
Forster, E.M., *Howards End*; compared to DeLillo on "connectivity" 70, 105
Eliot, George, *Middlemarch* 70
Elsaesser, Thomas; on the "mind-game film" 23 n.6,
Epstein, Jean 55, 61
extratext; in *The Fermata* 183, 196, 199. *See also* aftertext, *Generosity*

Faulkner, William 3; *Sound and the Fury, The* 106
Federman, Raymond; "surfiction" 24 n.12
Fellini, Federico 2, 20
Fermata, The 4, 47; book-in-the-making trope compared to Powers 195; "chrononanistic" lure of Dictaphone transcription 209; erotics of the book object 206; imagined autobiographic publication 193–94; masturbation as diagnostic cover story 189–92;

narratographic reading of salacious detail 215; obscene neologisms and word play 195–96, 211–12; porno text within the text 207–08, 21; sci-fi magic of "drop"/ "fold" / "hold" as trope for writing and slow reading as well as orgasm 191–93, 209–10, 223–24; textual phenomenology eroticized 210

Franzen, Jonathan 79, 82

freeze-frame; as traumatic flashback in *Spider-Man: Far From Home* 57. *See also* Kubrick, *Barry Lyndon*

Gain (Powers) 108
Galatea 2.0 (Powers) 88
Gass, William H; "metafiction" 14, 17, 219
Gauguin, Paul 112, 122
Generosity: An Enhancement (Powers) 18, 66, 85, 223; burden of plot 159–62; cinematic tropes 142; conflation of hero and narrator 143–45; edutainment as parody of Powers's infofiction 139; etymology of the title 152–53; freeplay vs. counterplay in *Plowing the Dark* 168; "genetically modified" Second City as setting 142; "hall of mirrors avant-garde novels" 151–52, 164, 170; human evolution troped as the history of writing 155–6; narrative reading as transport 148; as novel in the works 109–10, 149–50; pivotal pun on "penned" 157, 164; plotting's "defeat of time" 140–41, 158–59, 164, 191; "rapid gene signature reading" 149–51; in relation to "constructivism" 143, 168; stranglehold of sexual plotting 154; terminal wordplay as in *The Overstory* and *Plowing the Dark* 167; transhumanist masterplot 152; valedictory closure 164–67; writing as rewriting 162–63

Gilbert, Elliot L. 219

Gold Bug Variations, The (Powers) 15, 16, 69, 115; closure (as self-enclosure) 115, 195; erotic style in 197–201, 215; genomics in 223; phone sex compared to *Vox* 201; phonetic slant rhyme 198; prose friction 201

Hamlet; "mirror up to nature" 12
House of Holes, The (Baker) 5, 213–14
Hutcheon, Linda 23 n. 11

Jameson, Fredric 103 n.2
Jenkins, Henry 139
Joyce, James; "phonemanon" 203–04

Kubrick, Stanley; *Barry Lyndon* 53–4; *2001: A Space Odyssey* 57

LaRocca, David 48 n.5
Lawrence, D.H. 213
LeClair, Tom 23 n.7

Mars-Jones, Adam 216 n.2
Matrix, The; liquid mirror in, compared to *Spider-Man: Far From Home* 57
McCarthy, Cormac 3
McHale, Brian; modernist epistemology vs. postmodernist ontology 7–8; shift since to phenomenology 8–9, 79
meta; in relation to metaphor 6, 12; etymology 13–14, 15, 33; linked to wordplay 219–20; revival in contemporary fiction 12; summarized by chapter 220–21
metatextuality revisited across media 4–5
Metz, Christian; *trucage* 41
The Mezzanine (Baker) 159; arcane vocabulary 73–74; reflexive figure for writing 75
Mieszkowski, Jan 23 n.8
mind-game film 6, 19; as "puzzle film" 9; related to tests of reading Powers and Baker 54–5; *The Sixth Sense* and *The Others* as prototypical 137. *See Spider-Man: Far From Home*
Mitchell, Lee Clark 21 n.1
Morrison, Toni 3

Nabokov, Vladimir *194*
narratography 7, 29
Nolan, Christopher 5, 47. *See Tenet*

Operation Wandering Soul (Powers) 103 n.2
Orfeo (Powers) 87
Overstory, The (Powers); "constructivism" 83; "echology" in 18, 88, 90, 91; legibility of arboreal nature 88, 90, 105; multi-plot narrative 18, 19, 81–82, 85; phonetic punning 98–101; protocinematic trope 93–4; style of a wordsmith 83–4; word play 85–7; understory in 2

Paris Review 10–11, 83–4; interviews by Powers and DeLillo compared 83–84
Picasso, Pablo; women reading 216 n.11
Plowing the Dark (Powers); compared to narrative's scalar shifts in Steinbeck 106, 107; counter-plotting 18, 19, 83, 85, 104–09, 223; disembodied climax compared to *Generosity* 135; metanarrative word play in closure 136, 220; newspaper photos in 169; regress of recitation 120, 126, 134; Sheherazade motif 136, 220; traumatic second person narration 118–21, 125, 130; virtual reality (Realization) lab 109, 111–13, 117, 122–3, 126; VR Cavern vs. prophet's cave 119–23; weaponized imaging 131
Poe, Edgar Allen 16
Poulet, Georges 175, 210–11
Powers, Richard; "constructivist fiction" 9–10; dictated prose approximating reader's inner ear 99, 134, 210; encyclopedic reference 80; maximalism versus Baker's detailism 3; *meta* in 1–2, 10, 26–7, 219; medium made readable 169; scientific infofiction 8, 10; sentences approximating mental states 84. See also *The Echo Maker, Gain, Galatea 2.0, Generosity: An Enhancement, The Gold Bug Variations, Orfeo, The Overstory, Plowing the Dark, The Time of Our Singing, Three Farmers on the Way to a Dance*

puns 1, 87; as modeling structural doubleness in Powers 9. See also *The Overstory*
Pynchon, Thomas 17, 20, 88

Ramis, Harold, *Groundhog Day* 55–56
Reflex action 1; aftertext as extratext 15, 17, 51, 129, 225; function versus effect 4, 5–6; in relation to formalism's "baring the device" 31; as stimulus-response aesthetic 215;
Resnais, Alain 2

Sander, August 64
Scott, Tony, *Déjà vu* 59
Smith, Zadie; erotic wordplay in *NW* 201
Spider-Man: Far From Home 5; CGI allegory 40–46, 56; climate crisis thematic 42; internet vindication in 45–6; mind-game format 40, 45, 54, 55; mirror parable 56–7; narratively incorporated Columbia logo 39; typical Marvel franchise tag-scene 40; and sci-fi as reflexive genre 46–47; Trump-era satire 41, 42, 56
Spielberg, Steven; Paramount logo in *Indiana Jones and the Temple of Doom* 38; *Ready Player One* 48 n.7
Stam, Robert 7, 76
Steinbeck, John, *Grapes of Wrath*. See *Plowing the Dark*
Stewart, Garrett; *Dear Reader* 23 n.10; four-book sequence on the evolution of the screen medium 29; *Novel Violence* 22 n.3; *The Value of Style in Fiction* 23 n.8
Strawson, Galen; episodic versus narrative self 177 n.2
suture in cinema 68
syntax of viewing compared to reading 7

technique\text/context paradigm, defined 28; alternately conceived as technique/text\context 39; configured as style\plot/theme 70, 132; lexicon\text\sex 215;

micro\plot/macro 137 n.1; prose\narrative/audience 225; prose\plot/premise 71

Tenet 5; compared to *Spider-Man* 62; film-within-the film 61–2; metanarrative mind-game of "the protagonist" 57–8; "proving window" in 60–61, 76; reflexive text of the algorithm 61

Thackeray, William Makepeace. *See* Kubrick, *Barry Lyndon*

Three Farmers on the Way to a Dance (Powers) 50; hyperprogress and its "trigger points" 62–4, 133; "metaself-consciousness" 66, 149; spectator as synthesizer of screen montage 68–9; "constructivist novels about fiction" 64; ekphrasis in 64–5; selfhood as narrative 66

Transformers: The Last Knight; Paramount logo 38

Villeneuve, Denis, *Arrival* 59–60; *Blade Runner 2049* 36–7

visual special effects (VFX) 30

Vollman, William 23 n. 7

Vox (Baker); anonymity redoubled by pseudonyms in closure 206; compare phone sex in *The Gold Bug Variations 201*; invented dirty words 202–04; palpated books 204–05; phonics of sex 202–04; telepathic desire 205

Wallace, David Foster 3, 23 n.7, 103 n.2

Watts, Jon. See *Spider-Man: Far From Home*

Waugh, Patricia 23 n.11

Welles, Orson; mirror scene in *Lady from Shanghai* 50. See also *Citizen Kane*

Whitehead, Colson 3

Williams, Evan Calder 77

Lightning Source UK Ltd.
Milton Keynes UK
UKHW020628170622
404565UK00006B/294